Fourth Conference on Machine Translation (WMT 2019)

Volume 1: Research Papers

Florence, Italy
1-2 August 2019

ISBN: 978-1-5108-9289-7

WMT 2019

**Fourth Conference on
Machine Translation**

Proceedings of the Conference

Volume 1: Research Papers

Introduction

The Fourth Conference on Machine Translation (WMT 2019) took place on Thursday, August 1 and Friday, August 2, 2019 in Florence, Italy, immediately following the 57th Annual Meeting of the Association for Computational Linguistics (ACL 2019).

This is the fourth time WMT has been held as a conference. The first time WMT was held as a conference was at ACL 2016 in Berlin, Germany, the second time at EMNLP 2017 in Copenhagen, Denmark, and the third time at EMNLP 2028 in Brussels, Belgium. Prior to being a conference, WMT was held 10 times as a workshop. WMT was held for the first time at HLT-NAACL 2006 in New York City, USA. In the following years the Workshop on Statistical Machine Translation was held at ACL 2007 in Prague, Czech Republic, ACL 2008, Columbus, Ohio, USA, EACL 2009 in Athens, Greece, ACL 2010 in Uppsala, Sweden, EMNLP 2011 in Edinburgh, Scotland, NAACL 2012 in Montreal, Canada, ACL 2013 in Sofia, Bulgaria, ACL 2014 in Baltimore, USA, and EMNLP 2015 in Lisbon, Portugal.

The focus of our conference is to bring together researchers from the area of machine translation and invite selected research papers to be presented at the conference.

Prior to the conference, in addition to soliciting relevant papers for review and possible presentation, we conducted 8 shared tasks. This consisted of four translation tasks: Machine Translation of News, Biomedical Translation, Robust Machine Translation, and Similar Language Translation, two evaluation tasks: Metrics and Quality Estimation, as well as the Automatic Post-Editing and Parallel Corpus Filtering tasks.

The results of all shared tasks were announced at the conference, and these proceedings also include overview papers for the shared tasks, summarizing the results, as well as providing information about the data used and any procedures that were followed in conducting or scoring the tasks. In addition, there are short papers from each participating team that describe their underlying system in greater detail.

Like in previous years, we have received a far larger number of submissions than we could accept for presentation. WMT 2019 has received 48 full research paper submissions (not counting withdrawn submissions). In total, WMT 2019 featured 12 full research paper oral presentations and 102 shared task poster presentations.

The invited talk was given by Marine Carpuat from the University of Maryland, College Park, USA. It was titled "Semantic, Style & Other Data Divergences in Neural Machine Translation".

We would like to thank the members of the Program Committee for their timely reviews. We also would like to thank the participants of the shared task and all the other volunteers who helped with the evaluations.

Ondřej Bojar, Rajen Chatterjee, Christian Federmann, Mark Fishel, Yvette Graham, Barry Haddow, Matthias Huck, Antonio Jimeno Yepes, Philipp Koehn, André Martins, Christof Monz, Matteo Negri, Aurélie Névéol, Mariana Neves, Matt Post, Marco Turchi, and Karin Verspoor

Co-Organizers

Organizers:

Ondřej Bojar (Charles University in Prague)
Rajen Chatterjee (FBK)
Christian Federmann (MSR)
Mark Fishel (University of Tartu)
Yvette Graham (DCU)
Barry Haddow (University of Edinburgh)
Matthias Huck (LMU Munich)
Antonio Jimeno Yepes (IBM Research Australia)
Philipp Koehn (University of Edinburgh / Johns Hopkins University)
André Martins (Unbabel)
Christof Monz (University of Amsterdam)
Matteo Negri (FBK)
Aurélie Névéol (LIMSI, CNRS)
Mariana Neves (German Federal Institute for Risk Assessment)
Matt Post (Johns Hopkins University)
Marco Turchi (FBK)
Karin Verspoor (University of Melbourne)

Invited Speaker:

Marine Carpuat (University of Maryland, College Park)

Program Committee:

Tamer Alkhouli (RWTH Aachen University)
Antonios Anastasopoulos (Carnegie Mellon University)
Yuki Arase (Osaka University)
Mihael Arcan (INSIGHT, NUI Galway)
Duygu Ataman (Fondazione Bruno Kessler - University of Edinburgh)
Eleftherios Avramidis (German Research Center for Artificial Intelligence (DFKI))
Amittai Axelrod (Didi Chuxing)
Parnia Bahar (RWTH Aachen University)
Ankur Bapna (Google AI)
Petra Barancikova (Charles University in Prague, Faculty of Mathematics and Physics)
Joost Bastings (University of Amsterdam)
Rachel Bawden (University of Edinburgh)
Meriem Beloucif (University of Hamburg)
Graeme Blackwood (IBM Research AI)
Frédéric Blain (University of Sheffield)
Chris Brockett (Microsoft Research)
Bill Byrne (University of Cambridge)
Elena Cabrio (Université Côte d'Azur, Inria, CNRS, I3S, France)

Marine Carpuat (University of Maryland)
Francisco Casacuberta (Universitat Politècnica de València)
Sheila Castilho (Dublin City University)
Rajen Chatterjee (Apple Inc)
Boxing Chen (Alibaba)
Colin Cherry (Google)
Mara Chinea-Rios (Universitat Politècnica de València)
Chenhui Chu (Osaka University)
Ann Clifton (Spotify)
Marta R. Costa-jussà (Universitat Politècnica de Catalunya)
Josep Crego (SYSTRAN)
Raj Dabre (NICT)
Steve DeNeefe (SDL Research)
Michael Denkowski (Amazon)
Mattia A. Di Gangi (Fondazione Bruno Kessler)
Miguel Domingo (Universitat Politècnica de València)
Kevin Duh (Johns Hopkins University)
Marc Dymetman (Naver Labs Europe)
Hiroshi Echizen'ya (Hokkai-Gakuen University)
Sergey Edunov (Faceook AI Research)
Marcello Federico (Amazon AI)
Yang Feng (Institute of Computing Technology, Chinese Academy of Sciences)
Andrew Finch (Apple Inc.)
Orhan Firat (Google AI)
George Foster (Google)
Alexander Fraser (Ludwig-Maximilians-Universität München)
Atsushi Fujita (National Institute of Information and Communications Technology)
Juri Ganitkevitch (Google)
Mercedes García-Martínez (Pangeanic)
Ekaterina Garmash (KLM Royal Dutch Airlines)
Jesús González-Rubio (WebInterpret)
Isao Goto (NHK)
Miguel Graça (RWTH Aachen University)
Roman Grundkiewicz (School of Informatics, University of Edinburgh)
Mandy Guo (Google)
Jeremy Gwinnup (Air Force Research Laboratory)
Thanh-Le Ha (Karlsruhe Institute of Technology)
Nizar Habash (New York University Abu Dhabi)
Gholamreza Haffari (Monash University)
Greg Hanneman (Amazon)
Christian Hardmeier (Uppsala universitet)
Eva Hasler (SDL Research)
Yifan He (Alibaba Group)
John Henderson (MITRE)
Christian Herold (RWTH Aachen University)
Felix Hieber (Amazon Research)
Hieu Hoang (University of Edinburgh)

Vu Cong Duy Hoang (The University of Melbourne)
Bojie Hu (Tencent Research, Beijing, China)
Junjie Hu (Carnegie Mellon University)
Mika Hämäläinen (University of Helsinki)
Gonzalo Iglesias (SDL)
Kenji Imamura (National Institute of Information and Communications Technology)
Aizhan Imankulova (Tokyo Metropolitan University)
Julia Ive (University of Sheffield)
Marcin Junczys-Dowmunt (Microsoft)
Shahram Khadivi (eBay)
Huda Khayrallah (Johns Hopkins University)
Douwe Kiela (Facebook)
Yunsu Kim (RWTH Aachen University)
Rebecca Knowles (Johns Hopkins University)
Julia Kreutzer (Department of Computational Linguistics, Heidelberg University)
Shankar Kumar (Google)
Anoop Kunchukuttan (Microsoft AI and Research)
Surafel Melaku Lakew (University of Trento and Fondazione Bruno Kessler)
Ekaterina Lapshinova-Koltunski (Universität des Saarlandes)
Alon Lavie (Amazon/Carnegie Mellon University)
Gregor Leusch (eBay)
William Lewis (Microsoft Research)
Jindřich Libovický (Charles University)
Patrick Littell (National Research Council of Canada)
Qun Liu (Huawei Noah's Ark Lab)
Samuel Läubli (University of Zurich)
Pranava Madhyastha (Imperial College London)
Andreas Maletti (Universität Leipzig)
Saab Mansour (Apple)
Sameen Maruf (Monash University)
Arne Mauser (Google, Inc)
Arya D. McCarthy (Johns Hopkins University)
Antonio Valerio Miceli Barone (The University of Edinburgh)
Paul Michel (Carnegie Mellon University)
Aaron Mueller (The Johns Hopkins University)
Kenton Murray (University of Notre Dame)
Tomáš Musil (Charles University)
Mathias Müller (University of Zurich)
Masaaki Nagata (NTT Corporation)
Toshiaki Nakazawa (The University of Tokyo)
Preslav Nakov (Qatar Computing Research Institute, HBKU)
Graham Neubig (Carnegie Mellon University)
Jan Niehues (Maastricht University)
Nikola Nikolov (University of Zurich and ETH Zurich)
Xing Niu (University of Maryland)
Tsuyoshi Okita (Kyushuu institute of technology)
Daniel Ortiz-Martínez (Technical University of Valencia)

Myle Ott (Facebook AI Research)
Santanu Pal (Saarland University)
Carla Parra Escartín (Unbabel)
Pavel Pecina (Charles University)
Stephan Peitz (Apple)
Sergio Penkale (Lingo24)
Mārcis Pinnis (Tilde)
Martin Popel (Charles University, Faculty of Mathematics and Physics, UFAL)
Maja Popović (ADAPT Centre @ DCU)
Matīss Rikters (Tilde)
Annette Rios (Institute of Computational Linguistics, University of Zurich)
Jan Rosendahl (RWTH Aachen University)
Raphael Rubino (DFKI)
Devendra Sachan (CMU / Petuum Inc.)
Elizabeth Salesky (Carnegie Mellon University)
Hassan Sawaf (Amazon Web Services)
Jean Senellart (SYSTRAN)
Rico Sennrich (University of Edinburgh)
Patrick Simianer (Lilt)
Linfeng Song (University of Rochester)
Felix Stahlberg (University of Cambridge, Department of Engineering)
Dario Stojanovski (LMU Munich)
Katsuhito Sudoh (Nara Institute of Science and Technology (NAIST))
Felipe Sánchez-Martínez (Universitat d'Alacant)
Aleš Tamchyna (Charles University in Prague, UFAL MFF)
Gongbo Tang (Uppsala University)
Jörg Tiedemann (University of Helsinki)
Antonio Toral (University of Groningen)
Ke Tran (Amazon)
Marco Turchi (Fondazione Bruno Kessler)
Ferhan Ture (Comcast Applied AI Research)
Nicola Ueffing (eBay)
Masao Utiyama (NICT)
Dušan Variš (Charles University, Institute of Formal and Applied Linguistics)
David Vilar (Amazon)
Ivan Vulić (University of Cambridge)
Ekaterina Vylomova (University of Melbourne)
Wei Wang (Google Research)
Weiyue Wang (RWTH Aachen University)
Taro Watanabe (Google)
Philip Williams (University of Edinburgh)
Hua Wu (Baidu)
Joern Wuebker (Lilt, Inc.)
Hainan Xu (Johns Hopkins University)
Yinfei Yang (Google)
François Yvon (LIMSI/CNRS)
Dakun Zhang (SYSTRAN)
Xuan Zhang (Johns Hopkins University)

Table of Contents

Conference Program

Thursday, August 1, 2019

8:45–9:00   *Opening Remarks*

9:00–10:30   **Session 1: Shared Tasks Overview Presentations I (chair: Barry Haddow)**

9:00–9:35   *Findings of the 2019 Conference on Machine Translation (WMT19)*
Loïc Barrault, Ondřej Bojar, Marta R. Costa-jussà, Christian Federmann, Mark Fishel, Yvette Graham, Barry Haddow, Matthias Huck, Philipp Koehn, Shervin Malmasi, Christof Monz, Mathias Müller, Santanu Pal, Matt Post and Marcos Zampieri

9:35–9:50   *Test Suites*

9:50–10:10   *Results of the WMT19 Metrics Shared Task: Segment-Level and Strong MT Systems Pose Big Challenges*
Qingsong Ma, Johnny Wei, Ondřej Bojar and Yvette Graham

10:10–10:30   *Findings of the First Shared Task on Machine Translation Robustness*
Xian Li, Paul Michel, Antonios Anastasopoulos, Yonatan Belinkov, Nadir Durrani, Orhan Firat, Philipp Koehn, Graham Neubig, Juan Pino and Hassan Sajjad

10:30-11:00   *Coffee Break*

11:00–12:30   **Session 2: Shared Task Poster Session I**

11:00–12:30   *Shared Task: News Translation*

The University of Edinburgh's Submissions to the WMT19 News Translation Task
Rachel Bawden, Nikolay Bogoychev, Ulrich Germann, Roman Grundkiewicz, Faheem Kirefu, Antonio Valerio Miceli Barone and Alexandra Birch

GTCOM Neural Machine Translation Systems for WMT19
Chao Bei, Hao Zong, Conghu Yuan, Qingming Liu and Baoyong Fan

Machine Translation with parfda, Moses, kenlm, nplm, and PRO
Ergun Biçici

CUNI System for the WMT19 Robustness Task
Jindřich Helcl, Jindřich Libovický and Martin Popel

NTT's Machine Translation Systems for WMT19 Robustness Task
Soichiro Murakami, Makoto Morishita, Tsutomu Hirao and Masaaki Nagata

JHU 2019 Robustness Task System Description
Matt Post and Kevin Duh

Robust Machine Translation with Domain Sensitive Pseudo-Sources: Baidu-OSU WMT19 MT Robustness Shared Task System Report
Renjie Zheng, Hairong Liu, Mingbo Ma, Baigong Zheng and Liang Huang

Improving Robustness of Neural Machine Translation with Multi-task Learning
Shuyan Zhou, Xiangkai Zeng, Yingqi Zhou, Antonios Anastasopoulos and Graham Neubig

12:30–14:00 **Lunch**

14:00–15:30 **Panel on "Open Problems in Machine Translation" (chair Ondrej Bojar): Alex Fraser (Ludwig-Maximilians-Universität München), Alon Lavie (Unbabel), Marcin Junczys-Dowmunt (Microsoft), Yvette Graham (Dublin City University)**

15:30–16:00 **Coffee Break**

16:00–17:30 **Session 4: Research Papers on Modeling and Analysis (chair: Matthias Huck)**

16:00–16:15 *Saliency-driven Word Alignment Interpretation for Neural Machine Translation*
Shuoyang Ding, Hainan Xu and Philipp Koehn

16:15–16:30 *Improving Zero-shot Translation with Language-Independent Constraints*
Ngoc-Quan Pham, Jan Niehues, Thanh-Le Ha and Alexander Waibel

16:30–16:45 *Incorporating Source Syntax into Transformer-Based Neural Machine Translation*
Anna Currey and Kenneth Heafield

USAAR-DFKI – The Transference Architecture for English–German Automatic Post-Editing
Santanu Pal, Hongfei Xu, Nico Herbig, Antonio Krüger and Josef van Genabith

APE through Neural and Statistical MT with Augmented Data. ADAPT/DCU Submission to the WMT 2019 APE Shared Task
Dimitar Shterionov, Joachim Wagner and Félix do Carmo

Effort-Aware Neural Automatic Post-Editing
Amirhossein Tebbifakhr, Matteo Negri and Marco Turchi

UdS Submission for the WMT 19 Automatic Post-Editing Task
Hongfei Xu, Qiuhui Liu and Josef van Genabith

11:00–12:30   *Shared Task: Biomedical Translation*

Terminology-Aware Segmentation and Domain Feature for the WMT19 Biomedical Translation Task
Casimiro Pio Carrino, Bardia Rafieian, Marta R. Costa-jussà and José A. R. Fonollosa

Exploring Transfer Learning and Domain Data Selection for the Biomedical Translation
Noor-e- Hira, Sadaf Abdul Rauf, Kiran Kiani, Ammara Zafar and Raheel Nawaz

Huawei's NMT Systems for the WMT 2019 Biomedical Translation Task
Wei Peng, Jianfeng Liu, Liangyou Li and Qun Liu

UCAM Biomedical Translation at WMT19: Transfer Learning Multi-domain Ensembles
Danielle Saunders, Felix Stahlberg and Bill Byrne

BSC Participation in the WMT Translation of Biomedical Abstracts
Felipe Soares and Martin Krallinger

11:00–12:30   *Shared Task: Similar Languages*

The MLLP-UPV Spanish-Portuguese and Portuguese-Spanish Machine Translation Systems for WMT19 Similar Language Translation Task
Pau Baquero-Arnal, Javier Iranzo-Sánchez, Jorge Civera and Alfons Juan

Friday, August 2, 2019 (continued)

14:00–15:30   Session 7: Invited Talk (chair: Matt Post)

14:00–15:30   *Marine Carpuat (University of Maryland): Semantic, Style and Other Data Divergences in Neural Machine Translation*

15:30–16:00   *Coffee Break*

16:00–17:30   Session 8: Research Papers on Applications (chair: Marco Turchi)

16:00–16:15   *Hierarchical Document Encoder for Parallel Corpus Mining*
Mandy Guo, Yinfei Yang, Keith Stevens, Daniel Cer, Heming Ge, Yun-hsuan Sung, Brian Strope and Ray Kurzweil

16:15–16:30   *The Effect of Translationese in Machine Translation Test Sets*
Mike Zhang and Antonio Toral

16:30–16:45   *Customizing Neural Machine Translation for Subtitling*
Evgeny Matusov, Patrick Wilken and Yota Georgakopoulou

16:45–17:00   *Integration of Dubbing Constraints into Machine Translation*
Ashutosh Saboo and Timo Baumann

17:00–17:15   *Widening the Representation Bottleneck in Neural Machine Translation with Lexical Shortcuts*
Denis Emelin, Ivan Titov and Rico Sennrich

17:15–17:30   *A High-Quality Multilingual Dataset for Structured Documentation Translation*
Kazuma Hashimoto, Raffaella Buschiazzo, James Bradbury, Teresa Marshall, Richard Socher and Caiming Xiong

Saliency-driven Word Alignment Interpretation for Neural Machine Translation

Shuoyang Ding   Hainan Xu   Philipp Koehn
Center for Language and Speech Processing
Johns Hopkins University
`{dings, hxu31, phi}@jhu.edu`

Abstract

Despite their original goal to jointly learn to align and translate, Neural Machine Translation (NMT) models, especially Transformer, are often perceived as not learning interpretable word alignments. In this paper, we show that NMT models do learn interpretable word alignments, which could only be revealed with proper interpretation methods. We propose a series of such methods that are model-agnostic, are able to be applied either offline or online, and do not require parameter update or architectural change. We show that under the force decoding setup, the alignments induced by our interpretation method are of better quality than fast-align for some systems, and when performing free decoding, they agree well with the alignments induced by automatic alignment tools.

1 Introduction

Neural Machine Translation (NMT) has made lots of advancements since its inception. One of the key innovations that led to the largest improvements is the introduction of the attention mechanism (Bahdanau et al., 2014; Luong et al., 2015), which jointly learns word alignment and translation. Since then, the attention mechanism has gradually become a general technique in various NLP tasks, including summarization (Rush et al., 2015; See et al., 2017), natural language inference (Parikh et al., 2016) and speech recognition (Chorowski et al., 2015; Chan et al., 2016).

Although word alignment is no longer a integral step like the case for Statistical Machine Translation (SMT) systems (Brown et al., 1993; Koehn et al., 2003), there is a resurgence of interest in the community to study word alignment for NMT models. Even for NMT, word alignments are useful for error analysis, inserting external vocabularies, and providing guidance for human translators

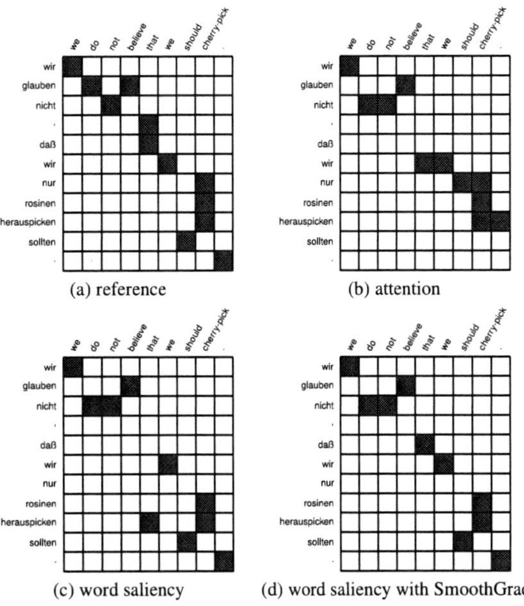

(a) reference   (b) attention

(c) word saliency   (d) word saliency with SmoothGrad

Figure 1: Comparison of our saliency-based word alignment interpretation of convolutional NMT model with reference and attention interpretation.

in computer-aided translation. When aiming for the most accurate alignments, the state-of-the-art tools include GIZA++ (Brown et al., 1993; Och and Ney, 2003) and fast-align (Dyer et al., 2013), which are all external models invented in SMT era and need to be run as a separate post-processing step after the full sentence translation is complete. As a direct result, they are not suitable for analyzing the internal decision processes of the neural machine translation models. Besides, these models are hard to apply in the online fashion, i.e. in the middle of left-to-right translation process, such as the scenario in certain constrained decoding algorithms (Hasler et al., 2018) and in computer-aided translation (Bouma and Parmentier, 2014; Arcan et al., 2014).

Proceedings of the Fourth Conference on Machine Translation (WMT), Volume 1: Research Papers, pages 1–12
Florence, Italy, August 1-2, 2019. ©2019 Association for Computational Linguistics

For these cases, the current common practice is to simply generate word alignments from attention weights between the encoder and decoder. However, there are problems with this practice. Koehn and Knowles (2017) showed that attention-based word alignment interpretation may be subject to "off-by-one" errors. Zenkel et al. (2019); Tang et al. (2018b); Raganato and Tiedemann (2018) pointed out that the attention-induced alignment is particularly noisy with Transformer models. Because of this, some studies, such as Nguyen and Chiang (2018); Zenkel et al. (2019) proposed either to add extra modules to generate higher quality word alignments, or to use these modules to further improve the model performance or interpretability.

This paper is a step towards interpreting word alignments from NMT without relying on external models. We argue that using only attention weights is insufficient for generating clean word alignment interpretations, which we demonstrate both conceptually and empirically. We propose to use the notion of *saliency* to obtain word alignment interpretation of NMT predictions. Different from previous alignment models, our proposal is a pure interpretation method and *does not require any parameter update or architecture change*. Nevertheless, we are able to reduce Alignment Error Rate (AER) by 10-20 points over the attention weight baseline under two evaluation settings we adopt (see Figure 1 for an example), and beat fast-align (Dyer et al., 2013) by as much as 8.7 points. Not only have we proposed a superior model interpretation method, but our empirical results also uncover that, contrary to common beliefs, architectures such as convolutional sequence-to-sequence models (Gehring et al., 2017) have already implicitly learned highly interpretable word alignments, which sheds light on how future improvement should be made on these architectures.

2 Related Work

We start with work that combines word alignments with NMT. Research in this area generally falls into one of three themes: (1) employing the notion of word alignments to interpret the prediction of NMT; (2) making use of word alignments to improve NMT performance; (3) making use of NMT to improve word alignments. We mainly focus on related work in the first theme as this is the problem we are addressing in this work. Then we briefly introduce work in the other themes that is relevant to our study. We conclude by briefly summarizing related work to our proposed interpretation method.

For the attention in RNN-based sequence-to-sequence model, the first comprehensive analysis is conducted by Ghader and Monz (2017). They argued that the attention in such systems agree with word alignment to a certain extent by showing that the RNN-based system achieves comparable alignment error rate comparable to that of bi-directional GIZA++ with symmetrization. However, they also point out that they are not exactly the same, as training the attention with alignments would occasionally cause the model to forget important information. Lee et al. (2017) presented a toolkit that facilitates study for the attention in RNN-based models.

There is also a number of other studies that analyze the attention in Transformer models. Tang et al. (2018a,b) conducted targeted evaluation of neural machine translation models in two different evaluation tasks, namely subject-verb agreement and word sense disambiguation. During the analysis, they noted that the pattern in Transformer model (what they refer to as *advanced attention mechanism*) is very different from that of the attention in RNN-based architecture, in that a lot of the probability mass is focused on the last input token. They did not dive deeper in this phenomenon in their analysis. Raganato and Tiedemann (2018) performed a brief but more refined analysis on each attention head and each layer, where they noticed several different patterns inside the modules, and concluded that Transformer tends to focus on local dependencies in lower layers but finds long dependencies on higher ones.

Beyond interpretation, in order to improve the translation of rare words, Nguyen and Chiang (2018) introduced LexNet, a feed-forward neural network that directly predicts the target word from a weighted sum of the source embeddings, on top of an RNN-based Seq2Seq models. Their goal was to improve translation output and hence they did not empirically show AER improvements on manually-aligned corpora. There are also a few other studies that inject alignment supervision during NMT training (Mi et al., 2016; Liu et al., 2016). In terms of improvements in word alignment quality, Legrand et al. (2016); Wang et al. (2018); Alkhouli et al. (2018) proposed neural word alignment modules decoupled from NMT systems, while Zenkel et al. (2019) introduced a separate module to extract alignment from NMT decoder states, with which they achieved comparable AER with fast-align with Transformer models.

The saliency method we propose in this work draws its inspiration from visual saliency proposed by Simonyan et al. (2013); Springenberg et al. (2014); Smilkov et al. (2017). It should be noted that these methods were mostly applied to computer vision tasks. To the best of our knowledge, Li et al. (2016) presented the only work that directly employs saliency methods to interpret NLP models. Most similar to our work in spirit, Ding et al. (2017) used Layer-wise Relevance Propagation (LRP; Bach et al. 2015), an interpretation method resembling saliency, to interpret the internal working mechanisms of RNN-based neural machine translation systems. Although conceptually LRP is also a good fit for word alignment interpretation, we have some concerns with the mathematical soundness of LRP when applied to attention models. Our proposed method is also considerably more flexible and easier to implement than LRP.

3 The Interpretation Problem

Formally, by interpreting model prediction, we are referring to the following problem: given a trained MT model and input tokens $\mathcal{S} = \{s_0, s_1, \ldots, s_{I-1}\}$, at a certain time step j when the models predicts t_j, we want to know which source word in $\mathcal{S}$ "contributed" most to this prediction. Note that the prediction t_j might not be $\arg\max_{t_j} p(t_j \mid \mathbf{t}_{1:j-1})$, as the locally optimal option may be pruned during beam search and not end up in the final translation.

Under this framework, we can see an important conceptual problem regarding interpreting attention weights as word alignment. Suppose for the same source sentence, there are two alternative translations that diverge at target time step j, generating t_j and t_j' which respectively correspond to different source words. Presumably, the source word that is aligned to t_j and t_j' should changed correspondingly. However, this is not possible with the attention weight interpretation, because the attention weight is computed *before* prediction of t_j or t_j'. With that, we argue that an ideal interpretation algorithm should be able to adapt the interpretation with the specified output label, regard-

less of whether it is the most likely label predicted by the model.

As a final note, the term "attention weights" here refers to the weights of the attention between encoder and decoder (the "encoder-decoder attention" in Vaswani et al. (2017)). Specifically, they do not refer to the weight of *self-attention* modules that only exist in the Transformer architecture, which do not establish alignment between the source and target words.

4 Method

Our proposal is based on the notion of visual saliency (Simonyan et al., 2013) in computer vision. In brief, the saliency of an input feature is defined by the partial gradient of the output score with regard to the input. We propose to extend this idea to NMT by drawing analogy between input pixels and the embedding look-up operation.

4.1 Visual Saliency

Suppose we have an image classification example $(\mathbf{x_0}, y_0)$, with y_0 being a specific image class and $\mathbf{x_0}$ being an $|\mathcal{X}|$-dimensional vector. Each entry of $\mathbf{x_0}$ is an input feature (i.e., a pixel) to the classifier. Given the input $\mathbf{x_0}$, a trained classifier can generate a prediction score for class y_0, denoted as $p(y_0 \mid \mathbf{x_0})$. Consider the first-order Taylor expansion of a perturbed version of this score at the neighborhood of input $\mathbf{x_0}$:

$$p(y_0 \mid \mathbf{x}) \approx p(y_0 \mid \mathbf{x_0}) + \left.\frac{\partial p(y_0 \mid \mathbf{x})}{\partial \mathbf{x}}\right|_{\mathbf{x_0}} \cdot (\mathbf{x} - \mathbf{x_0}) \tag{1}$$

This is essentially re-formulating the perturbed prediction score $p(y_0 \mid \mathbf{x})$ as an affine approximation of the input features, while the "contribution" of each feature to the final prediction being the partial derivative of the prediction score with regard to the feature. Assuming a feature that is deemed as salient for the local perturbation of the prediction score would also be globally salient, the saliency of an input feature is defined as follows:

Definition 1 *Denoted as* $\mathbf{\Psi}(\mathbf{x}, y)$, *the saliency of feature vector* $\mathbf{x}$ *with regard to output class* y *is defined as* $\dfrac{\partial p(y \mid \mathbf{x})}{\partial \mathbf{x}}$.

Note that $\mathbf{\Psi}(\mathbf{x}, y)$ is also a vector, with each entry corresponding to the saliency of a single input feature in $\mathbf{x}$. Such formulation has following nice properties:

- The saliency of an input feature is related to the choice of output class y, as model scores of different output classes correspond to a different set of parameters, and hence resulting in different partial gradients for the input features. This makes up for the aforementioned deficiency of attention weights in addressing the interpretation problem.

- The partial gradient could be computed by back-propagation, which is efficiently implemented in most deep learning frameworks.

- The formulation is agnostic to the model that generates $p(y \mid \mathbf{x})$, so it could be applied to any deep learning architecture.

4.2 Word Saliency

In computer vision, the input feature is a 3D Tensor corresponding to the level in each channel. The key question to apply such method to NMT is what constitutes the input feature to a NMT system. Li et al. (2016) proposed to use the embedding of of the input words as the input feature to formulate saliency score, which results in the saliency of an input word being a vector of the same dimension as embedding vectors. To obtain a scalar saliency value, they computed the mean of the absolute value of the embedding gradients. We argue that there is a more mathematically principled way to approach this.

To start, we treat the word embedding look-up operation as a dot product between the embedding weight matrix $\mathbf{W}$ and an one-hot vector $\mathbf{z}$. The size of $\mathbf{z}$ is the same as the source vocabulary size. Similarly, the input sentence could be formulated as a matrix $\mathbf{Z}$ with only 0 and 1 entries. Notice that $\mathbf{z}$ has certain resemblance to the pixels of an image, with each cell representing the pixel-wise activation level of the words in the vocabulary. For the output word t_j at time step j, we can similarly define the saliency of the one-hot vector $\mathbf{z}$ as:

$$\Psi(\mathbf{z}, t_j) = \frac{\partial p(t_j \mid \mathbf{Z})}{\partial \mathbf{z}} \quad (2)$$

where $p(t_j \mid \mathbf{Z})$ is the probability of word t_j generated by the NMT model given source sentence $\mathbf{Z}$. $\Psi(\mathbf{z}, t_j)$ is a vector of the same size as $\mathbf{z}$.

However, note that there is a key difference between $\mathbf{z}$ and pixels. If the pixel level is 0, it means that the pixel is black, while a 0-entry in $\mathbf{z}$ means that the input word is not the word denoted by the corresponding cell. While the black region of

an input image may still carry important information, we are not interested in the saliency of the 0-entries in $\mathbf{z}$.[1] Hence, we only take the 1-entries of matrix $\mathbf{Z}$ as the input to the NMT model. For a source word s_i in the source sentence, this means we only care about the saliency of the 1-entries, i.e., the entry corresponding to source word s_i:

$$
\begin{aligned}
\psi(s_i, t_j) &= \left[\frac{\partial p(t_j \mid \mathbf{Z})}{\partial \mathbf{z}} \right]_{s_i} \\
&= \left[\frac{\partial p(t_j \mid \mathbf{Z})}{\partial \mathbf{W}_{\mathbf{s_i}}} \cdot \frac{\partial \mathbf{W}_{\mathbf{s_i}}}{\partial \mathbf{z}} \right]_{s_i} \\
&= \left[\frac{\partial p(t_j \mid \mathbf{Z})}{\partial \mathbf{W}_{\mathbf{s_i}}} \cdot \mathbf{W} \right]_{s_i} \\
&= \frac{\partial p(t_j \mid \mathbf{Z})}{\partial \mathbf{W}_{\mathbf{s_i}}} \cdot \mathbf{W}_{\mathbf{s_i}} \quad (3)
\end{aligned}
$$

where $[\cdot]_i$ denotes the i-th row of a matrix or the i-th element of a vector. In other words, the saliency $\psi(s_i, t_j)$ is a weighted sum of the word embedding of input word s_i, with the partial gradient of each cell as the weight. By comparison, the word saliency[2] in Li et al. (2016) is defined as:

$$\psi'(s_i, t_j) = \text{mean}\left(\left| \frac{\partial p(t_j \mid \mathbf{Z})}{\partial \mathbf{W}_{\mathbf{s_i}}} \right| \right) \quad (4)$$

There are two implementation details that we would like to call for the reader's attention:

- When the same word occurs multiple times in the source sentence, multiple copies of embedding for such word need to be made to ensure that the gradients flowing to different instances of the same word are not merged;

- Note that $\psi(s_i, t_j)$ is not a probability distribution, which does not affect word alignment results because we are taking $\arg \max$. For visualizations presented herein, we normalized the distribution by $p(s_i \mid t_j) \propto \max(0, \psi(s_i, t_j))$. One may also use softmax function for applications that need more well-formed probability distribution.

---

[1] Although we introduce $\mathbf{z}$ to facilitate presentation, note that word embedding look-up is never implemented as a matrix multiplication. Instead, it is implemented as a table look-up, so for each input word, only one row of the word embedding is fed into the subsequent computation. As a consequence, during training, since the other rows are not part of the computation graph, only parameters in the rows corresponding to the 1-entries will be updated. This is another reason why we choose to discard the saliency of 0-entries.

[2] Li et al. (2016) mostly focused on studying saliency on the level of word embedding dimensions. This word-level formulation is proposed as part of the analysis in Section 5.2 and Section 6 of that work.

4.3 SmoothGrad

There are two scenarios where the naïve gradient-based saliency may make mistakes:

- For highly non-linear models, the saliency obtained from local perturbation may not be a good representation of the global saliency.
- If the model fits the distribution nearly perfectly, some data points or input features may become *saturated*, i.e. having a partial gradient of 0. This does not necessarily mean they are not salient with regard to the prediction.

We alleviate these problems with SmoothGrad, a method proposed by Smilkov et al. (2017). The idea is to augment the input to the network into n samples by adding random noise generated by normal distribution $\mathcal{N}(0, \sigma^2)$. The saliency scores of each augmented sample are then averaged to cancel out the noise in the gradients.

We made one small modification to this method in our experiments: rather than adding noise to the word inputs that are represented as one-hot vectors, we instead add noise to the queried embedding vectors. This allows us to introduce more randomness for each word input.

5 Experiments

5.1 Evaluation Method

The best evaluation method would compare predicted word alignments against manually labeled word alignments between source sentences and NMT output sentences, but this is too costly for our study. Instead, we conduct two automatic evaluations for our proposed method using resources available:

- *force decoding*: take a human-annotated corpus, run NMT models to force-generate the target side of the corpus and measure AER against the human alignment;
- *free decoding*: take the NMT prediction, obtain reasonably clean reference alignments between the prediction and the source and measure AER against this reference.[3]

Notice that both automatic evaluation methods have their respective limitation: the force decoding method may force the model to predict something it deems unlikely, and thus generating noisy

alignment; whereas the free decoding method lacks authentic references.

5.2 Setup

We follow Zenkel et al. (2019) in data setup and use the accompanied scripts of that paper[4] for preprocessing. Their training data consists of 1.9M, 1.1M and 0.4M sentence pairs for German-English (de-en), English-French (en-fr) and Romanian-English (ro-en) language pairs, respectively, whereas the manually-aligned test data contains 508, 447 and 248 sentence pairs for each language pair. There is no development data provided in their setup, and it is not clear what they used for NMT system training, so we set aside the last 1,000 sentences of the training data for each language as the development set.

For our NMT systems, we use fairseq[5] to train attention-based RNN systems (**LSTM**) (Bahdanau et al., 2014), convolution systems (**FConv**) (Gehring et al., 2017), and Transformer systems (**Transformer**) (Vaswani et al., 2017). We use the pre-configured model architectures for IWSLT German-English experiments[6] to build all NMT systems. Our experiments cover the following interpretation methods:

- *Attention*: directly take the attention weights as soft alignment scores. For transformer, we follow the implementation in fairseq and used the attention weights from the final layer averaged across all heads;
- *Smoothed Attention*: obtain multiple version of attention weights with the same data augmentation procedure as SmoothGrad and average them. This is to prove that smoothing itself does not improve the interpretation quality, and has to be used together with effective interpretation method;
- (Li et al., 2016): applied with normal back-propagation (*Grad*) and *SmoothGrad*;
- Ours: applied with normal back-propagation (*Grad*) and *SmoothGrad*.

For all the methods above, we follow the same procedure in (Zenkel et al., 2019) to convert soft alignment scores to hard alignment.

---

[3] Our reference alignment construction process is as follows: we first run automatic alignment on both sides, and take the intersection of the two outputs as "sure" alignments and the rest as "possible" alignments.

[4] https://github.com/lilt/alignment-scripts
[5] https://github.com/pytorch/fairseq
[6] The exact model options we used are respectively fconv_iwslt_de_en, lstm_wiseman _iwslt_de_en, transformer_iwslt_de_en.

	de<>en			fr<>en			ro<>en		
	de-en	en-de	bidir	en-fr	fr-en	bidir	ro-en	en-ro	bidir
FConv									
Attention	38.5	40.1	37.5	23.8	27.4	22.0	40.9	38.6	39.1
Smoothed Attention	40.2	43.9	41.2	24.1	27.4	22.5	41.5	39.6	40.4
(Li et al., 2016) Grad	39.0	39.6	35.3	26.8	29.2	21.1	41.9	42.1	38.6
(Li et al., 2016) SmoothGrad	40.7	44.5	39.3	27.3	28.1	21.6	43.5	43.5	40.0
Ours Grad	33.1	40.5	26.8	25.2	22.7	11.9	37.1	39.4	29.8
Ours SmoothGrad	<u>27.3</u>	<u>33.0</u>	<u>22.3</u>	<u>21.2</u>	<u>18.1</u>	<u>8.5</u>	<u>32.4</u>	<u>34.2</u>	<u>27.2</u>
LSTM									
Attention	42.8	47.5	36.9	33.7	38.0	25.8	47.1	47.0	40.9
Smoothed Attention	47.3	50.7	40.0	35.4	40.2	27.5	50.7	50.2	43.5
(Li et al., 2016) Grad	41.0	43.9	33.5	32.9	37.1	23.5	44.5	44.9	37.5
(Li et al., 2016) SmoothGrad	39.4	43.1	31.5	32.2	36.2	22.0	45.7	46.8	37.7
Ours Grad	47.5	50.2	38.6	41.1	41.6	30.4	54.2	55.8	42.8
Ours SmoothGrad	<u>31.4</u>	<u>36.8</u>	<u>23.7</u>	<u>27.2</u>	<u>25.0</u>	<u>13.8</u>	<u>40.4</u>	<u>39.9</u>	<u>32.0</u>
Transformer									
Attention	53.4	58.6	42.3	48.1	48.7	33.8	51.6	51.1	43.3
Smoothed Attention	55.8	56.1	48.6	42.5	47.5	32.9	57.5	57.6	51.5
(Li et al., 2016) Grad	51.1	56.2	43.7	43.6	47.9	39.9	46.7	48.4	35.5
(Li et al., 2016) SmoothGrad	<u>36.4</u>	45.8	30.3	<u>27.0</u>	<u>25.5</u>	15.6	41.3	<u>39.9</u>	33.7
Ours Grad	77.7	78.2	77.4	69.1	72.5	74.5	74.6	75.2	71.0
Ours SmoothGrad	*<u>36.4</u>	<u>43.0</u>	*<u>29.0</u>	29.7	25.9	<u>15.3</u>	<u>41.2</u>	41.4	<u>32.7</u>
fast-align Offline	28.4	32.0	27.0	16.4	15.9	10.5	33.8	35.5	32.1
fast-align Online	30.8	34.4	30.0	18.8	16.8	13.6	37.1	41.1	35.9
(Zenkel et al., 2019)	26.6	30.4	**21.2**	23.8	20.5	10.0	32.3	34.8	**27.6**
GIZA++	**21.0**	**23.1**	21.4	**8.0**	**9.8**	**5.9**	**28.7**	**32.2**	27.9

Table 1: Alignment Error Rate (AER) with different saliency methods, under *force decoding* setting. GIZA++ and fast-align Offline results are quoted from Zenkel et al. (2019), whereas fast-align Online stands for our online alignment result (c.f. Section 5.2). *bidir* refers to the symmetrized alignment results. Best results for each architecture are marked with underlines, and best interpretation/alignment results are respectively marked with boldface. Numbers affected by hyper-parameter tuning are marked with *.

For *force decoding* experiments, we generate symmetrized alignment results with `grow-diag-final`. We also include AER results[7] of fast-align (Dyer et al., 2013), GIZA++[8] and the best model (Add+SGD) from Zenkel et al. (2019) on the same dataset for comparison. However, the readers should be aware that there are certain caveats in this comparison:

- All of these models are specifically designed and optimized to generate high-quality alignments, while our method is an *interpretation* method and is not making any architecture modifications or parameter updates;
- fast-align and GIZA++ usually need to update model with full sentence to generate optimal alignments, while our system and Zenkel et al. (2019) can do so on-the-fly.

Realizing the second caveat, we also run fast-align under the *online* alignment scenario, where we first train a fast-align model and decode on the test set. This is a real-world scenario in applications such as computer-aided translation (Bouma and Parmentier, 2014; Arcan et al., 2014), where we cannot practically update alignment models on-the-fly. On the other hand, we believe this is a slightly better comparison for methods with online alignment capabilities such as Zenkel et al. (2019) and this work.

The data used in Zenkel et al. (2019) did not provide a manually-aligned development set, so we tune the SmoothGrad hyperparameters (noise standard deviation σ and sample size n) on a 30-sentence subset of the German-English test data with the Transformer model. We ended up using the recommended $\sigma = 0.15$ in the original paper and a slightly smaller sample size $n = 30$ for speed. This hyperparameter setting is applied to the other SmoothGrad experiments as-is. For com-

---

[7] We reproduced the fast-align results as a sanity check and we were able to perfectly replicate their numbers with their released scripts.

[8] https://github.com/moses-smt/giza-pp

parison with previous work, we do not exclude these sentences from the reported results, we instead mark the numbers affected to raise caution.

5.3 Force Decoding Results

Table 1 shows the AER results under the *force decoding* setting. First, note that after applying our saliency method with normal back-propagation, AER is only reduced for FConv model but instead increases for LSTM and Transformer. The largest increase is observed for Transformer, where the AER increases by about 20 points on average. However, after applying SmoothGrad on top of that, we observe a sharp drop in AER, which ends up with 10-20 points lower than the attention weight baseline. We can also see that this is not just an effect introduced by input noise, as the same smoothing procedure for attention increases the AER most of the times. To summarize, at least under *force decoding* settings, our saliency method with SmoothGrad obtains word alignment interpretations of much higher quality than the attention weight baseline.

As for Li et al. (2016), for FConv and LSTM architectures, it is not only consistently worse than our method, but at times also worse than attention. Besides, the effect of SmoothGrad is also not as consistent on their saliency formulation as ours. Although with the Transformer model, the Li et al. (2016) method obtained better AER than our method under several settings, it is still pretty clear overall that the superior mathematical soundness of our method is translated into better interpretation quality.

While the GIZA++ model obtains the best alignment result in Table 1[9], most of our word alignment interpretation of FConv model with Smooth-Grad surpasses the alignment quality of fast-align (either Online or Offline), sometimes by as much as 8.7 points (symmetrized ro<>en result). Our best models are also largely on-par with (Zenkel et al., 2019). These are notable results as our method is an interpretation method and no extra parameter is updated to optimize the quality of alignment. On the other hand, this also indicates that it is possible to induce high-quality

---

[9]While Ghader and Monz (2017) showed that the AER obtained by LSTM model is close to that of GIZA++, our experiments yield a much larger difference. We think this is largely due to the fact that we choose to train our model with BPE, while Ghader and Monz (2017) explicitly avoided doing so.

alignments from NMT model without modifying its parameters, showing that it has acquired such information in an implicit way. Most interestingly, although NMT is often deemed as performing poorly under low-resource setting, our interpretation seems to work relatively well on ro<>en language pair, which happens to be the language pair that we have least training data for. We think this is a phenomenon that merits further exploration.

Besides, it can be seen that for all reported methods, the overall order for the number of alignment errors is FConv < LSTM < Transformer. To our best knowledge, this is also a novel insight, as no one has analyzed attention weights of FConv with other architectures before. We can also observe that while our method is not strong enough to fully bridge the gap of the attention noise level between different model architecture, it does manage to narrow the difference in some cases.

5.4 Free Decoding Results

Table 2 shows the result under *free decoding setting*. The trend in this group of experiment is similar to Table 1, except that Transformer occasionally outperforms LSTM. We think this is mainly due to the fact that Transformer generates higher quality translations, but could also be partially attributed to the noise in fast-align reference. Also, notice that the AER numbers are also generally lower compared to Table 1 under this setting. One reason is that our model is aligning output with which it is most confident, so less noise should be expected in the model behavior. On the other hand, by qualitatively comparing the reference translation in the test set and the NMT output, we find that it is generally easier to align the translation as it is often a more literal translation.

6 Analysis

6.1 Comparison with Li et al. (2016)

The main reason why the word saliency formulation in Li et al. (2016) does not work as well for word alignment is the lack of polarity in the formulation. In other words, it only quantifies how much the input influences the output, but does not specify *in what way* does the input influence. This is sufficient for error analysis, but does not suit the purpose of word alignment, as humans will only align a target word to the input words that constitute a translation pair, i.e. have positive influence.

	de-en	en-de	en-fr	fr-en	ro-en	en-ro
FConv						
Attention	27.4	24.2	20.7	23.6	32.5	25.6
Smoothed Attention	29.4	29.0	21.1	23.6	33.7	26.7
(Li et al., 2016) Grad	29.3	23.5	25.0	23.7	33.9	27.9
(Li et al., 2016) SmoothGrad	31.2	30.4	24.1	24.0	35.6	30.1
Ours Grad	18.2	20.0	20.2	14.3	24.9	22.8
Ours SmoothGrad	**13.7**	**14.2**	**17.0**	**10.6**	**21.4**	**17.4**
LSTM						
Attention	33.6	34.6	32.5	32.3	36.5	31.7
Smoothed Attention	38.2	39.5	34.3	35.2	41.2	36.3
(Li et al., 2016) Grad	34.1	32.5	33.6	33.7	36.6	32.1
(Li et al., 2016) SmoothGrad	30.8	29.4	31.8	32.1	38.9	34.8
Ours Grad	35.9	36.7	40.2	36.3	44.1	43.1
Ours SmoothGrad	<u>20.5</u>	<u>21.9</u>	<u>26.0</u>	<u>19.1</u>	<u>32.6</u>	<u>27.5</u>
Transformer						
Attention	50.2	53.0	50.4	48.5	44.9	41.9
Smoothed Attention	51.4	49.0	44.5	47.3	49.9	48.9
(Li et al., 2016) Grad	49.9	51.2	49.4	51.5	42.9	40.8
(Li et al., 2016) SmoothGrad	27.8	35.3	<u>28.3</u>	22.3	30.5	<u>26.5</u>
Ours Grad	76.7	76.6	77.1	78.9	71.9	74.0
Ours SmoothGrad	*26.6	<u>31.0</u>	30.0	<u>21.4</u>	<u>30.0</u>	28.2

Table 2: Alignment Error Rate (AER) with different saliency models, under *free decoding* setting. See the caption of Table 1 for notations.

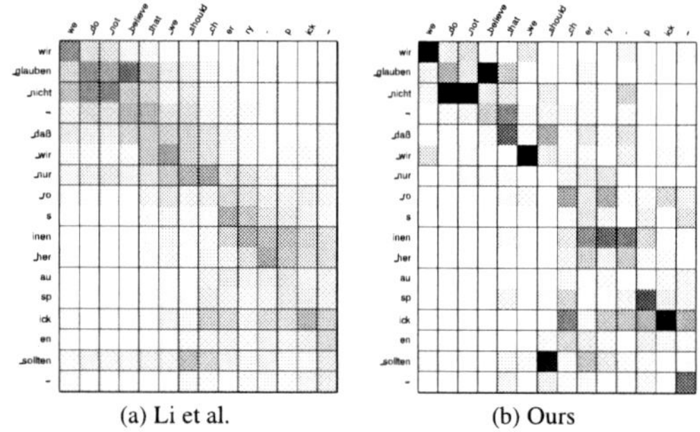

(a) Li et al.   (b) Ours

Figure 2: Saliency interpretation of FConv de-en model with the method in Li et al. (2016) and this paper. SmoothGrad ($\sigma = 0.15$, $n = 30$) is applied for both interpretations.

Figure 2 shows a case where this problem occurs in our German-English experiments. Note that in Subfigure (a), the source word *nur* has high saliency on several target words, e.g. *should*, but the word *nur* is actually not translated in the reference. On the other hand, as shown in Subfigure (b), our method correctly assigns negative (shown as white) or small positive values at all time steps for this source word. Specifically, the saliency value of *nur* for *should* is negative with large magnitude, indicating significant negative contributions to the prediction of that target word. Hence, a good word alignment interpreta-

tion should strongly avoid aligning them.

6.2 SmoothGrad

Tables 1 and 2 show that SmoothGrad is a crucial factor to reduce AER, especially for Transformer. Figure 3 shows the interpretation of the same German-English sentence pair by our proposed method, but with Transformer and different SmoothGrad noise levels. Specifically, Subfigures (a) and (c) corresponds to our Grad and SmoothGrad experiments in Table 1. By comparing Subfigures (a) and (c), we notice that (1) without SmoothGrad, the word saliency obtained from the Transformer model is extremely noisy, and (2) the output of SmoothGrad is not only a smoother version of the naïve gradient output, but also gains new information by performing extra forward and backward evaluations with the noisy input. For example, compare the alignment point between source word *wir* and target word *we*: in Subfigure (a), this word pair has very low saliency, but in (c), they become the most likely alignment pair for that target word.

Referring back to our motivation for using SmoothGrad in Section 4.3, we think the observations above verify that the Transformer model is a case where very high non-linearities occur almost everywhere in the parameter space, such that the saliency obtained from local perturbation is a very

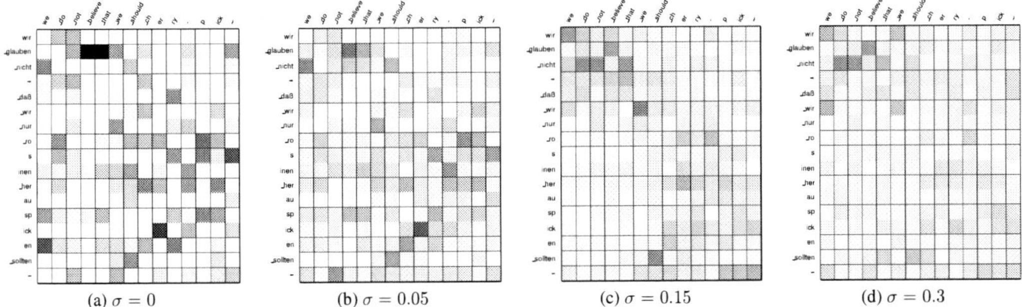

(a) $\sigma = 0$ (b) $\sigma = 0.05$ (c) $\sigma = 0.15$ (d) $\sigma = 0.3$

Figure 3: Saliency interpretation of Transformer de-en model with different SmoothGrad noise values σ ($n = 30$).

	att	$\sigma = 0$	$\sigma = 0.05$	$\sigma = 0.15$	$\sigma = 0.3$
FConv					
force	2.09	1.36	1.48	1.89	2.59
free	2.00	1.34	1.43	1.79	2.54
LSTM					
force	1.75	1.63	2.02	2.54	2.89
free	1.65	1.57	1.91	2.46	2.88
Transformer					
force	1.73	1.91	2.63	2.76	2.85
free	1.69	1.89	2.62	2.74	2.84

Table 3: Alignment distribution entropy for selected de-en models. **att** stands for attention in Table 1.

poor representation of the global saliency almost all the time. On the other hand, this is also why the Transformer especially relies on SmoothGrad to work well, as the perturbation will give a better estimation of the global saliency.

It could also be observed from Subfigures (b) and (d) that when the noise is too moderate, the evaluation does not deviate enough from the original spot to gain non-local information, and at (d) it deviates too much and hence the resulting alignment is almost random. Intuitively, the noise parameter σ should be sensitive to the model architecture or even specific input feature values, but interestingly we end up finding that a single choice from the computer vision literature works well with all of our systems. We encourage future work to conduct more comprehensive analysis of the effect of SmoothGrad on more complicated architectures beyond convolutional neural nets.

6.3 Alignment Dispersion

We run German-English alignments under several different SmoothGrad noise deviation σ and report their dispersion as measured by entropy of the (soft) alignment distribution averaged by number of target words. Results are summarized in Ta-

ble 3, where lower entropy indicates more peaky alignments. First, we observe that dispersion of word saliency gets higher as we increase σ, which aligns with the observations in Figure 3. It should also be noted that the alignment dispersion is consistently lower for *free decoding* than *force decoding*. This verifies our conjecture that the *force decoding* setting might introduce more noise in the model behavior, but judging from this result, that gap seems to be minimal. Comparing different architectures, the dispersion of attention weights does not correlate well with the dispersion of word saliency. We also notice that, while the Transformer attention interpretation consistently results in higher AER, its dispersion is lower than the other architectures, indicating that with attention, a lot of the probability mass might be concentrated in the wrong place more often. This corroborates the finding in Raganato and Tiedemann (2018).

7 Discussion And Future Work

There are several extensions to this work that we would like to discuss in this section. First, in this paper we only explored two saliency methods among many others available (Montavon et al., 2018). In our preliminary study, we also experimented with guided back-propagation (Springenberg et al., 2014), a frequently used saliency method in computer vision, which did not work well for our problem. We suspect that there is a gap between applying these methods on mostly-convolutional architectures in computer vision and architectures with more non-linearities in NLP. We hope the future research from the NLP and machine learning communities could bridge this gap.

Secondly, the alignment errors in our method comes from three different sources: the limitation of NMT models on learning word alignments, the

9

limitation of interpretation method on recovering interpretable word alignments, and the ambiguity in word alignments itself. Although we have shown that high quality alignment could be recovered from NMT systems (thus pushing our understanding on the limitation of NMT models), we are not yet able to separate these sources of errors in this work. While exploration on this direction will help us better understand both NMT models and the capability of saliency methods in NLP, researchers may want to avoid using word alignment as a benchmark for saliency methods because of its ambiguity. For such purpose, simpler tasks with clear ground truth, such as subject-verb agreement, might be a better choice.

Finally, as mentioned before, we are only conducting approximate evaluation to measure the ability of our interpretation method. An immediate future work would be evaluating this on human-annotated translation outputs generated by the NMT system.

8 Conclusion

We propose to use word saliency and SmoothGrad to interpret word alignments from NMT predictions. Our proposal is model-agnostic, is able to be applied either offline or online, and does not require any parameter updates or architectural change. Both *force decoding* and *free decoding* evaluations show that our method is capable of generating word alignment interpretations of much higher quality compared to its attention-based counterpart. Our empirical results also probe into the NMT black-box and reveal that even without any special architecture or training algorithm, some NMT models have already implicitly learned interpretable word alignments of comparable quality to fast-align. The model and code for our experiments are available at `https://github.com/shuoyangd/meerkat`.

Acknowledgements

The authors would like to thank Matt Post for helpful feedback on an earlier draft of this work, and the authors of Zenkel et al. (2019) for efforts in making their results easily reproducible. This material is based upon work supported in part by the DARPA LORELEI and IARPA MATERIAL programs.

References

Tamer Alkhouli, Gabriel Bretschner, and Hermann Ney. 2018. On the alignment problem in multi-head attention-based neural machine translation. In *Proceedings of the Third Conference on Machine Translation: Research Papers, WMT 2018, Belgium, Brussels, October 31 - November 1, 2018*, pages 177–185.

Mihael Arcan, Marco Turchi, Sara Tonelli, and Paul Buitelaar. 2014. Enhancing statistical machine translation with bilingual terminology in a cat environment. In *Proceedings of the 11th Biennial Conference of the Association for Machine Translation in the Americas (AMTA 2014)*, pages 54–68.

Sebastian Bach, Alexander Binder, Grégoire Montavon, Frederick Klauschen, Klaus-Robert Müller, and Wojciech Samek. 2015. On pixel-wise explanations for non-linear classifier decisions by layer-wise relevance propagation. *PloS one*, 10(7):e0130140.

Dzmitry Bahdanau, Kyunghyun Cho, and Yoshua Bengio. 2014. Neural machine translation by jointly learning to align and translate. *CoRR*, abs/1409.0473.

Gosse Bouma and Yannick Parmentier, editors. 2014. *Proceedings of the 14th Conference of the European Chapter of the Association for Computational Linguistics, EACL 2014, April 26-30, 2014, Gothenburg, Sweden*. The Association for Computer Linguistics.

Peter F. Brown, Stephen Della Pietra, Vincent J. Della Pietra, and Robert L. Mercer. 1993. The mathematics of statistical machine translation: Parameter estimation. *Computational Linguistics*, 19(2):263–311.

William Chan, Navdeep Jaitly, Quoc V. Le, and Oriol Vinyals. 2016. Listen, attend and spell: A neural network for large vocabulary conversational speech recognition. In *2016 IEEE International Conference on Acoustics, Speech and Signal Processing, ICASSP 2016, Shanghai, China, March 20-25, 2016*, pages 4960–4964.

Jan Chorowski, Dzmitry Bahdanau, Dmitriy Serdyuk, Kyunghyun Cho, and Yoshua Bengio. 2015. Attention-based models for speech recognition. In *Advances in Neural Information Processing Systems 28: Annual Conference on Neural Information Processing Systems 2015, December 7-12, 2015, Montreal, Quebec, Canada*, pages 577–585.

Yanzhuo Ding, Yang Liu, Huanbo Luan, and Maosong Sun. 2017. Visualizing and understanding neural machine translation. In *Proceedings of the 55th Annual Meeting of the Association for Computational Linguistics, ACL 2017, Vancouver, Canada, July 30 - August 4, Volume 1: Long Papers*, pages 1150–1159.

Chris Dyer, Victor Chahuneau, and Noah A. Smith. 2013. A simple, fast, and effective reparameterization of IBM model 2. In *Human Language Technologies: Conference of the North American Chapter of the Association of Computational Linguistics, Proceedings, June 9-14, 2013, Westin Peachtree Plaza Hotel, Atlanta, Georgia, USA*, pages 644–648.

Jonas Gehring, Michael Auli, David Grangier, Denis Yarats, and Yann N. Dauphin. 2017. Convolutional sequence to sequence learning. In *Proceedings of the 34th International Conference on Machine Learning, ICML 2017, Sydney, NSW, Australia, 6-11 August 2017*, pages 1243–1252.

Hamidreza Ghader and Christof Monz. 2017. What does attention in neural machine translation pay attention to? In *Proceedings of the Eighth International Joint Conference on Natural Language Processing, IJCNLP 2017, Taipei, Taiwan, November 27 - December 1, 2017 - Volume 1: Long Papers*, pages 30–39.

Eva Hasler, Adrià de Gispert, Gonzalo Iglesias, and Bill Byrne. 2018. Neural machine translation decoding with terminology constraints. In *Proceedings of the 2018 Conference of the North American Chapter of the Association for Computational Linguistics: Human Language Technologies, NAACL-HLT, New Orleans, Louisiana, USA, June 1-6, 2018, Volume 2 (Short Papers)*, pages 506–512.

Philipp Koehn and Rebecca Knowles. 2017. Six challenges for neural machine translation. In *Proceedings of the First Workshop on Neural Machine Translation, NMT@ACL 2017, Vancouver, Canada, August 4, 2017*, pages 28–39.

Philipp Koehn, Franz Josef Och, and Daniel Marcu. 2003. Statistical phrase-based translation. In *Human Language Technology Conference of the North American Chapter of the Association for Computational Linguistics, HLT-NAACL 2003, Edmonton, Canada, May 27 - June 1, 2003*.

Jaesong Lee, Joong-Hwi Shin, and Jun-Seok Kim. 2017. Interactive visualization and manipulation of attention-based neural machine translation. In *Proceedings of the 2017 Conference on Empirical Methods in Natural Language Processing, EMNLP 2017, Copenhagen, Denmark, September 9-11, 2017 - System Demonstrations*, pages 121–126.

Joël Legrand, Michael Auli, and Ronan Collobert. 2016. Neural network-based word alignment through score aggregation. In *Proceedings of the First Conference on Machine Translation, WMT 2016, colocated with ACL 2016, August 11-12, Berlin, Germany*, pages 66–73.

Jiwei Li, Xinlei Chen, Eduard H. Hovy, and Dan Jurafsky. 2016. Visualizing and understanding neural models in NLP. In *NAACL HLT 2016, The 2016 Conference of the North American Chapter of the Association for Computational Linguistics: Human Language Technologies, San Diego California, USA, June 12-17, 2016*, pages 681–691.

Lemao Liu, Masao Utiyama, Andrew M. Finch, and Eiichiro Sumita. 2016. Neural machine translation with supervised attention. In *COLING 2016, 26th International Conference on Computational Linguistics, Proceedings of the Conference: Technical Papers, December 11-16, 2016, Osaka, Japan*, pages 3093–3102.

Thang Luong, Hieu Pham, and Christopher D. Manning. 2015. Effective approaches to attention-based neural machine translation. In *Proceedings of the 2015 Conference on Empirical Methods in Natural Language Processing, EMNLP 2015, Lisbon, Portugal, September 17-21, 2015*, pages 1412–1421.

Haitao Mi, Zhiguo Wang, and Abe Ittycheriah. 2016. Supervised attentions for neural machine translation. In *Proceedings of the 2016 Conference on Empirical Methods in Natural Language Processing, EMNLP 2016, Austin, Texas, USA, November 1-4, 2016*, pages 2283–2288.

Grégoire Montavon, Wojciech Samek, and Klaus-Robert Müller. 2018. Methods for interpreting and understanding deep neural networks. *Digital Signal Processing*, 73:1–15.

Toan Q. Nguyen and David Chiang. 2018. Improving lexical choice in neural machine translation. In *Proceedings of the 2018 Conference of the North American Chapter of the Association for Computational Linguistics: Human Language Technologies, NAACL-HLT 2018, New Orleans, Louisiana, USA, June 1-6, 2018, Volume 1 (Long Papers)*, pages 334–343.

Franz Josef Och and Hermann Ney. 2003. A systematic comparison of various statistical alignment models. *Computational Linguistics*, 29(1):19–51.

Ankur P. Parikh, Oscar Täckström, Dipanjan Das, and Jakob Uszkoreit. 2016. A decomposable attention model for natural language inference. In *Proceedings of the 2016 Conference on Empirical Methods in Natural Language Processing, EMNLP 2016, Austin, Texas, USA, November 1-4, 2016*, pages 2249–2255.

Alessandro Raganato and Jörg Tiedemann. 2018. An analysis of encoder representations in transformer-based machine translation. In *Proceedings of the Workshop: Analyzing and Interpreting Neural Networks for NLP, BlackboxNLP@EMNLP 2018, Brussels, Belgium, November 1, 2018*, pages 287–297.

Alexander M. Rush, Sumit Chopra, and Jason Weston. 2015. A neural attention model for abstractive sentence summarization. In *Proceedings of the 2015 Conference on Empirical Methods in Natural Language Processing, EMNLP 2015, Lisbon, Portugal, September 17-21, 2015*, pages 379–389.

Abigail See, Peter J. Liu, and Christopher D. Manning. 2017. Get to the point: Summarization with pointer-generator networks. In *Proceedings of the 55th Annual Meeting of the Association for Computational*

Linguistics, ACL 2017, Vancouver, Canada, July 30 - August 4, Volume 1: Long Papers, pages 1073–1083.

Karen Simonyan, Andrea Vedaldi, and Andrew Zisserman. 2013. Deep inside convolutional networks: Visualising image classification models and saliency maps. *CoRR*, abs/1312.6034.

Daniel Smilkov, Nikhil Thorat, Been Kim, Fernanda B. Viégas, and Martin Wattenberg. 2017. Smoothgrad: removing noise by adding noise. *CoRR*, abs/1706.03825.

Jost Tobias Springenberg, Alexey Dosovitskiy, Thomas Brox, and Martin A. Riedmiller. 2014. Striving for simplicity: The all convolutional net. *CoRR*, abs/1412.6806.

Gongbo Tang, Mathias Müller, Annette Rios, and Rico Sennrich. 2018a. Why self-attention? A targeted evaluation of neural machine translation architectures. In *Proceedings of the 2018 Conference on Empirical Methods in Natural Language Processing, Brussels, Belgium, October 31 - November 4, 2018*, pages 4263–4272.

Gongbo Tang, Rico Sennrich, and Joakim Nivre. 2018b. An analysis of attention mechanisms: The case of word sense disambiguation in neural machine translation. In *Proceedings of the Third Conference on Machine Translation: Research Papers, WMT 2018, Belgium, Brussels, October 31 - November 1, 2018*, pages 26–35.

Ashish Vaswani, Noam Shazeer, Niki Parmar, Jakob Uszkoreit, Llion Jones, Aidan N. Gomez, Lukasz Kaiser, and Illia Polosukhin. 2017. Attention is all you need. In *Advances in Neural Information Processing Systems 30: Annual Conference on Neural Information Processing Systems 2017, 4-9 December 2017, Long Beach, CA, USA*, pages 6000–6010.

Weiyue Wang, Derui Zhu, Tamer Alkhouli, Zixuan Gan, and Hermann Ney. 2018. Neural hidden markov model for machine translation. In *Proceedings of the 56th Annual Meeting of the Association for Computational Linguistics, ACL 2018, Melbourne, Australia, July 15-20, 2018, Volume 2: Short Papers*, pages 377–382.

Thomas Zenkel, Joern Wuebker, and John DeNero. 2019. Adding interpretable attention to neural translation models improves word alignment. *CoRR*, abs/1901.11359.

Improving Zero-shot Translation with Language-Independent Constraints

Ngoc-Quan Pham[*] and **Jan Niehues**[+] and **Thanh-Le Ha**[+] and **Alex Waibel**[+]
[*] Karlsruhe Institute of Technology
{ngoc.pham, thanh-le.ha, alex.waibel}@kit.edu
[+] Maastricht University
jan.niehues@maastrichtuniversity.nl

Abstract

An important concern in training multilingual neural machine translation (NMT) is to translate between language pairs unseen during training, i.e zero-shot translation. Improving this ability kills two birds with one stone by providing an alternative to pivot translation which also allows us to better understand how the model captures information between languages.

In this work, we carried out an investigation on this capability of the multilingual NMT models. First, we intentionally create an encoder architecture which is independent with respect to the source language. Such experiments shed light on the ability of NMT encoders to learn multilingual representations, in general. Based on such proof of concept, we were able to design regularization methods into the standard Transformer model, so that the whole architecture becomes more robust in zero-shot conditions. We investigated the behaviour of such models on the standard IWSLT 2017 multilingual dataset. We achieved an average improvement of 2.23 BLEU points across 12 language pairs compared to the zero-shot performance of a state-of-the-art multilingual system. Additionally, we carry out further experiments in which the effect is confirmed even for language pairs with multiple intermediate pivots.

1 Introduction

Neural machine translation (NMT) exploits neural networks to directly learn to transform sentences from a source language to a target language (Sutskever et al., 2014; Bahdanau et al., 2014). Universal multilingual NMT discovered that a neural translation system can be trained on datasets containing source and target sentences in multiple languages (Firat et al., 2016; Johnson et al., 2016). Successfully trained models using this approach can be used to translate arbitrar-

ily between any languages included in the training data. In low-resource scenarios, multilingual NMT has proven to be an extremely useful regularization method since each language direction benefits from the information of the others (Ha et al., 2016; Gu et al., 2018).

An important research focus of multilingual NMT is zero-shot translation (ZS), or translation between languages included in multilingual data for which no directly parallel training data exists. Application-wise, ZS offers a faster and more direct path between languages compared to pivot translation, which requires translation to one or many intermediate languages. This can result in large latency and error propagation, common issues in non-end-to-end pipelines.From a representation learning point of view, there is evidence of NMT's ability to capture language-independent features, which have proved useful for cross-lingual transfer learning (Zoph et al., 2016; Kim et al., 2019) and provide motivation for ZS translation. However it is still unclear if minimizing the difference in representations between languages is beneficial for zero-shot learning.

On the other hand, the current neural architecture and learning mechanisms of multilingual NMT is not geared towards having a common representation. Different languages are likely to convey the same semantic content with sentences of different lengths (Kalchbrenner et al., 2016), which makes the desiderata difficult to achieve. Moreover, the loss function of the neural translation model does not favour having sentences encoded in the same representation space regardless of the source language. As a result, if the network capacity is large enough, it may partition itself into different sub-spaces for different language pairs (Arivazhagan et al., 2019).

Our work here focuses on the zero-shot translation aspect of universal multilingual NMT.

Proceedings of the Fourth Conference on Machine Translation (WMT), Volume 1: Research Papers, pages 13–23
Florence, Italy, August 1-2, 2019. ©2019 Association for Computational Linguistics

First, we attempt to investigate the relationship of encoder representation and ZS performance. By modifying the Transformer architecture of Vaswani et al. (2017) to afford a fixed-size representation for the encoder output, we found that we can significantly improve zero-shot performance at the cost of a lower performance on the supervised language pairs. To the best of our knowledge, this is the first empirical evidence showing that the multilingual model can capture both language-independent and language-dependent features, and that the former can be prioritized during training.

This observation leads us to the most important contribution in this work, which is to propose several techniques to learn a joint semantic space for different languages in multilingual models without any architectural modification. The key idea is to prefer a source language-independent representation in the decoder using an additional loss function. As a result, the NMT architecture remains untouched and the technique is scalable to the number of languages in the training data. The success of this method is shown by significant gains on zero-shot translation quality in the standard IWSLT 2017 multilingual benchmark (Cettolo et al., 2017). Finally, we introduce a more challenging scenario that involves more than one bridge language between source and target languages. This challenging setup confirms the consistency of our zero-shot techniques while clarifying the disadvantages of pivot-based translation.

2 Background: Multilingual Neural Machine Translation

Given an input sequence X and its translation Y, neural machine translation (NMT) uses sequence-to-sequence models (Sutskever et al., 2014) to directly model the posterior probability of generating Y from X.

Universal multilingual NMT expands the original bilingual setting by combining parallel corpora from multiple language pairs into one single corpus. By directly training the NMT model on this combined corpus, the model can be made to translate sentences from any seen source language into any seen target language. Notably, this multilingual framework does not yield any difference in the training objective, i.e maximizing the likelihood of the target sentence Y given the source

sentence X:

$$Loss(X, Y) = -P(Y|X) \qquad (1)$$

Previous work on universal NMT proposed different methods to control language generation. While source language identity may not be the concern, the decoder requires a target language signal to generate sentences in any desired language. Work from Ha et al. (2016) and Johnson et al. (2016) used the addition of language identity tokens in order to minimize architectural changes while controlling generation. Subsequently, stronger constraints were bestowed upon the decoder to force the correct language to be generated through language features or vocabulary filtering during decoding (Ha et al., 2017).

In practice, the number of language pairs in a multilingual corpus increases exponentially over the size of the language set. Therefore, a multilingual corpus rarely covers all of the language pairs involved, resulting in a need to investigate translation between the missing directions. The missing directions are referred as 'zero-shot translation' as the model has no access to any explicit parallel samples, naturally or artificially.

3 Proof of concept: Fixed-size encoder representations for language-independence

As the length of encoder representations depends on the source language, current architectures are not ideal to learn language-independent encoder representations. Therefore, we propose different architectures with fixed-size encoder representations. This also allows us to directly compare encoder representations of different languages, and to enforce such similarity through an additional loss function. This modification comes with the price of an information bottleneck due to the process of removing the length variability. On the other hand, it adds additional regularization which would naturally prioritize the features shared between languages.

Motivated by the literature in sentence embeddings (Schwenk and Douze, 2017; Wang et al., 2017), we take the average over time of the encoder states. Specifically, assume that X is the set of source embeddings input to the encoder:

$$\begin{aligned} H_v &= Encoder(X) \\ H_f &= mean\_pooling(H_v) \end{aligned} \qquad (2)$$

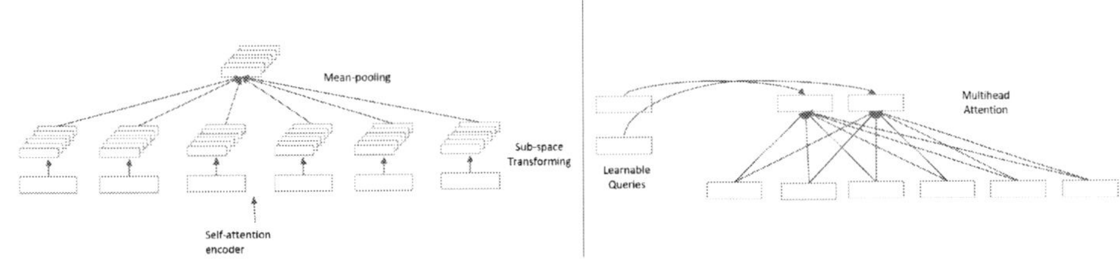

Figure 1: Fixed-size representations using multi-head mean-pooling (left) and attention-pooling (right).

The purpose of this modification is two-fold. First, this model explicitly opens more possibilities for language-independent representation to occur, because every sentence is compressed into a consistent number of states. Second, we can observe the balance between language-independent and language-dependent information in the encoder; if zero-shot performance is minimally affected, then the encoder is in general able to capture language-independent information, and this restricted encoder retains this information.

However, this model naturally has a disadvantage due to the introduced information bottleneck, similar to non-attention models (Sutskever et al., 2014; Kalchbrenner and Blunsom, 2013). We alleviate this problem by expanding the number of hidden states of the encoder output. As a result we investigate two variations of pooling as follows:

Multi-head Mean-Pooling While taking the average over time significantly reduces the model capacity, we can allocate more capacity for the model by linearly projecting the variable-length representation. By concatenating the pooled values from different sub-spaces, we obtain a fixed-size representation with the size $N \times H$. However, instead of learning to pay attention to input tokens normally, this decoder learns to distribute its focus into each mean-pooled embedding.

Multi-head Attention-Pooling The attention model is notable for its ability to extract relevant information from a sequence, which is an alternative to using pooling operators. However, self-attention is not within our architectural choices because the self-attention output has the same number of states with the input, while we need to restrict to a fixed set. We instead propose to set a fixed number of queries as learnable parameters for the model, so it will learn to extract necessary information from the sequence to include in the limited space. It is possible for this model to

converge to mean-pooling because these parameters are not as informative as either encoder or decoder states. However, our experiments later on have proven this does not occur in practice.

These two variations are illustrated in Figure 1. Here we investigate these models for the purpose of observing the relationship between encoder representations and zero-shot performance. Section 5 shows that, despite the fact that this model falls short against the baseline Transformer in non-zero-shot tests, we observed that the retained information in the bottleneck does not affect the performance of zero-shot translation, our motivation for the upcoming objectives.

Language-Independent Objective With constant length encoder output, we can now design an objective function using this advantage for language-independent representation. Hypothetically, for true multi-parallel data in which sentences from different languages are aligned, we can force the encoder outputs to be the same for the aligned sentences (newly enabled by the fixed state size). In other multilingual frameworks in which each data sample is bilingual, we exploit the fact that certain languages are shared between multiple language pairs (in order to enable zero-shot translation). As a result, by using such languages as a bridge, we can simply minimize the squared root deviation (i.e Min Squared Error - MSE) of the encoder representations between the bridge and other languages, and adding the regularization term $R(X, Y)$ to the loss function:

$$Loss(X, Y) = -P(Y|X) + \alpha(R(X, Y))$$
$$R(X, Y) = -(Encoder(X) - Encoder(Y))^2$$
$$(3)$$

In Equation 3, we ran the encoder on both languages. Assuming sentence X belongs to the bridge language, the loss function will lead to the similar representation of different sentences in other languages that were aligned with X. The difficulty lies in optimizing two objectives at once:

the second acts as a regularization because it prevents language-specific information from being included in the encoder output. As well, many multilingual corpora may not contain perfectly aligned sentences, which is a hindrance for language bridging.

4   Source Language-Independent Decoders

We have so far described our proposed method to learn language-independent features. We introduce the fixed-size states for the encoder and adds a regularization term to the NMT loss function to encourage similarity between encoder states. The problem with this method is the limiting factor of the fixed-size representations. With the standard architecture, while the length of the encoder states always depends on the source sentence, at each timestep the decoder only has access to a fixed representation of the encoder (context vector from attention). This observation suggests that forcing a decoder state to be independent of the source language and maintaining the variable-size representation for the encoder is possible. In this section, we navigate the target NMT architecture back to the popular variable-length sequential encoder in which no such compromise was made.

Starting from the above motivation, the key idea is to force a source language-independent representation in the decoder using an additional loss function. We achieve this by operating the encoder-decoder flow not only from the source sentence to the target, but also from the source to itself to recreate the source sentence. While this resembles an auto-encoder which can be combined with translation (He et al., 2016; Domhan and Hieber, 2017), it is not necessary to minimize the auto-encoder likelihood as in the multi-task approach (Niehues and Cho, 2017), but only the decoder-level similarity between the true target sentence and the auto-encoded source sentence. Due to the lack of true parallel data, this method serves as a bridge between the different languages.

An important feature of the NMT attention mechanism is that it extracts relevant information in encoded memory (the keys and queries, in this case they are the source sentence hidden states) and compresses them into one single state. More importantly, in the decoder operation this operator dynamically repeats every timestep. By using the encoder to encode both (source and target)

sentences and operate the attentive decoder on top of both encoded sentences, we obtain two attentive representations of the two sentences which are equally long. This is the key to enabling forced-length representations in our model.

Given the described model, the question is about where in the model we can apply our representation-forcing from Equation 3. Due to the nature of many translation models being multi-layered, it is not as straightforward as in the pooled encoder models. Hence, we investigate three different locations where this regularization method can be applied. Their illustration is depicted in Figure 2.

Attention Forcing   We can force each attention context vector[1] to be the same between two decoding outputs. As a Transformer has N decoder layers, we take N attention vectors of each decoder and apply MSE element-wise[2]. This **MSE-Attention** method is naturally the most immediate derivative of forcing encoder states to be similar. Here we annotate $Att^n(Y_t, X)$ to be the context vector from attention of layer n between decoder state of token Y_t and source sentence X.

$$R(X, Y) = -\sum_{n=0}^{N-1}\sum_{t=0}^{T-1}(Att^n(Y_t, X) - Att^n(Y_t, Y))^2$$
$$(4)$$

Decoder Forcing   Instead of optimizing for each context vector, we can also regularize the final decoder layer (before the Softmax layer), because this state summarizes the information gathered in the decoder at each timestep. This approach will be referred as **MSE-Decoder**. Similar to Equation 4, we denote the decoder state of the conditional probability at time t as $Dec(Y_t|X, Y_{1..t-1})$.

$$R(X, Y) = \sum_{t=0}^{T-1}(Dec(Y_t|X, Y_{1..t-1}) - Dec(Y_t|Y, Y_{1..t-1}))^2 \qquad (5)$$

Softmax Forcing   Similar to our second variation, the restriction is now put at the final layer. By running the decoder twice for translation and auto-encoder, we can force the output distribution of each step $P(Y_t|X, Y_{1..t-1})$ to be equal using KL

---

[1]As in (Luong et al., 2015) the context vector denotes the weighted sum of the encoder after the attention operation

[2]For multi-head attention we take the output after concatenating the heads.

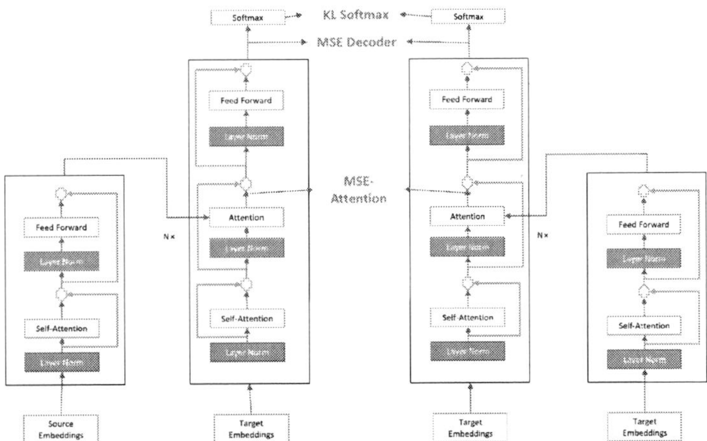

Figure 2: Three different constraints for language-independent decoders. The model is run twice as translation (left) and auto-encoder (right). The KL-Softmax is applied at the very top, while the MSE-Decoder minimizes difference between the layer-normalized states at the end of the decoder. The MSE-attention operates on non-normalized attention outputs.

divergence minimization. The purpose of this step is to enable the decoder to generate the same target sentence with source sentences in different languages. We denote this approach as **KL-Softmax**.

$$R(X,Y) = \sum_{t=0}^{T-1} KL(P(Y_t|X, Y_{1..t-1}), \quad (6)$$
$$P(Y_t|Y, Y_{1..t-1}))$$

These three different strategies have the same theoretical derivatives from semantically equivalent encoder states, but allow different freedoms for optimization.

5 Experiments

5.1 Experimental Setup

Our experiments use the standard IWSLT2017 benchmark in multilingual translation (Cettolo et al., 2017), which established a standardized multilingual corpora in different languages {English, German, Dutch, Romanian and Italian}. The data is around 60% true parallel, i.e. the same sentences translated in multiple languages (Dabre et al., 2017). With the target of zero-shot translation in mind, we designed two different setups which challenge multilingual models but are also industrially practical.

First, it is typical that English is the most commonly spoken language in the language set, leading the multilingual model to use English

as the bridge language participating in all language pairs. Our first setup therefore consists of English⟷{German, Dutch, Italian, Romanian} language pairs, with 8 language pairs in total having supervision during training and the remaining 12 dedicated to the ZS setup.[3]

It is notable that zero-shot (or zero-resource, if the method used generates artificial data to fill the language gap) setups which have been carried out in previous works were mostly concerned language connection with only one bridge (English). However, more realistically, data between local languages or dialects (such as Indian or Vietnamese languages) may more abundant than English. The connectivity in this case demands more than one language for bridging, which is simulated in our second setup by setting a "Chain" of languages. This setup also contains 8 supervised languages and 12 for zero-shot. Figure 3 shows the connections between languages in our setups.

The data is preprocessed using standard MT procedures including tokenization and true-casing[4] and byte-pair encoding with $40K$ codes. For model selection, the checkpoints performing best on the validation data (dev2010 and tst2010 combined) are averaged, which is then used to translate the tst2017 test set (including all 20 lan-

---

[3]This is different from the ZS setup of the IWSLT evaluation campaign in which only 4 out of 20 directions were not present during training.

[4]From the Moses toolkit: https://github.com/moses-smt/mosesdecoder

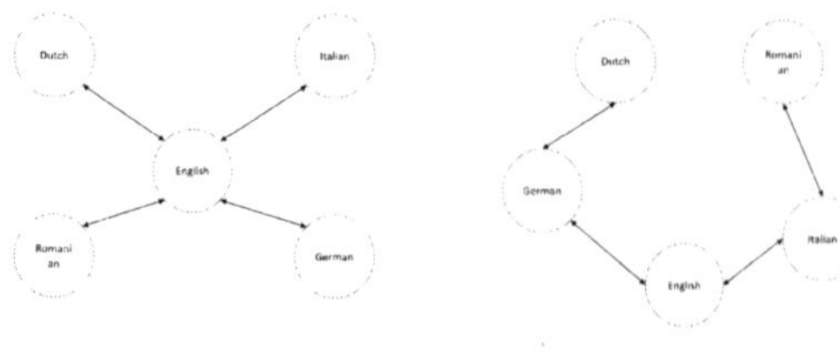

Figure 3: The STAR setup (left) with English as the sole bridge language, and the CHAIN setup (right) with 3 different bridge languages and more than 2 steps for zero-shot translation.

guage pairs).

5.2 Model Configuration

Our baseline model is the Transformer following the *Base* configuration in (Vaswani et al., 2017). Empirically, we increased the number of layers to 8 for both encoder and decoder, keeping the layer sizes at 512 for embedding and 2048 for the inner layers, and combined with word-dropout of $P_drop = 0.1$ (Gal and Ghahramani, 2016) to improve the potency of the baseline for this task. Layer dropout is also added according to the original work with $P_drop = 0.2$. The learning rate follows the adaptive learning rate proposed with the Transformer; we use the base learning rate 2 and the number of warm-up steps is 8192. The Transformer is trained for around 60000 steps before overfitting.

For multilingual functionality, the model uses language embeddings as a feature[5] (Ha et al., 2017). Our fixed-size models with pooling use 16 heads for the multi-head pooling models and 16 attention heads for the attention-pooling models.

5.3 Training Details

For all three variations of the decoder, the most important factor is the coefficient α of the second loss term (as in Equation 3 which decides the importance of this term during the training process. In the beginning of training, it is more important to focus on the main translation tasks, while the regularization term has more effect when the model is converging. To make training stable, repeatable, and reduce the necessity of hyperparameter tuning, we always take the Transformer baseline as the pretrained model and then continue training with the 2nd loss term with constant α. Based on

initial experiments for MSE-Decoder and MSE-Attention, we set $\alpha = 0.2$ while it is set to 0.01 for KL-Softmax. As a result, all of our variations have the same baseline as common ground. Further, when models are trained from the baseline checkpoint, we reset the learning rate and learning rate on an adaptive schedule and continue training for around 50000 steps[6].

An important detail during training is that, it is crucial to free the gradient-path in the decoder from the 2nd loss term for all three variations. In other words, the encoder only receives gradients from regularization. While we saw little difference for the development data with or without this constraint, we noticed that zero-shot translation performance can worsen if gradients flow through the decoder normally[7].

Our model is implemented in PyTorch (Paszke et al., 2017) and is publicly available [8].

5.4 Baseline and Fixed-size Source Language Representation Results

First, as outlined in Section 3, our goals are to set a competitive baseline and more importantly verify the behaviour of the encoder when the output space is limited to a fixed size instead of variable states. As shown in Table 1, while the two pooling models suffered from information bottleneck and lost $1 - 2$ BLEU for each language pair compared to the base Transformer model, the Mean-Pooling model is surprisingly better than the baseline at zero-shot tests. The Attention-Pooling model outperformed the Mean-Pooling at non-zero-shot tests, yet is worse at zero-shot conditions. Compared to other published works on this dataset (which are trained on all 20 directions), our supervised directions set the state-of-the-art for these directions while the zero-shot results approach the best supervised models in the literature (Dabre et al., 2017; Platanios et al., 2018)). Furthermore, by training these two models with a loss function including MSE-loss for encoder similarity, we found noticeable gains on zero-shot performance. More importantly, the zero-shot performance of our Mean-Pooling model with MSE-encoder not only outperforms the baseline, but also rivals the

---

[5] We tried the simpler method with the input token as in (Johnson et al., 2016), but our model could not consistently produce the correct output language in zero-shot tests, which is in-line with (Ha et al., 2017)

[6] Prolonging training of the baseline is not beneficial because it will begin to overfit.

[7] This can be done in PyTorch by creating a second decoder with (frozen) separate parameters from the main model decoder and then synchronizing them after each update.

[8] The implementation is available at *https://github.com/quanpn90/NMTGMinor/tree/DbMajor*

Transformer model competitively trained with all language pairs in Dabre et al. (2017). This gain is also noticed with the Attention-Pooling model.

These preliminary experiments shed light on several findings. First, when limited in representation size, the multilingual NMT models can selectively focus on features shared between languages; this is our hypothesis for the improvement in zero-shot translation from the baseline to the *Mean-Pooling* model (on average +1.28 BLEU points). Second, by applying the MSE-loss to both pooling variations, they significantly improve in zero-shot performance. This is, to the best of our knowledge, the first empirical proof that a multilingual model is able to learn a common representation space.

5.5 Transformer with Language-Independent Regularization

In Section 4 we showed three different strategies to achieve a decoder that is source language-independent, which theoretically may have the same effect to minimize encoded representation differences: directly equalizing the Softmax outputs, the decoder outputs, and the attention output of each layer. It is important to note that no architectural modification was necessary to include these strategies, thus all of the advantages of the Transformer model and the overall number of parameters are maintained.

5.5.1 Results for the STAR Configuration

The results are shown in table 2 for the *STAR* configuration. Because MSE-attention is the closest derivative to having the same encoder representation, we first investigate the effects of this variation. All zero-shot translation pairs receive noticeable improvement, with the average of 1.71 BLEU points. The most significant gain belongs to It-Nl pair, which achieves a 2.7 BLEU gain. More importantly, unlike the pooling models, we did not have a performance compromise for the non-zero tests. Specifically, the results in the 8 supervised language pairs are nearly identical to the baseline (except for the En-Nl direction, which decreases by 0.8 points). On average, the benefit for the zero-shot tests greatly outweighs any potential compromise.

The MSE-Decoder allows more freedom during optimization compared to the MSE-attention, as it only requires the final state of the decoder which looks at both encoded sentences to be the same.

In this case, we found significant improvement for zero-shot translation with +2.21 BLEU points on average. The previously most-improved language pair, It-Nl, is further improved by 0.4 for a total of 3.1 BLEU. Moreover, we found that this addition is also helpful for the pooling models, as reflected in the final column of the Table 2, significantly increasing the averaged BLEU scores from 17.22 to 19.81 points.

Finally, we found that regularizing on Softmax level is extremely difficult to optimize, and the resulting model deteriorates in performance for both zero-shot and normal tests. We found that the gradient norm is much bigger than the other two cases, so possibly optimization can be done with appropriate coefficients. However, this model is the most computationally expensive among the three investigated, due to the second Sofmax function required to be computed, making hyperparameter tuning expensive.

Even with the significant gain from regularizing the encoder representation, there is still a distance (0.4 BLEU point on average) between the best zero-shot model and pivot translation. While pivot translation can theoretically suffer from error cascading, we argue that this is a very strong baseline because the language-specific information, which is possibly negated by finding a language-independent encoder, can be transferred during the pivot process. On the other hand, pivot translation is twice as slow because multiple translation phases are required.

Our results also proved that our approach does not induce bias toward any language pair, as evidenced by the fact that our improvements (or deterioration) is nearly uniform across language pairs.

5.6 Results for the CHAIN configuration

In this particularly challenging setting where we have multiple bridge languages and different zero-shot distances, we experience different behavior from both pivot techniques and our techniques.

For the closest language pairs (with 2-step distance), the pivot translation method yields better results than both standard and our methods. The exception is the Romanian-English direction, in which case the pivot language is Italian being closer to Romanian than English.

It is important to note that most works in the literature used English as the common bridge language; these results indicate that zero-shot per-

Pair/Model	Transformer (ours)	Mean-Pooling	+ MSE	Attn-Pooling	+ MSE	Transformer (Dabre et al., 2017)
en-de	27.51	23.74	25.51	26.04	26.2	23.25
de-en	30.73	27.53	28.44	28.68	29.34	26.45
en-ro	27.45	23.48	25.08	25.37	26.03	24.66
ro-en	33.65	30.25	30.95	32.1	32.02	29.58
en-it	31.84	27.71	29.11	30.14	30.08	30.79
it-en	35.84	32.50	33.75	34.16	34.23	34.73
en-nl	32.15	28.58	29.86	30.9	30.68	28.80
nl-en	34.81	31.00	32.1	32.81	33.02	30.49
de-nl	19.04	19.68	20.46	18.36	19.41	19.64
nl-de	20.46	19.89	21.10	19.48	20.44	20.27
it-ro	18.45	18.16	19.73	17.42	18.74	20.60
ro-it	19.84	19.70	20.96	18.73	19.92	21.89
de-it	16.59	16.40	17.53	15.23	16.59	17.54
it-de	17.55	16.91	18.89	16.89	18.36	19.10
nl-ro	16.89	16.63	17.85	15.77	16.94	17.65
ro-nl	18.12	18.65	19.79	17.41	18.8	20.24
nl-it	18.11	18.31	19.78	17.45	18.54	19.86
it-nl	18.71	19.31	21.08	18.31	19.91	22.32
de-ro	15.33	15.07	16.13	14.56	15.31	16.27
ro-de	17.92	17.19	19.02	17.04	18.16	17.94
Avg.	18.08	18.0	19.36	17.22	18.43	
Δ		-0.08	**+1.28**	-0.86	+0.35	

Table 1: IWSLT 2017 STAR configuration: Baseline vs (Mean/Attention) Pooling. The top section shows 8 language pairs involved in training, while the bottom section shows the zero-shot results for 12 language pairs. We also present results for this dataset from previous work for reference.

formance can be more favourable when language similarity is taken into account.

When the distance increases, zero-shot translation with forced language-independence using an additional loss clearly outperforms pivot-based translation. We see improvements of more than 1 BLEU over pivoting for languages with several bridge languages. In this case, both of our techniques still bring improvements for every direction compared to the baseline zero-shot, while potential disadvantages of pivoting, namely error propagation, become clearer. It is important to note that our regularization techniques scale to settings with multiple bridges. We found the performance enhancement to be most significant for the language pairs which are furthest in the chain (4), with +1.54 BLEU points difference compared to the baseline. On the other hand, the Nl⟺It language pairs were most difficult to improve. This is also the setting in which pivot suffered the heaviest loss. To summarize, these multi-steps experiments showed the drawbacks of pivot while at the same

time confirm the consistency of our approach.

6 Related Work

Zero-shot translation is of considerable concern among the multilingual translation community. By sharing network parameters across languages, ZS was proven feasible for universal multilingual MT (Ha et al., 2016; Johnson et al., 2016). There are many variations of multilingual models geared towards zero-shot translation. Lu et al. (2018) proposed to explicitly define a recurrent layer with a fixed number of states as "Interlingua" which resembles our attention-pooling models. However, they compromise the model compactness by having separate encoder-decoder per language, which linearly increases the model size across languages. On the other hand, Platanios et al. (2018) shares all parameters, but utilized a parameter generator to generate specific parameters for the LSTMs in each language pair using language embeddings. The closest to our work is probably Arivazhagan et al. (2019). The authors aimed to regularize

Pair/Model	Transformer	+Pivot	+MSE-Attn	+MSE-dec	+KL-Sofmax	Mean-Pooling	Attn-Pooling
en-de	27.51		27.44	27.21	25.52	25.64	25.51
de-en	30.73		30.6	30.37	29.32	29.34	28.44
en-ro	27.45		27.32	27.1	25.40	25.84	25.08
ro-en	33.65		33.24	33.62	31.89	32.12	30.95
en-it	31.84		31.61	31.84	29.55	30.03	29.11
it-en	35.84		35.76	35.93	34.34	34.72	33.75
en-nl	32.15		31.85	31.38	29.78	30.46	29.86
nl-en	34.81		34.3	34.52	32.97	33.25	32.1
de-nl	19.04	21.59	20.93	21.47	19.44	20.95	20.46
nl-de	20.46	22.14	21.99	21.9	19.93	21.51	21.1
it-ro	18.45	20.68	20.25	20.56	18.01	20.23	19.73
ro-it	19.84	22.32	21.44	22.19	20.02	21.48	20.96
de-it	16.59	19.08	18.12	18.44	17.01	18.18	17.53
it-de	17.55	20.68	19.09	19.92	18.21	19.47	18.89
nl-ro	16.89	19.25	18.41	18.8	16.97	18.12	17.85
ro-nl	18.12	21.38	20.16	20.8	19.33	20.34	19.79
nl-it	18.11	21.7	20.04	20.91	18.93	20.15	19.78
it-nl	18.71	22.67	21.41	21.8	19.75	21.52	21.08
de-ro	15.33	17.69	16.77	17.12	15.47	16.56	16.13
ro-de	17.92	20.84	19.89	19.84	18.35	19.31	19.02
avg	18.08	20.83	19.88	20.31	18.45	19.36	19.81
Δ		+2.64	+1.80	**+2.23**	+0.37	+1.28	+1.73

Table 2: IWSLT 2017 STAR configuration result. Here we showed the Mean Pooling model that is enhanced with MSE-Encoder, and the Attn-Pooling model with MSE-Decoder.

Pair/Model	Distance	Transformer	Pivot	+MSE-Decoder	+MSE-Attn
en-ro	2	21.88	24.38	24.04	23.3
ro-en	2	29.82	29.29	30.79	30.92
de-it	2	17.5	19.45	19.3	18.57
it-de	2	18.22	20.97	19.84	19.02
en-nl	2	25.98	27.07	28.22	27.38
nl-en	2	31.24	29.22	31.65	32.08
nl-it	3	20.51	19.12	20.94	20.64
it-nl	3	20.87	20.39	21.47	21.17
de-ro	3	16.55	16.61	17.06	16.71
ro-de	3	19.35	19.15	20.18	19.65
nl-ro	4	16.37	16.81	17.33	16.92
ro-nl	4	17.55	18.55	19.66	18.88
Avg.	all	19.86	20.47	**21.06**	20.58
Avg.	2	24.10	25.06	**25.64**	25.21
Avg.	3	19.32	18.81	**19.91**	19.54
Avg.	4	16.96	17.68	**18.50**	17.90

Table 3: IWSLT 2017 CHAIN configuration results (12 zero-shot directions).

the model into a common encoding space by taking the mean-pooling of the encoder states and minimize the cosine similarity between the source and the target sentence encodings. In comparison, our approach is more generalized because the decoder is also taken into account during regularization, which is shown by our results on the

IWSLT benchmark[9]. Also, we proposed stronger representation-forcing since the cosine similarity minimizes the angle between two representational vectors, while the MSE forces them to be exactly equal. In addition, zero-resource techniques which generate artificial data for the missing directions have been proposed as an alternative to zero-shot translation (Chen et al., 2018; Al-Shedivat and Parikh, 2019; Chen et al., 2017). The main disadvantage, however, is the requirement of computationally expensive sampling during training which makes the algorithm less scalable to the number of languages. In our work, we focus on minimally affecting the training paradigm of universal multilingual NMT.

7 Conclusion

This work provides a through investigation of zero-shot translation in multilingual NMT. We conduct an analysis of neural architectures for zero-shot through two three different modifications showing that a beneficial shared representation can be learned for zero-shot translation. Furthermore, we provide a regularization scheme to encourage the model to capture language-independent features for the Transformer model which increases zero-shot performance by 2.23 BLEU points, achieving the state-of-the-art zero-shot performance in the standard benchmark IWSLT2017 dataset. We also proposed an alternative setting with more than one language as a bridge. In this challenging setup for zero-shot translation, we confirmed the consistent effects of our method by showing that the benefit is still significant when languages are far from each other in the pivot path. This result also motivates future works to apply the same strategy for other end-to-end tasks such as speech translation where there may be more variability in domains and modalities.

Acknowledgments

The project ELITR leading to this publication has received funding from the European Unions Horizon 2020 Research and Innovation Programme under grant agreement № 825460. We thank Elizabeth Salesky for the constructive comments.

---

[9]They used the same STAR setup but only reported the average BLEU score across all language pairs

References

Maruan Al-Shedivat and Ankur P Parikh. 2019. Consistency by agreement in zero-shot neural machine translation. *arXiv preprint arXiv:1904.02338.*

Naveen Arivazhagan, Ankur Bapna, Orhan Firat, Roee Aharoni, Melvin Johnson, and Wolfgang Macherey. 2019. The missing ingredient in zero-shot neural machine translation. *arXiv preprint arXiv:1903.07091.*

D. Bahdanau, K. Cho, and Y. Bengio. 2014. Neural machine translation by jointly learning to align and translate. *CoRR*, abs/1409.0473.

Mauro Cettolo, Marcello Federico, Luisa Bentivogli, Niehues Jan, Stüker Sebastian, Sudoh Katsuitho, Yoshino Koichiro, and Federmann Christian. 2017. Overview of the iwslt 2017 evaluation campaign. In *International Workshop on Spoken Language Translation*, pages 2–14.

Yun Chen, Yang Liu, Yong Cheng, and Victor OK Li. 2017. A teacher-student framework for zero-resource neural machine translation. *arXiv preprint arXiv:1705.00753.*

Yun Chen, Yang Liu, and Victor OK Li. 2018. Zero-resource neural machine translation with multi-agent communication game. In *Thirty-Second AAAI Conference on Artificial Intelligence.*

Raj Dabre, Fabien Cromieres, and Sadao Kurohashi. 2017. Kyoto university mt system description for iwslt 2017. *Proc. of IWSLT, Tokyo, Japan.*

Tobias Domhan and Felix Hieber. 2017. Using target-side monolingual data for neural machine translation through multi-task learning. In *Proceedings of the 2017 Conference on Empirical Methods in Natural Language Processing*, pages 1500–1505.

Orhan Firat, Kyunghyun Cho, and Yoshua Bengio. 2016. Multi-way, multilingual neural machine translation with a shared attention mechanism. *arXiv preprint arXiv:1601.01073.*

Yarin Gal and Zoubin Ghahramani. 2016. A theoretically grounded application of dropout in recurrent neural networks. In *Advances in neural information processing systems*, pages 1019–1027.

Jiatao Gu, Hany Hassan, Jacob Devlin, and Victor OK Li. 2018. Universal neural machine translation for extremely low resource languages. *arXiv preprint arXiv:1802.05368.*

Thanh-Le Ha, Jan Niehues, and Alexander Waibel. 2016. Toward multilingual neural machine translation with universal encoder and decoder. In *Proceedings of the 13th International Workshop on Spoken Language Translation (IWSLT 2016)*, Seattle, USA.

Thanh-Le Ha, Jan Niehues, and Alexander Waibel. 2017. Effective strategies in zero-shot neural machine translation. *arXiv preprint arXiv:1711.07893*.

Di He, Yingce Xia, Tao Qin, Liwei Wang, Nenghai Yu, Tie-Yan Liu, and Wei-Ying Ma. 2016. Dual learning for machine translation. In *Advances in Neural Information Processing Systems*, pages 820–828.

M. Johnson, M. Schuster, Q. V. Le, M. Krikun, Y. Wu, Z. Chen, N. Thorat, F. B. Viegas, M. Wattenberg, G. Corrado, M. Hughes, and J. Dean. 2016. Google's multilingual neural machine translation system: Enabling zero-shot translation. *CoRR*, abs/1611.04558.

Nal Kalchbrenner and Phil Blunsom. 2013. Recurrent continuous translation models. In *EMNLP*, volume 3, page 413.

Nal Kalchbrenner, Lasse Espeholt, Karen Simonyan, Aaron van den Oord, Alex Graves, and Koray Kavukcuoglu. 2016. Neural machine translation in linear time. *arXiv preprint arXiv:1610.10099*.

Yunsu Kim, Yingbo Gao, and Hermann Ney. 2019. Effective cross-lingual transfer of neural machine translation models without shared vocabularies. In *Proceedings of the Annual Meeting on Association for Computational Linguistics (ACL 2019)*.

Yichao Lu, Phillip Keung, Faisal Ladhak, Vikas Bhardwaj, Shaonan Zhang, and Jason Sun. 2018. A neural interlingua for multilingual machine translation. *arXiv preprint arXiv:1804.08198*.

Minh-Thang Luong, Hieu Pham, and Christopher D Manning. 2015. Effective approaches to attention-based neural machine translation. *arXiv preprint arXiv:1508.04025*.

Jan Niehues and Eunah Cho. 2017. Exploiting linguistic resources for neural machine translation using multi-task learning. In *Proceedings of the Second Conference on Machine Translation*, pages 80–89.

Adam Paszke, Sam Gross, Soumith Chintala, Gregory Chanan, Edward Yang, Zachary DeVito, Zeming Lin, Alban Desmaison, Luca Antiga, and Adam Lerer. 2017. Automatic differentiation in pytorch.

Emmanouil Antonios Platanios, Mrinmaya Sachan, Graham Neubig, and Tom Mitchell. 2018. Contextual parameter generation for universal neural machine translation. *arXiv preprint arXiv:1808.08493*.

Holger Schwenk and Matthijs Douze. 2017. Learning joint multilingual sentence representations with neural machine translation. *arXiv preprint arXiv:1704.04154*.

I. Sutskever, O. Vinyals, and Q. V. Le. 2014. Sequence to sequence learning with neural networks. In *Advances in Neural Information Processing Systems 27: Annual Conference on Neural Information Processing Systems 2014*, pages 3104–3112, Quebec, Canada.

Ashish Vaswani, Noam Shazeer, Niki Parmar, Jakob Uszkoreit, Llion Jones, Aidan N Gomez, Lukasz Kaiser, and Illia Polosukhin. 2017. Attention is all you need. *arXiv preprint arXiv:1706.03762*.

Rui Wang, Andrew Finch, Masao Utiyama, and Eiichiro Sumita. 2017. Sentence embedding for neural machine translation domain adaptation. In *Proceedings of the 55th Annual Meeting of the Association for Computational Linguistics (Volume 2: Short Papers)*, pages 560–566, Vancouver, Canada. Association for Computational Linguistics.

Barret Zoph, Deniz Yuret, Jonathan May, and Kevin Knight. 2016. Transfer learning for low-resource neural machine translation. In *Proceedings of the Conference on Empirical Methods in Natural Language Processing (EMNLP 2016)*, pages 1568–1575, Austin, USA.

Incorporating Source Syntax into Transformer-Based Neural Machine Translation

Anna Currey
University of Edinburgh
a.currey@sms.ed.ac.uk

Kenneth Heafield
University of Edinburgh
kheafiel@ed.ac.uk

Abstract

Transformer-based neural machine translation (NMT) has recently achieved state-of-the-art performance on many machine translation tasks. However, recent work (Raganato and Tiedemann, 2018; Tang et al., 2018; Tran et al., 2018) has indicated that Transformer models may not learn syntactic structures as well as their recurrent neural network-based counterparts, particularly in low-resource cases. In this paper, we incorporate constituency parse information into a Transformer NMT model. We leverage linearized parses of the source training sentences in order to inject syntax into the Transformer architecture without modifying it.

We introduce two methods: a multi-task machine translation and parsing model with a single encoder and decoder, and a mixed encoder model that learns to translate directly from parsed and unparsed source sentences. We evaluate our methods on low-resource translation from English into twenty target languages, showing consistent improvements of 1.3 BLEU on average across diverse target languages for the multi-task technique. We further evaluate the models on full-scale WMT tasks, finding that the multi-task model aids low- and medium-resource NMT but degenerates high-resource English→German translation.

1 Introduction

Transformer-based neural machine translation (NMT) (Vaswani et al., 2017) has recently outperformed recurrent neural network (RNN)-based models (Bahdanau et al., 2015; Cho et al., 2014) in many tasks (Bojar et al., 2018). However, there is still room for improvement for NMT, particularly for low- and moderate-resource language pairs. Enriching NMT with syntactic information has the potential to improve generalization in low-resource scenarios, and adding syntax to Transformer-based NMT is currently an underexplored research area.

Transformer-based NMT may in fact stand to benefit even more from explicit syntactic annotations than RNN-based NMT, particularly in low-resource settings. On the one hand, the Transformer model already learns some syntax without explicit supervision in high-resource cases. Vaswani et al. (2017) visualized a few encoder self-attentions in a trained NMT model and found that they seemed to capture syntactic structure. This was formalized by Raganato and Tiedemann (2018), who found that Transformer encoders trained on high-resource NMT tasks were able to perform reasonably well at part-of-speech tagging, chunking, and other tasks. However, for Transformers trained on low-resource NMT, the results on these tasks were not as strong. Additionally, Tran et al. (2018) found that an RNN language model did better at predicting subject-verb agreement than a Transformer language model; Tang et al. (2018) saw similar results for Transformer vs. RNN NMT models.

Thus, the goal of this paper is to improve Transformer-based NMT using source-side syntactic supervision. We propose two methods that incorporate source-side linearized constituency parses into Transformer-based NMT. The first, multi-task, uses the Transformer to learn to parse and translate the source sentence simultaneously. The second, mixed encoder, learns to translate directly from both parsed and unparsed source sentences. This paper makes the following contributions:

- This is one of the first attempts at using syntax to improve Transformer-based NMT

- We introduce two methods for adding syntax

Proceedings of the Fourth Conference on Machine Translation (WMT), Volume 1: Research Papers, pages 24–33
Florence, Italy, August 1-2, 2019. ©2019 Association for Computational Linguistics

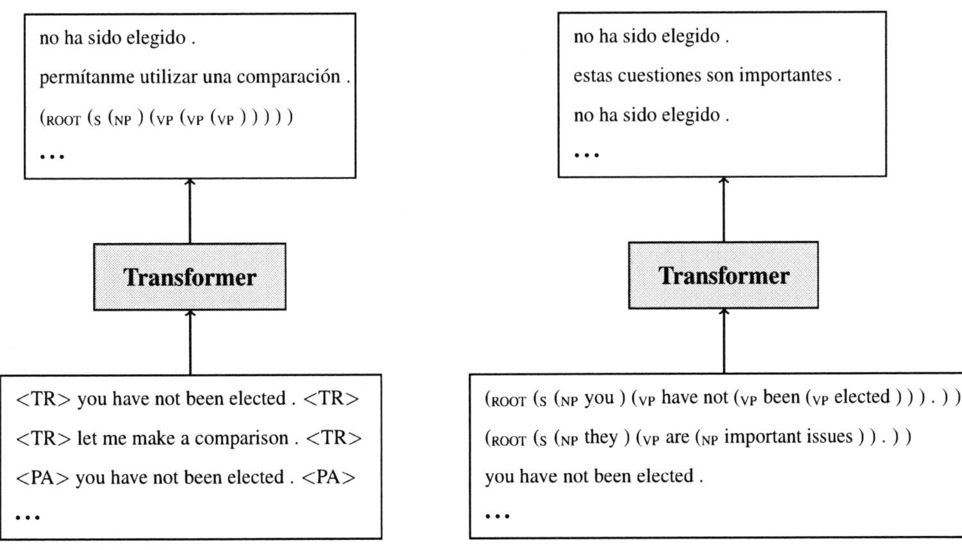

(a) Multi-task syntactic NMT model. The system is trained to translate (<TR>) and parse (<PA>) source sentences using the same architecture.

(b) Mixed encoder syntactic NMT model. The system learns to translate directly from both parsed and unparsed source sentences into unparsed target sentences.

Figure 1: Illustrations of the two proposed syntactic NMT methods.

to NMT that are straightforward to incorporate in practice

- We empirically evaluate both methods on translation from English into 21 diverse target languages, finding that the multi-task method improves consistently over a non-syntactic baseline

2 Transformer-Based NMT with Linearized Parses

We propose two models for incorporating linearized parses into Transformer-based NMT: a *multi-task* model and a *mixed encoder* model. Figure 1 summarizes the two proposed methods; they are discussed in detail in sections 2.2 and 2.3, respectively.

2.1 Linearized Constituency Parses

Both of our proposed methods make use of linearized parses of the source sentences to inject source syntax into Transformer-based NMT. Linearizing the parses allows us to add syntactic information without modifying the Transformer architecture. Here, we describe how these parses are created. We generate and format the parsed data as follows:

1. In order to generate syntactically parsed training data, we use the Stanford CoreNLP constituency parser (Manning et al., 2014) to parse the source side of the parallel corpus. This technique of parsing the parallel data instead of using gold parses is common in syntactic NMT (Eriguchi et al., 2016) and in neural parsing (Vinyals et al., 2015). For the multi-task model, it would be possible to incorporate gold parses into training as well, but we leave this for future work.

2. We linearize the resulting parses similarly to Vinyals et al. (2015) by using a depth-first tree traversal. We tokenize the opening parenthesis of each phrase with its phrase label.

3. Since neural machine translation already struggles with long sentences (Bahdanau et al., 2015), and adding the phrase nodes has the potential to make the sentences much longer, we remove part-of-speech tags from the parses (as was done by Aharoni and Goldberg, 2017).

4. For our multi-task model (section 2.2), we remove words from the linearized parses. We do this in order to further shorten the length of the target sequences. We do not expect that this will make the parsing task too difficult, as a similar technique was used for neural pars-

translation	<TR> you have not been elected . <TR> → no ha sido elegido .
parsing	<PA> you have not been elected . <PA> → (ROOT (S (NP) (VP (VP (VP)))))

Table 1: Example of English→Spanish training data for parsing and translation tasks in the multi-task system.

(ROOT (S (NP you) (VP have not (VP been (VP elected))) .)) → no ha sido elegido .
you have not been elected .   → no ha sido elegido .

Table 2: Example of English→Spanish training data for the mixed encoder system.

ing by Vinyals et al. (2015).

5. For our mixed encoder model (section 2.3), we convert the words in the parses into subwords using byte pair encoding (Sennrich et al., 2016). We do not allow the parse labels to be broken into subwords.

Tables 1 and 2 give examples of the resulting parse formats.

2.2 Multi-Task NMT and Parsing with Shared Decoder

Our first method for incorporating source-side syntax into Transformer-based NMT adopts a multi-task framework. The main task is translating the source sentence into the target language; the secondary task is parsing the source sentence. For the parsing task, we employ the same encoder-decoder framework as for NMT, with the sequential source sentence as input and the linearized, unlexicalized parsed source sentence as output. Thus, both tasks are trained using a single model with a shared encoder and decoder. This is similar to the multi-task framework proposed by Luong et al. (2016), with three main differences: 1) we do not use separate decoders for each task, 2) we use the same source data for both parsing and translation, and 3) we use a Transformer rather than recurrent neural network-based architecture.

We do not directly use gold parses to train the parsing task, nor do we split the training data between the two tasks. The reason for using the same source data for both tasks is that we expect it to be difficult to find a sufficiently large amount of in-domain gold parses for training; additionally, our main goal is to improve NMT, so we do not expect the lower quality of the synthetic parses to matter.

In order to generate the training data for this model, we first create linearized parses of the source side of the training corpus as described above. Next, we add a tag at the beginning and end of each source sentence indicating the desired

task, similar to what was done by Johnson et al. (2017) for multilingual NMT. Table 1 gives an example of the data format. Finally, we shuffle the parsing and translation training data together and train the shared encoder and decoder on both tasks, making no further distinction between the tasks during training. Since we parse all of the training data, each source sentence appears twice: once with a target language sentence and once with a parse of the source sentence. These copies are shuffled separately.

2.3 Mixed Encoder Transformer

Our second method for augmenting the NMT Transformer with syntax is the mixed encoder model. This model learns to translate both from unparsed and parsed source sentences into unparsed target sentences.

In order to train the mixed encoder model, we create two copies of the training data, one with parsed source sentences and the other with unparsed source sentences. We then shuffle these training corpora together into a single corpus and train a standard Transformer NMT model on the final data, with a single encoder for both parsed and unparsed source sentences. The training data contains (parsed source, unparsed target) and (unparsed source, unparsed target) sentence pairs; Table 2 gives an example of the two types of training sentence pairs for the mixed encoder method. Since the data is shuffled, these two sentence pairs (with identical target sentences) will not necessarily be seen together during training.

Since the mixed encoder model is trained on both parsed and unparsed source sentences, during inference it is able to translate from either source sentence format. Inference on unparsed source sentences is slightly faster (since it does not require parsing of the source sentence) and achieves slightly higher BLEU scores, so we show results using unparsed source sentences for our experiments (sections 4.2 and 5.2).

3   Experimental Setup

We evaluate our multi-task and mixed encoder models compared to a standard (non-syntactic) Transformer baseline on translation from English into 21 target languages. Sections 4.1 and 5.1 contain detailed information on the target languages and data used. All models are implemented in Sockeye (Hieber et al., 2017). For hyperparameter settings, we follow the recommendations of Vaswani et al. (2017).

We preprocess our data for all experiments as follows. First, we tokenize and truecase the data using the Moses scripts (Koehn et al., 2007). We then train separate subword vocabularies (Sennrich et al., 2016) for the source and target languages, with 30k merge operations per language. We use the Stanford CoreNLP parser (Manning et al., 2014) to generate constituency parses of the source (English) sentences, and linearize and format the parses as described in section 2.1. We do not use any monolingual training data; however, our proposed models are amenable to adding monolingual data, and we expect that BLEU scores would strongly increase if monolingual training data were used.

4   Small-Scale Cross-Lingual Experiments

4.1   Data

We use the Europarl Parallel Corpus (Koehn, 2005) as the basis for our small-scale cross-lingual experiments. We consider translation from English (EN) into each of the twenty remaining target languages; Table 3 contains a full list of the target languages, as well as their language families or branches. By using this data set, we are able to evaluate the usefulness of syntactic information for several relatively diverse target languages, unlike most previous work on syntactic NMT (reviewed in section 7). However, all the languages in our experiments are Indo-European or Uralic due to using Europarl.

In order to facilitate comparison between the target languages, we follow Cotterell et al. (2018) by taking only the intersections of the Europarl training data. This means that the source (EN) data is identical for all experiments, and the targets are all translations of each other in the different target languages. This results in 170k parallel training sentences for each language pair. We reserve a

Family	Language	Abbrev.
Baltic	Latvian	LV
	Lithuanian	LT
Germanic	Danish	DA
	Dutch	NL
	German	DE
	Swedish	SV
Hellenic	Greek	EL
Romance	French	FR
	Italian	IT
	Portuguese	PT
	Romanian	RO
	Spanish	ES
Slavic	Bulgarian	BG
	Czech	CS
	Polish	PL
	Slovak	SK
	Slovene	SL
Uralic	Estonian	ET
	Finnish	FI
	Hungarian	HU

Table 3: Target languages used in our experiments, along with their language families or branches and their abbreviations (abbrev.).

random subset of 10k sentences from the original data to use as development data and an additional 10k sentences as test data; these development and test sets are not included in the training data.

4.2   Results

Table 4 displays BLEU scores on the test data for each target language for the proposed systems. The multi-task system outperforms the baseline for all target languages. In addition, for all but four target languages (SV, EL, SK, and ET), the multi-task system is at least 1 BLEU point better than the baseline. Thus, our proposed multi-task method consistently improves over a non-syntactic baseline across several diverse target languages in low-resource scenarios. Additionally, in all cases but two (EN→LT and EN→ET), multi-task achieves the highest BLEU score of all models.

The performance of the mixed encoder system in relation to the baseline is less consistent than that of the multi-task system. In most cases, the mixed encoder improves only slightly (less than 1 BLEU) over the baseline, although for LV, LT, RO, ES, PL, and FI, the improvements are stronger. However, for four target languages (NL, EL, BG,

EN→*	base	mixed enc.	multi-task
LV	26.5	28.1 (+1.6)	**28.2** (+1.7)
LT	23.5	**24.6** (+1.1)	24.8 (+1.3)
DA	39.5	40.1 (+0.6)	**40.7** (+1.2)
NL	28.8	28.7 (-0.1)	**30.6** (+1.8)
DE	30.5	30.6 (+0.1)	**32.1** (+1.6)
SV	35.9	36.4 (+0.5)	**36.4** (+0.5)
EL	38.9	38.8 (-0.1)	**39.7** (+0.8)
FR	38.3	38.5 (+0.2)	**40.4** (+2.1)
IT	31.3	31.3 (==)	**32.5** (+1.2)
PT	39.2	39.3 (+0.1)	**40.5** (+1.3)
RO	36.3	**37.8** (+1.5)	37.8 (+1.5)
ES	41.6	43.0 (+1.4)	**43.1** (+1.5)
BG	39.0	38.6 (-0.4)	**40.5** (+1.5)
CS	27.5	28.3 (+0.8)	**28.8** (+1.3)
PL	23.7	24.8 (+1.1)	**25.1** (+1.4)
SK	32.8	32.5 (-0.3)	**32.9** (+0.1)
SL	33.3	34.2 (+0.9)	**34.9** (+1.6)
ET	20.2	**20.9** (+0.7)	20.8 (+0.6)
FI	21.5	22.8 (+1.3)	**23.3** (+1.8)
HU	22.3	22.6 (+0.3)	**23.4** (+1.1)

Table 4: BLEU scores on the test set for small-scale cross-lingual experiments for the baseline (base), mixed encoder (mixed enc.), and multi-task models. Difference with the baseline is shown in parentheses.

System	newstest2017	newstest2018
baseline	9.6	8.8
mixed enc.	9.6 (==)	9.3 (+0.5)
multi-task	**10.6** (+1.0)	**10.4** (+1.6)

Table 5: BLEU scores (and improvement over the baseline) for EN→TR on the test (newstest2017) and held-out (newstest2018) datasets.

and SK), the mixed encoder system does worse than the non-syntactic baseline.

Target language family does not seem to have a noticeable effect on the performance of either the mixed encoder or the multi-task method; this could be due to the fact that the syntactic annotations were on the source sentence only. It remains to be seen whether certain source languages are particularly amenable to incorporating source syntax in NMT.

5 Full-Scale WMT Experiments

5.1 Data

The main goal of the previous section was to evaluate our proposed syntactic NMT methods on a wide range of target languages and compare the effect of target language on performance. In this section, we run additional experiments in order to evaluate the proposed methods on a standard benchmark. We train our models on the following tasks: English→Turkish (TR) from the WMT18 news translation shared task (Bojar et al., 2018), English→Romanian WMT16 (Bojar et al., 2016), and English→German WMT17 (Bo-

jar et al., 2017).

For each experiment, we use all available parallel training data from the task, but no monolingual data. This gives us 200k parallel training sentences for EN→TR, 600k for EN→RO, and 5.9M for EN→DE. Note that the EN→RO and EN→DE training corpora contain some overlaps with the training data in section 4.1, although the experiments in this section use significantly more training data. We validate EN→TR on newstest2016, EN→RO on newsdev2016, and EN→DE on newstest2015.

5.2 Results

The results for the EN→TR experiments are displayed in Table 5. These results mirror what was seen in the previous experiments: the mixed encoder method gives modest improvements over the non-syntactic baseline (0–0.5 BLEU), while the multi-task method yields the strongest results, with an improvement of 1.0–1.6 BLEU points over the baseline. Although Turkish is not related to any of the target languages studied in section 4, the amount of training data for EN→TR is similar to what was used in the previous section, which might be one explanation for the similar results.

Table 6 shows performance of each model on the WMT EN→RO experiments. Here, we see more modest improvements from adding the syntactic data: only 0.5 BLEU over the baseline for both the mixed encoder and multi-task methods. It is interesting to compare this with the results for the Europarl EN→RO experiments (section 4.2); there, we saw a much larger improvement over the baseline for both multi-task models (1.5 BLEU). This indicates that the effectiveness of these models may depend on amount of data (the WMT models were trained on about three times as much training data) rather than on target language family.

Finally, we display our WMT EN→DE results in Table 7. Here, we see that for very high-resource EN→DE translation, the multi-task

System	newstest2016
baseline	21.5
mixed enc.	**22.0** (+0.5)
multi-task	**22.0** (+0.5)

Table 6: BLEU scores (and improvement over the baseline) for EN→RO on the test set (newstest2016).

System	newstest2016	newstest2017
baseline	31.7	25.5
mixed enc.	**31.9** (+0.2)	**26.0** (+0.5)
multi-task	29.6 (-2.1)	23.4 (-2.1)

Table 7: BLEU scores (and difference with the baseline) for EN→DE on the test (newstest2016) and held-out (newstest2017) datasets.

EN→*	% Valid Parses
LV	96.8%
LT	99.2%
DA	70.8%
NL	93.3%
DE	87.2%
SV	95.4%
EL	85.2%
FR	92.3%
IT	78.8%
PT	89.4%
RO	96.3%
ES	86.5%
BG	97.5%
CS	95.9%
PL	98.1%
SK	98.5%
SL	97.3%
ET	98.2%
FI	95.1%
HU	93.6%

Table 8: Percent of valid parses of the parses generated by the Europarl multi-task systems.

method does much worse than the baseline (by 2.1 BLEU points). In addition, the mixed encoder method achieves comparable BLEU scores to the baseline (only 0.2–0.5 BLEU higher). Thus, neither proposed technique is particularly successful for high-resource EN→DE NMT. Again, we can contrast this with the Europarl EN→DE experiments, where we saw strong improvements from the multi-task model (1.6 BLEU). This lends further credence to the hypothesis that these NMT models with linearized source parses are helpful cross-linguistically in low-resource scenarios, but not in high-resource setups.

We further investigated the WMT EN→DE multi-task model to find reasons for the large drop in performance compared to the baseline. We found that while the multi-task model was able to generate reasonable (albeit lower-quality) translations, it did not successfully learn to parse. During parsing inference, the model always output the same parse regardless of the input sentence: $(_{ROOT}$ $(_S (_{NP}) (_{VP} (_{NP} (_{NP}) (_{PP} (_{NP} (_{NP}) (_{PP} (_{NP}))))$ $))))$. This was a common parse in the training data (it occurred 12k times in the data). This issue is partially due to the fact that validation is only done on the translation task, not on the parsing task. However, we do not see this issue with the other language pairs and experiments. This failure to learn to parse indicates that the WMT EN→DE multi-task model is not able to take advantage of the syntactic annotations.

6 Validity of Parses

The multi-task syntactic NMT models are trained both to translate and to parse the input sentences. The main goal of these models has been to improve translation; those results were reported in sections 4.2 and 5.2. In this section, we analyze the validity of the parses produced by the multi-task systems. We use a standard parsing benchmark, WSJ section 23 of the Penn Treebank (Marcus et al., 1993), as the evaluation dataset in this section. We preprocess this dataset as described in section 3 before using it as the source data for the multi-task systems.

The multi-task models were trained to generate unlexicalized parses. Since we removed part-of-speech tags from the parses during preprocessing, it is not possible to automatically relexicalize the parses. This is because there is no one-to-one correspondence between the leaves of the parse tree and the number of words in the sentence. Thus, rather than evaluating the parses directly, we count the number of valid parses (i.e. parses with balanced parentheses) per target language.

Table 8 shows the percent of generated parses that were valid for the Europarl multi-task models. For most target languages, over 90% of the generated parses are valid.

Unlike for the translation results, target language family does seem to have an effect on the

EN→*	% Valid Parses
TR	86.3%
RO	99.8%
DE	100%

Table 9: Percent of valid parses of the parses generated by the WMT multi-task systems.

parsing results. Overall, Romance, Germanic, and Hellenic target language systems generate the fewest valid parses. This indicates that Baltic, Slavic, and Uralic target languages are most helpful in learning to parse English in a multi-task system. Thus, from our cross-lingual experiments, it seems that the parsing performance of a multi-task system depends on the target language, whereas we saw in the previous sections that the translation success depends more on the amount of training data. Note, however, some caveats: 1) we did not perform validation on the parsing task (only on the translation task), and 2) we are measuring only parsing validity here, rather than parsing performance.

Table 9 shows the percent of valid parses for the three WMT multi-task experiments. For EN→DE, all of the generated parses are valid because they are all identical (as dicussed in section 5.2). For EN→RO, nearly all the parses are valid as well. However, this language pair did not have the same issue as EN→DE: the parses generated for each sentence were different, and a manual analysis indicated that the generated EN→RO parses were reasonable. The EN→TR system generated a large amount of valid parses, but fewer than the EN→RO system; it is possible that the EN→TR system would have done better with more training data.

7 Related Work

The performance of many RNN-based NMT paradigms has been improved by adding explicit syntactic annotations, particularly on the source side; we review some syntactic NMT models here. This paper is, along with Wu et al. (2018) and Zhang et al. (2019), among the first to add explicit syntax to Transformer-based NMT.

7.1 Linearized Parses in Neural Networks

In this work, we use linearized parse trees to add syntax into the Transformer. Vinyals et al. (2015) and Choe and Charniak (2016) introduced the idea of linearizing parse trees for neural parsing. Linearized parses are advantageous because they can be used anywhere that standard sequences can be used; in fact, Vaswani et al. (2017) showed that they can also be used by the Transformer to learn constituency parsing. Here, we leverage this idea by using linearized parses as an additional signal for the Transformer during NMT training.

7.2 Syntactic NMT with Modified Encoder

There have been several recent proposals to incorporate source-side syntax into RNN-based NMT by modifying the encoder architecture; we review some such models here. Eriguchi et al. (2016) augmented the RNN encoder with a tree-LSTM (Tai et al., 2015) to read in source-side HPSG parses, and combined this with a standard RNN decoder. Similarly, Bastings et al. (2017) used a graph convolutional encoder in combination with an RNN decoder to translate from dependency parsed source sentences. Although these models improved over non-syntactic RNN-based NMT systems, they relied heavily on parsed data during both training and inference, whereas our models are able to translate unparsed data. In addition, it is not clear how to incorporate such improvements into the state-of-the-art Transformer architecture.

7.3 Linearized Parses in NMT

This work fits with another line of research that uses linearized parses to incorporate syntax into neural machine translation without requiring a specific NMT architecture. Luong et al. (2016) used a single encoder and different decoders to train two tasks: parsing the source sentence and translating from source to target. Kiperwasser and Ballesteros (2018) also applied multi-task learning to syntactic NMT; they used a shared RNN decoder for translation, dependency parsing, and part-of-speech tagging and evaluated different scheduling techniques to combine the tasks. Our multi-task system builds off these two papers by training a joint NMT and parsing model using a single encoder and decoder in a Transformer framework, and further evaluates the multi-task framework on several language pairs.

Currey and Heafield (2018) leveraged a multi-source NMT system to learn to translate from both unparsed and parsed source sentences. Wu et al. (2018) similarly combined the standard bidirectional encoder with two additional encoders, one that encoded the pre-order traversal of the dependency parse of the sentence and one that encoded the post-order traversal. Unlike Currey and Heafield (2018), they joined the encoders on the word level and used a Transformer architecture. Our mixed encoder model is similar to these but instead uses a single Transformer encoder for both parsed and unparsed source sentences.

The mixed RNN encoder model of Li et al. (2017) is also similar to our mixed encoder model; their model used an RNN to encode a linearized parse of a source sentence, but attended only to the words of the parse. Our mixed encoder model is trained on both linearized parses and unparsed sentences, but for the linearized parses we attend to words and to parse labels. Zhang et al. (2019) used syntax to augment the word representations in both RNN-based and Transformer-based NMT; this was done by concatenating the hidden states of a dependency parser with the NMT word embeddings. Their method is complementary to ours and could be used along with our multi-task or mixed encoder models to enhance any NMT architecture.

In this work, we have concentrated on source-side syntax, but linearized parses have also been popular for incorporating target syntax into neural machine translation. Aharoni and Goldberg (2017) and Nadejde et al. (2017) both trained RNN-based neural machine translation systems to translate from sequential source sentences into linearized parses of target sentences; this could also be done using a Transformer.

8 Conclusions

In this paper, we proposed two methods for incorporating source-side syntactic annotations into a Transformer-based neural machine translation system. The first, multi-task, used a shared encoder and decoder to train two tasks: translation and constituency parsing. The second, mixed encoder, learned to translate linearized parses of the source sentences as well as unparsed source sentences directly into the target language. We performed experiments from English into twenty target languages in a low-resource setup; the multi-task system improved over the non-syntactic baseline for all target languages. We further demonstrated the success of this method on the EN→TR and EN→RO WMT datasets; however, for the very high-resource EN→DE WMT setup, the multi-task model performed poorly, while the mixed encoder model did only marginally better than the non-syntactic baseline.

In the future, we plan on extending these techniques to incorporate target-side syntax into Transformer-based NMT. In addition, we would like to experiment with different source languages in order to find out whether adding source-side syntax has a greater effect on some source languages than others. It would also be interesting to experiment with a multi-task, multilingual NMT framework with multiple target languages.

References

Roee Aharoni and Yoav Goldberg. 2017. Towards string-to-tree neural machine translation. In *Proceedings of the 55th Annual Meeting of the ACL*, pages 132–140. Association for Computational Linguistics.

Dzmitry Bahdanau, Kyunghyun Cho, and Yoshua Bengio. 2015. Neural machine translation by jointly learning to align and translate. In *3rd International Conference on Learning Representations*.

Joost Bastings, Ivan Titov, Wilker Aziz, Diego Marcheggiani, and Khalil Sima'an. 2017. Graph convolutional encoders for syntax-aware neural machine translation. In *Proceedings of the 2017 Conference on Empirical Methods in Natural Language Processing*, pages 1957–1967. Association for Computational Linguistics.

Ondřej Bojar, Rajen Chatterjee, Christian Federmann, Yvette Graham, Barry Haddow, Shujian Huang, Matthias Huck, Philipp Koehn, Qun Liu, Varvara Logacheva, Christof Monz, Matteo Negri, Matt Post, Raphael Rubino, Lucia Specia, and Marco Turchi. 2017. Findings of the 2017 Conference on Machine Translation (WMT17). In *Proceedings of the Second Conference on Machine Translation*, pages 169–214. Association for Computational Linguistics.

Ondřej Bojar, Rajen Chatterjee, Christian Federmann, Yvette Graham, Barry Haddow, Matthias Huck, Antonio Jimeno Yepes, Philipp Koehn, Varvara Logacheva, Christof Monz, Matteo Negri, Aurélie Névéol, Mariana Neves, Martin Popel, Matt Post, Raphael Rubino, Carolina Scarton, Lucia Specia, Marco Turchi, Karin Verspoor, and Marcos Zampieri. 2016. Findings of the 2016 Conference on Machine Translation. In *Proceedings of the First Conference on Machine Translation*, pages 131–198. Association for Computational Linguistics.

Ondřej Bojar, Christian Federmann, Mark Fishel, Yvette Graham, Barry Haddow, Philipp Koehn, and Christof Monz. 2018. Findings of the 2018 Conference on Machine Translation (WMT18). In *Proceedings of the Third Conference on Machine Trans-*

lation, pages 272–303. Association for Computational Linguistics.

Kyunghyun Cho, Bart Van Merriënboer, Caglar Gulcehre, Dzmitry Bahdanau, Fethi Bougares, Holger Schwenk, and Yoshua Bengio. 2014. Learning phrase representations using RNN encoder-decoder for statistical machine translation. In *Proceedings of the 2014 Conference on Empirical Methods in Natural Language Processing*, pages 1724–1734. Association for Computational Linguistics.

Do Kook Choe and Eugene Charniak. 2016. Parsing as language modeling. In *Proceedings of the 2016 Conference on Empirical Methods in Natural Language Processing*, pages 2331–2336. Association for Computational Linguistics.

Ryan Cotterell, Sebastian J. Mielke, Jason Eisner, and Brian Roark. 2018. Are all languages equally hard to language-model? In *Proceedings of NAACL-HLT*, pages 536–541. Association for Computational Linguistics.

Anna Currey and Kenneth Heafield. 2018. Multisource syntactic neural machine translation. In *Proceedings of the 2018 Conference on Empirical Methods in Natural Language Processing*, pages 2961–2966. Association for Computational Linguistics.

Akiko Eriguchi, Kazuma Hashimoto, and Yoshimasa Tsuruoka. 2016. Tree-to-sequence attentional neural machine translation. In *Proceedings of the 54th Annual Meeting of the ACL*, pages 823–833. Association for Computational Linguistics.

Felix Hieber, Tobias Domhan, Michael Denkowski, David Vilar, Artem Sokolov, Ann Clifton, and Matt Post. 2017. Sockeye: A toolkit for neural machine translation. *arXiv preprint arXiv:1712.05690.*

Melvin Johnson, Mike Schuster, Quoc V Le, Maxim Krikun, Yonghui Wu, Zhifeng Chen, Nikhil Thorat, Fernanda Viégas, Martin Wattenberg, Greg Corrado, Macduff Hughes, and Jeffrey Dean. 2017. Google's multilingual neural machine translation system: Enabling zero-shot translation. *Transactions of the Association for Computational Linguistics*, 5:339–351.

Eliyahu Kiperwasser and Miguel Ballesteros. 2018. Scheduled multi-task learning: From syntax to translation. *Transactions of the Association for Computational Linguistics*, 6:225–240.

Philipp Koehn. 2005. Europarl: A parallel corpus for statistical machine translation. In *10th Machine Translation Summit*, volume 5, pages 79–86.

Philipp Koehn, Hieu Hoang, Alexandra Birch, Chris Callison-Burch, Marcello Federico, Nicola Bertoldi, Brooke Cowan, Wade Shen, Christine Moran, Richard Zens, Chris Dyer, Ondřej Bojar, Alexandra Constantin, and Evan Herbst. 2007. Moses: Open source toolkit for statistical machine translation. In *Proceedings of the 45th Annual Meeting of the ACL*, pages 177–180. Association for Computational Linguistics.

Junhui Li, Deyi Xiong, Zhaopeng Tu, Muhua Zhu, Min Zhang, and Guodong Zhou. 2017. Modeling source syntax for neural machine translation. In *Proceedings of the 55th Annual Meeting of the ACL*, pages 688–697. Association for Computational Linguistics.

Minh-Thang Luong, Quoc V Le, Ilya Sutskever, Oriol Vinyals, and Lukasz Kaiser. 2016. Multi-task sequence to sequence learning. In *4th International Conference on Learning Representations*.

Christopher Manning, Mihai Surdeanu, John Bauer, Jenny Rose Finkel, Steven Bethard, and David McClosky. 2014. The Stanford CoreNLP natural language processing toolkit. In *Proceedings of the 52nd Annual Meeting of the ACL*, pages 55–60. Association for Computational Linguistics.

Mitchell P. Marcus, Beatrice Santorini, and Mary Ann Marcinkiewicz. 1993. Building a large annotated corpus of English: The Penn Treebank. *Computational Linguistics*, 19(2):313–330.

Maria Nadejde, Siva Reddy, Rico Sennrich, Tomasz Dwojak, Marcin Junczys-Dowmunt, Philipp Koehn, and Alexandra Birch. 2017. Predicting target language CCG supertags improves neural machine translation. In *Proceedings of the Second Conference on Machine Translation*, pages 68–79. Association for Computational Linguistics.

Alessandro Raganato and Jörg Tiedemann. 2018. An analysis of encoder representations in Transformer-based machine translation. In *Proceedings of the 2018 EMNLP Workshop BlackboxNLP: Analyzing and Interpreting Neural Networks for NLP*, pages 287–297. Association for Computational Linguistics.

Rico Sennrich, Barry Haddow, and Alexandra Birch. 2016. Neural machine translation of rare words with subword units. In *Proceedings of the 54th Annual Meeting of the ACL*, pages 1715–1725. Association for Computational Linguistics.

Kai Sheng Tai, Richard Socher, and Christopher Manning. 2015. Improved semantic representations from tree-structured long short-term memory networks. In *Proceedings of the 53rd Annual Meeting of the ACL and the 7th International Joint Conference on Natural Language Processing*, pages 1556–1566. Association for Computational Linguistics.

Gongbo Tang, Mathias Müller, Annette Rios, and Rico Sennrich. 2018. Why self-attention? A targeted evaluation of neural machine translation architectures. In *Proceedings of the 2018 Conference on Empirical Methods in Natural Language Processing*, pages 4263–4272. Association for Computational Linguistics.

Ke Tran, Arianna Bisazza, and Christof Monz. 2018. The importance of being recurrent for modeling hierarchical structure. In *Proceedings of the 2018*

Conference on Empirical Methods in Natural Language Processing, pages 4731–4736. Association for Computational Linguistics.

Ashish Vaswani, Noam Shazeer, Niki Parmar, Jakob Uszkoreit, Llion Jones, Aidan N Gomez, Łukasz Kaiser, and Illia Polosukhin. 2017. Attention is all you need. In *Advances in Neural Information Processing Systems 30*, pages 5998–6008.

Oriol Vinyals, Łukasz Kaiser, Terry Koo, Slav Petrov, Ilya Sutskever, and Geoffrey Hinton. 2015. Grammar as a foreign language. In *Advances in Neural Information Processing Systems 28*, pages 2773–2781.

Shuangzhi Wu, Dongdong Zhang, Zhirui Zhang, Nan Yang, Mu Li, and Ming Zhou. 2018. Dependency-to-dependency neural machine translation. *IEEE/ACM Transactions on Audio, Speech, and Language Processing*, 26(11):2132–2141.

Meishan Zhang, Zhenghua Li, Guohong Fu, and Min Zhang. 2019. Syntax-enhanced neural machine translation with syntax-aware word representations. In *Proceedings of NAACL*, pages 1151–1161. Association for Computational Linguistics.

APE at Scale and its Implications on MT Evaluation Biases

Markus Freitag, Isaac Caswell, Scott Roy
Google Research
{freitag,icaswell,hsr}@google.com

Abstract

In this work, we train an Automatic Post-Editing (APE) model and use it to reveal biases in standard Machine Translation (MT) evaluation procedures. The goal of our APE model is to correct typical errors introduced by the translation process, and convert the "translationese" output into natural text. Our APE model is trained entirely on monolingual data that has been round-trip translated through English, to mimic errors that are similar to the ones introduced by NMT. We apply our model to the output of existing NMT systems, and demonstrate that, while the human-judged quality improves in all cases, BLEU scores drop with forward-translated test sets. We verify these results for the WMT18 English→German, WMT15 English→French, and WMT16 English→Romanian tasks. Furthermore, we selectively apply our APE model on the output of the top submissions of the most recent WMT evaluation campaigns. We see quality improvements on all tasks of up to 2.5 BLEU points.

1 Introduction

Neural Machine Translation (NMT) (Bahdanau et al., 2015; Gehring et al., 2017; Vaswani et al., 2017) is currently the most popular approach in Machine Translation leading to state-of-the-art performance for many tasks. NMT relies mainly on parallel training data, which can be an expensive and scarce resource. There are several approaches to leverage monolingual data for NMT: Language model fusion for both phrase-based (Brants et al., 2007) and neural MT (Gülçehre et al., 2015, 2017), back-translation (Sennrich et al., 2016b), unsupervised NMT (Lample et al., 2018a; Artetxe et al., 2018a), dual learning (Cheng et al., 2016; He et al., 2016; Xia et al., 2017), and multi-task learning (Domhan and Hieber, 2017).

In this paper, we present a different approach to leverage monolingual data, which can be used as a post-processor for any existing translation. The idea is to train an Automatic Post-Editing (APE) system that is only trained on a large amount of synthetic data, to fix typical errors introduced by the translation process. During training, our model uses a noisy version of each sentence as input and learns how to reconstruct the original sentence. In this work, we model the noise with round-trip translations (RTT) through English, translating a sentence in the target language into English, then translating the result back into the original language. We train our APE model with a standard transformer model on the WMT18 English→German, WMT15 English→French and WMT16 English→Romanian monolingual News Crawl data and apply this model on the output of NMT models that are either trained on all available bitext or trained on a combination of bitext and back-translated monolingual data. Furthermore, we show that our APE model can be used as a post-processor for the best output of the recent WMT evaluation campaigns, where it improves even the output of these well engineered translation systems.

In addition to measuring quality in terms of BLEU scores on the standard WMT test sets, we split each test set into two subsets based on whether the source or target is the original sentence (each sentence is either originally written in the source or target language and human-translated into the other). We call these the source-language-original and target-language-original halves, respectively. We find that evaluating our post-edited output on the source-language-original half actually decreases the BLEU scores, whereas the BLEU scores improve for the target-language-original half. This is in line with results from Koppel and Ordan (2011), who demonstrate

Proceedings of the Fourth Conference on Machine Translation (WMT), Volume 1: Research Papers, pages 34–44
Florence, Italy, August 1-2, 2019. ©2019 Association for Computational Linguistics

that the mere fact of being translated plays a crucial role in the makeup of a translated text, making the actual (human) translation a less natural example of the target language. We hypothesize that, given these findings, the consistent decreases in BLEU scores on test sets whose source side are natural text does not mean that the actual output is of lower quality. To verify this hypothesis, we run human evaluations for different outputs with and without APE. The human ratings demonstrate that the output of the APE model is both consistently more accurate and consistently more fluent, regardless of whether the source or the target language is the original language, contradicting the corresponding BLEU scores.

To summarize the contributions of the paper:

- We introduce an APE model trained only on synthetic data generated with RTT for fixing typical translation errors from NMT output and investigate its scalability. To the best of our knowledge, this paper is the first to study the effect of an APE system trained at scale and only on synthetic data.

- We improve the BLEU of top submissions of the recent WMT evaluation campaigns.

- We show that the BLEU scores of the APE output only correlate well with human ratings when they are calculated with target-original references.

- We propose separately reporting scores on test sets whose source sentences are translated and whose target sentences are translated, and call for higher-quality test sets.

2 APE with RTT

2.1 Definition and Training

We formalize our APE model as a translation model from synthetic "translationese" (Gellerstam, 1986) text in one language to natural text in the same language. For a language pair (X, Y) and a monolingual corpus M_Y in language Y, the training procedure is as follows:

1. Train two translation models on bitext for $X{\to}Y$ and $Y{\to}X$

2. Use these models to generate round-trip translations for every target-language sentence y in M_Y, resulting in the synthetic dataset $\text{RTT}(M_Y)$.

3. Train a translation model on pairs of $(\text{RTT}(y), y)$, that translates from the round-tripped version of a sentence to its original form.

This procedure is illustrated in Figure 1.

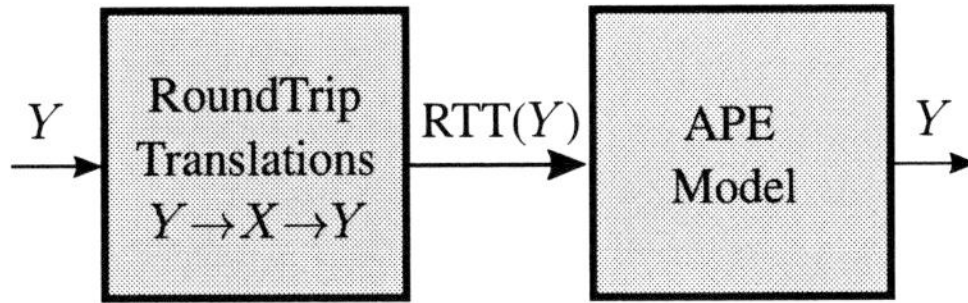

Figure 1: Training procedure of our APE model with RTT in language Y.

2.2 Application

Given a trained translation model and a trained APE model, the procedure is simply to a) translate any source text from language X to language Y with the translation model, and b) post-edit the output of the translation by passing it through the APE model. In this sense, the APE model may also be viewed as a paraphrasing model to produce "naturalized" text. This procedure is illustrated in Figure 2.

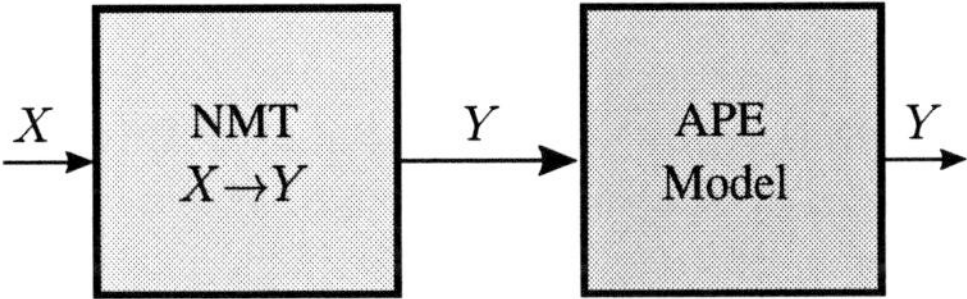

Figure 2: Automatic Post-Editing (APE) as post-processor of NMT.

3 Experimental Setup

3.1 Architecture

For the translation models, we use the transformer implementation in *lingvo* (Shen et al., 2019), using the transformer-base model size for Romanian→English and transformer-big model size (Vaswani et al., 2017) for German→English and French→English. The reverse models, English→Romanian, English→German and English→French, are all transformer-big. All use a vocabulary of 32k subword units, and exponentially moving averaging of checkpoints (EMA decay) with the weight decrease parameter set to $\alpha = 0.999$ (Buduma and Locascio, 2017).

The APE models are also transformer models with 32k subword units and EMA decay trained with lingvo. For the German and the French APE models, we use the transformer-big size, whereas for the Romanian APE model, we use the smaller transformer-base setup as we have less monolingual data.

3.2 Evaluation

We report BLEU (Papineni et al., 2002) and human evaluations. All BLEU scores are calculated with sacreBLEU (Post, 2018)[1].

Since 2014, the organizers of the WMT evaluation campaign (Bojar et al., 2017) have created test sets with the following method: first, they crawled monolingual data in both English and the target language from news stories from online sources. Thereafter they took about 1500 English sentences and translated them into the target language, and an additional 1500 sentences from the target language and translated them into English. This results in test sets of about 3000 sentences for each English-X language pair. The sgm files of each WMT test set include the original language for each sentence.

Therefore, in addition to reporting overall BLEU scores on the different test sets, we also report results on the two subsets (based on the original language) of each newstest20XX, which we call the {German,French,Romanian}-original and English-original halves of the test set. This is motivated by Koppel and Ordan (2011), who demonstrated that they can train a simple classifier to distinguish human-translated text from natural text with high accuracy. These text categorization experiments suggest that both the source language and the mere fact of being translated play a crucial role in the makeup of a translated text. One of the major goals of our APE model is to rephrase the NMT output in a more natural way, aiming to remove undesirable translation artifacts that have been introduced.

To collect human rankings, we present each output to crowd-workers, who were asked to score each sentence on a 5-point scale for:

- **fluency:** How do you judge the overall naturalness of the utterance in terms of its grammatical correctness and fluency?

Further, we included the source sentence and asked the raters to evaluate each sentence on a 2-point scale (binary decision) for:

- **accuracy:** Does the statement factually contradict anything in the reference information?

Each task was given to three different raters. Consequently, each output has a separate score for each question that is the average of 3 different ratings.

3.3 Data

For the round-trip experiments we use the monolingual News Crawl data from the WMT evaluation campaign. We remove duplicates and apply a max-length filter on the source sentences and the round-trip translations, filtering to the minimum of 500 characters or 70 tokens. For German, we concatenate all News Crawl data from 2007 to 2017, comprising 216.5M sentences after filtering and removing duplicates. For Romanian, we use News Crawl '16, comprising 2.2M sentences after filtering and deduplication. For French, we concatenate News Crawl data from 2007 to 2014, comprising 34M sentences after filtering.

Our translation models are trained on WMT18 ($\sim$5M sentences for German after filtering), WMT16 ($\sim$0.5M sentences for Romanian after filtering) and WMT15 ($\sim$41M sentences for French) bitext. For Romanian and German we filter sentence pairs that have empty source or target, that have source or target longer than 250 tokens, or the ratio of whose length is greater than 2.0. For English$\rightarrow$German and English$\rightarrow$French, we also build a system based on noised back-translation, as in Edunov et al. (2018). We use the same monolingual sentences that we used for the APE model to generate the noisy back-translation data.

4 Experiments

4.1 English$\rightarrow$German

The results of our English$\rightarrow$German experiments are shown in Table 1. We trained the APE model on RTT produced by English$\rightarrow$German and German$\rightarrow$English NMT models that are only trained on bitext. Applying the APE model on the output of our NMT model also trained on only bitext improves the BLEU scores by up to 1.5 BLEU points for newstest2014 and 0.7 BLEU points for newstest2017. Nevertheless, the score drops by 1.4 points on newstest2016. To investigate the differing impact on the test sets, we split each test set by its original language (Table 2). The APE model consistently increases the BLEU on the German-original half of the test set, but decreases the BLEU

---

[1] sacreBLEU signatures: BLEU+case.mixed+lang.en-LANG+numrefs.1+smooth.exp+SET+tok.intl+version.1.2.20

	newstest2014	newstest2015	newstest2016	newstest2017	average
Vaswani et al. (2017)	28.4	-	-	-	
Shaw et al. (2018)	29.2	-	-	-	
our bitext	29.2	31.4	35.0	29.4	31.2
+ RTT APE	30.7	31.2	33.6	30.1	31.4
+ RTT APE de-orig only	31.7	32.9	37.2	31.9	33.4
our NBT	33.5	34.4	38.3	32.5	34.7
+ RTT APE	32.5	32.7	35.2	31.3	32.9
+ RTT APE de-orig only	34.0	34.5	38.7	33.2	35.1

Table 1: BLEU scores for WMT18 English→German. We apply the same APE model (trained on RTT with bitext models) for both an NMT system based on pure bitext and an NMT system that uses noised back-translation (NBT) in addition to bitext.

	newstest2014		newstest2015		newstest2016		newstest2017		average	
	orig-de	orig-en	orig-de	orig-en	orig-de	orig-en	orig-de	orig-en	orig-de	orig-en
our bitext	28.4	29.4	26.5	33.3	29.9	38.2	25.9	31.6	27.7	33.1
+ RTT APE	34.1	27.6	31.3	30.9	35.7	32.2	32.1	28.5	33.3	29.8
our NBT	35.6	31.3	32.6	34.7	37.6	38.7	31.7	32.6	34.4	34.3
+ RTT APE	36.9	28.8	33.5	32.0	38.5	32.9	33.8	29.2	35.7	30.7

Table 2: BLEU scores for WMT18 English→German. Test sets are divided by their original source language (either German or English).

	newstest2016				newstest2017			
	fluency		accuracy		fluency		accuracy	
	orig-de	orig-en	orig-de	orig-en	orig-de	orig-en	orig-de	orig-en
baseline bitext	4.65	4.49	95.6%	94.4%	4.74	4.52	97.2%	94.6%
+ RTT APE	4.77	4.59	98.4%	95.0%	4.84	4.58	98.0%	94.8%
our NBT	4.79	4.64	98.2%	95.8%	4.79	4.65	98.2%	95.4%
+ RTT APE	4.82	4.63	98.0%	96.2%	4.86	4.68	98.0%	96.4%
reference	4.85	4.67	98.6%	98.6%	4.83	4.70	98.0%	99.2%

Table 3: English→German human evaluation results split by original language of the test set.

on the English-original half. Consequentially, we applied our APE model only on the sentences with original language in German (*+RTT APE de-orig only* in Table 1) and see consistent improvements over all test sets with an average BLEU improvement of 2.2 points.

To verify that the drop in BLEU score is because of the unnatural reference translations, we run a human evaluation (see Section 3.2) for both fluency/grammatical correctness and accuracy. Based on the human ratings (Table 3), our APE model also improves on the English-original half of the test set (which is a more realistic use case).

Without re-training, we use the APE model that is trained on the bitext RTT and apply it to a stronger NMT system that also includes all the available monolingual data in the form of noised back-translation. We see a very similar pattern to the previous experiments. Regarding automatic scores, our APE model only improves on the German-original part of the test sets, with an average improvement of 1.3 BLEU points. The human evaluations show the same inconsistency with the automatic scores for the English-original half. As with the weaker baseline, humans rate the output of our APE model at least as fluent and accurate as the original output of the NMT model (Table 3). Further, we also run a human evaluation on the reference sentences and found that the scores for both fluency and accuracy are only minimally higher than for our APE NBT output.

Comparing only the BLEU scores from our bitext and NBT models in Table 2 reveals that augmenting the parallel data with back-translated data also mostly improves the BLEU scores on the German-original half of the test set. This is in line with the results of our APE model and opens the question of how much of the original bitext data is natural on the target side.

As our APE model seems agnostic to the model which produced the RTT, we applied it to the best submissions of the recent WMT18 evaluation campaign, applying to German-original half of the test set only. Table 4 shows the results for the 2 top submissions of Microsoft (Junczys-Dowmunt, 2018) and Cambridge (Stahlberg et al., 2018). Both systems improved by up to 0.8 points in BLEU.

	Microsoft	Cambridge
WMT18 submission	48.7	47.2
+ APE only de-orig	49.5	47.7

Table 4: BLEU scores for WMT18 English→German newstest2018. We apply our APE model only on the German-original half of the test set. BLEU scores are calculated on the full newstest2018 set and the English-original half is just copied from the submission.

Finally, we train our APE model on different random subsets of the available 216.5M monolingual data (see Figure 3). The average BLEU scores on newstest2014-newstest2017 show that we can achieve similar performance by using 24 million training examples only, and that large improvements are seen using as few as 4M training examples.

4.2 English→Romanian

Experimental results for the WMT16 English→Romanian task are summarized in Table 5. By applying our APE model on top of a baseline that is only trained on bitext, we see improvements of 3.0 BLEU (dev) and 0.3 BLEU (test) over our baseline system when we automatically post edit only to the Romanian-original half of the test set. Similar to English→German, we apply our APE model on the top 2 submissions of the WMT16 evaluation campaign (Table 6). Both the QT21 submission (Peter et al., 2016), which is a system combination of several NMT systems,

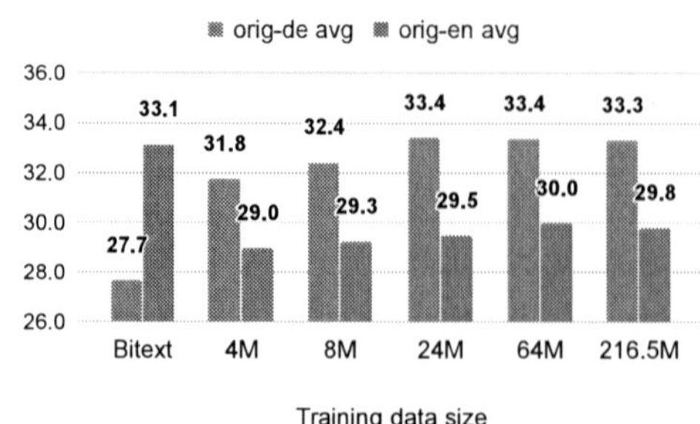

Figure 3: English→German - Average BLEU scores for newstest2014-newstest2017: Our APE model is trained on different subsets of the monolingual data.

and the ensemble of the University of Edinburgh (Sennrich et al., 2016a) improve, by 0.3 BLEU and 0.2 BLEU on test, respectively.

	dev	test
Sennrich et al. (2016a)	-	28.8
our bitext	27.0	28.9
+ RTT APE	27.3	29.0
+ RTT APE only ro-orig	30.0	29.2

Table 5: BLEU scores for our models on WMT16 English→Romanian.

	QT21	Edinburgh
WMT16 submission	29.4	28.8
+ RTT APE only ro-orig	29.7	29.0

Table 6: BLEU scores for WMT16 English→Romanian test set. Our APE model was applied on top of the best WMT16 submissions.

4.3 English→French

Experimental results for English→French are summarized in Table 7. We see the same tendency as we saw for German and Romanian. When applying our APE system on the output of the bitext baseline, we get a small improvement of 0.1 BLEU. By only post-editing the French-original half, we get an improvement of 1.0 BLEU points. The same effect can be seen on the English→French system that is trained with Noised BT. We yield quality improvements of 0.8 BLEU by applying our APE model on the French-original half of the test set only.

	newstest2014
our bitext	43.2
+ RTT APE	43.3
+ RTT APE only fr-orig	44.2
our NBT	45.3
+ RTT APE	44.6
+ RTT APE only fr-orig	46.1

Table 7: BLEU scores for WMT15 English→French.

5 Example Output

We would like to highlight a few short examples where our APE model improves the NMT translation in German. Although our APE model is also quite helpful for long sentences, we will focus on short examples for the sake of simplicity. In Table 8 there are examples from the English→German noised back-translated (NBT) setup (see Table 1), with and without automatic post editing. In the first example, NMT translates *club* (i.e. cudgel) incorrectly into *Club* (i.e. organization). Based on the context of the sentence, our APE model learned that *club* has to be translated into *Schlagstock* (i.e. cudgel). The next two examples are very similar as our APE model improves the word choice of the translations by taking the context of the sentence into account. The NMT translations of the last two examples make little sense and our APE model rephrases the output into a fluent, meaningful sentence.

6 Discussion

In this section, we focus on the results on target-language-original test sets, like the English-original subset of newstest2016 (Table 2 and Table 3), where the APE model lowered the score by 6 BLEU, yet improved human evaluations. A naïve take-away from this result would be that evaluation sets whose target side is natural text are inherently superior. However, translating *from* translationese also has its own problems, including 1) it does not represent any real-world translation task, and 2) translationese sources may be much easier to translate "correctly", and reward MT biases like word-for-word translation. The take-away, therefore, must be to report scores both on the source-language-original and the target-language-original test sets, rather than lumping two test-sets together into one as has heretofore been done. This gives a higher-precision glimpse into the strengths and weaknesses of different modeling techniques, and may prevent some effects (like improvements in naturalness of output) from being hidden.

Going forward, our results should also be seen as a call for higher-quality test sets. Multi reference BLEU is one option and less likely to suffer these biases as acutely, and has previously been used in the NIST projects. Another option could be to align sentence pairs from monolingual data sets in two languages and run human evaluation to exclude bad sentence pairs.

7 Related Work

Automatic Post-Editing

Probably most similar to our work, Junczys-Dowmunt and Grundkiewicz (2016, 2018) uses RTT as additional training data for the automatic post-editing (APE) task of the WMT evaluation campaign (Chatterjee et al., 2018). They claimed that the provided post-editing data is orders of magnitude too small to train neural models, and combined the training data with artificial training data generated with RTT. They found that the additional artificial data helps against early overfitting and makes it possible to overcome the problem of too little training data. In contrast to our work, they do not report results for models only trained on the artificial RTT data. Further, their RTT data is much smaller (10M sentences) compared to ours (up to 200M sentences) and they only report results for the APE subtask.

There have been several earlier approaches using RTT for APE. Hermet and Alain (2009) used RTT to improve a standard preposition error detection system. Although their evaluation corpus was limited to 133 prepositions, the hybrid system outperformed their standard method by roughly 13%. Madnani et al. (2012) combined RTT obtained from Google Translate via 8 different pivot languages into a lattice for grammatical error correction. Similar to system combination, their final output is extracted by the shortest path scored by different features. They claimed that their preliminary experiments yield fairly satisfactory results but leave significant room for improvement.

Back-translation

Back-translation (Sennrich et al., 2016b; Poncelas et al., 2018) augments relatively scarce parallel data with plentiful monolingual data, allowing one to train source-to-target (S2T) models with the help of target-to-source (T2S) models. Specif-

source	Using a **club**, they **beat** the victim in the face and upper leg.
NBT	Mit einem **Club schlagen** sie das Opfer in Gesicht und Oberschenkel.
+ RTT APE	Mit einem **Schlagstock schlugen** sie dem Opfer ins Gesicht und in den Oberschenkel.
source	Müller put another one in with a **with a penalty**.
NBT	Müller setzte einen weiteren **mit einer Strafe** ein.
+ RTT APE	Müller netzte einen weiteren **per Elfmeter** ein.
source	Obama **receives** Netanyahu
NBT	Obama **erhält** Netanjahu
+ RTT APE	Obama **empfängt** Netanjahu
source	At least one Bayern fan was **taken injured from the stadium**.
NBT	Mindestens ein Bayern-Fan wurde **vom Stadion verletzt**.
+ RTT APE	Mindestens ein Bayern-Fan wurde **verletzt aus dem Stadion gebracht**.
source	The archaeologists **made a find in the third construction phase** of the Rhein Boulevard.
NBT	Die Archäologen **haben in der dritten Bauphase** des Rheinboulevards **gefunden**.
+ RTT APE	Die Archäologen **sind im dritten Bauabschnitt** des Rheinboulevards **fündig geworden**.

Table 8: Example output for English→German.

ically, given a set of sentences in the target language, a pre-constructed T2S translation system is used to generate translations to the source language. These synthetic sentence pairs are combined with the original bilingual data when training the S2T NMT model.

Iterative Back-translation
Iterative back-translation (Zhang et al., 2018; Cotterell and Kreutzer, 2018; Hoang et al., 2018) is a joint training algorithm to enhance the effect of monolingual source and target data by iteratively boosting the source-to-target and target-to-source translation models. The joint training method uses the monolingual data and updates NMT models through several iterations. A variety of flavors of iterative back-translation have been proposed, including Niu et al. (2018), who simultaneously perform iterative S2T and T2S back-translation in a multilingual model, and He et al. (2016); Xia et al. (2017), who combine dual learning with phases of back- and forward-translation.

Artetxe et al. (2018a,b) and Lample et al. (2018a,b) used iterative back-translation to train two unsupervised translation systems in both directions ($X \rightarrow Y$ and $Y \rightarrow X$) in parallel. Further, they used back-translation to generate a synthetic source to construct a dev set for tuning the parameters of their unsupervised statistical machine translation system. In a similar formulation, Cheng et al. (2016) jointly learn a translation system with a round-trip autoencoder.

Round-tripping and Paraphrasing
Round-trip translation has seen success as a method to generate paraphrases. Bannard and Callison-Burch (2005) extracted paraphrases by using alternative phase translations from bilingual phrase tables from Statistical Machine Translation. Mallinson et al. (2017) presented PARANET, a neural paraphrasing model based on round-trip translations with NMT. They showed that their paraphrase model outperforms all traditional paraphrase models.

Wu et al. (2018) train a paraphrasing model on $(X, \mathrm{RTT}(X))$ pairs, translating from natural text into a simplified version. They apply this sentence-simplifier on the source sentences of the training data and report quality gains for IWSLT.

Translationese and Artifacts from NMT
The difference between translated sentence pairs based on whether the source or the target is the original sentence has long been recognized by the human translation community, but only partially investigated by the machine translation community. An introduction to the latter is presented in Koppel and Ordan (2011), who train a high-accuracy classifier to distinguish human-translated text from natural text in the Europarl corpus. This is in line with research from the professional translation community, which has seen various works investigating both systematic biases inherent to translated texts (Baker, 1993; Selinker, 1972), as well as biases resulting specifically from interference from the source text (Toury, 1995). There has similarly long been a focus on the conflict between *Fidelity* (the extent to which the translation is faithful to the source) and *Transparency* (the ex-

tent to which the translation appears to be a natural sentence in the target language) (Warner, 2018; Schleiermacher, 1816; Dryden, 1685). To frame our hypotheses in these terms, the present work hypothesizes that outputs from NMT systems often err on the side of disfluent fidelity, or word-by-word translation.

There are a few papers that discuss the effect of translationese on MT models. Lembersky et al. (2012); Stymne (2017) explored how the translation direction for statistical machine translation affects the translation result. They found that using training and tuning data translated in the same direction as the translation systems tends to give the best results. Holmqvist et al. (2009) noted that the original language of the test sentences influences the BLEU score of translations. They showed that the BLEU scores for target-original sentences are on average higher than sentences that have their original source in a different language. Popel (2018) split the WMT Czech-English test set based on the original language. They found that when training on synthetic data, the model performs much better on the Czech-original half than on the non Czech-original half. When trained on authentic data, it is the other way round. Fomicheva et al. (2017) found that both the average score and Pearson correlation with human judgments is substantially higher when both the MT output and human translation were generated from the same source language.

8 Ablation

8.1 Iterative APE

We can apply our APE model in an iterative fashion several times on the same output. In Table 9, we applied our APE model on the already post-edited output to see if we can further naturalize the sentences. As a result, 75% of the sentences did not change. The remaining sentences lowered the BLEU scores on average by 0.1 points for German-original half and by 0.7 points for the English-original half of the test sets.

8.2 Reverse APE

Instead of training an APE model on $(\text{RTT}(y), y)$ sentence pairs (see Section 2), we train in this section a `reverse APE` model that flips source and target and is trained on $(y, \text{RTT}(y))$ sentence pairs. Experimental results can be seen in Table 10. Overall, the performance decreases on

	average	
	orig-de	orig-en
our bitext	27.7	33.1
+ APE	33.3	29.8
+ 2xAPE	33.2	29.1

Table 9: Average BLEU scores for WMT18 English→German newstest2014-2017. We run our APE model a second time on the output of the already post-editied output.

both the German-original half and the English-original half. Interestingly, the BLEU scores of the reverse APE model on the English-original half are higher than those of the normal APE model. This demonstrates again that sentences evaluated on the English-original half prefer output that is biased by the translation process.

	average	
	orig-de	orig-en
our bitext	27.7	33.1
+ RTT APE	33.3	29.8
+ Reverse APE	25.1	30.6
our NBT	34.4	34.3
+ RTT APE	35.7	30.7
+ Reverse APE	27.0	31.3

Table 10: Average BLEU scores for WMT18 English→German newstest2014-2017.

8.3 Inside the black box of RTT

In this subsection we are interested in how much RTT changes translation outputs. We calculate the BLEU scores of all English→German test sets (11,175 sentences in total) by taking the original German sentences as references and their RTT as hypotheses. Although the RTT hypotheses are a less clean (paraphrased) version of the references, having been forward-translated from an already noisy back-translated source, the BLEU score is 40.9, with unigram precision of 72.3%, bigram precision of 48.9%, trigram precision of 35.6% and 4gram precision of 26.6%.

We further found that the original sentences use a larger vocabulary than the artificial RTT data. While the output of the RTT has only 29,635 unique tokens, the original sentences contain 33,814 unique tokens. Even more interesting, the NMT output (from the model trained only on bitext) of the same test sets has a vocabulary size of 30,540, but after running our APE on the same test sets the vocabulary size increases to 31,471. The NMT output from the NBT model has a vocabulary size of 32,170 and its post-edited version increases the number of unique words to 32,283. Overall, we see that both the RTT and the NMT output have a smaller vocabulary size than the original or post-edited versions, and that BLEU score grows directly with increased number of unique tokens in the target side.

9 Conclusion

We propose an APE model that is only trained on RTT and increases the quality of NMT translations, measured both by BLEU and human evaluation. We see improvements both when automatically post editing our model translations and when automatically post editing outputs from the winning submissions to the WMT competition. Our APE has the advantage that it is agnostic to the model which produced the translations, and so can be used on top of any new advance in the field, without need for re-training. Further, we demonstrate that we need only a subset of 24M training examples to train our APE model. We furthermore use this model as a tool to reveal systematic problems with reference translations, and propose finer-grained BLEU reporting on both source-language-original test sets and target-language-original test sets, as well as calling for higher-quality and multi-reference test sets.

References

Mikel Artetxe, Gorka Labaka, and Eneko Agirre. 2018a. Unsupervised Statistical Machine Translation. In *Proceedings of the 2018 Conference on Empirical Methods in Natural Language Processing*, pages 3632–3642.

Mikel Artetxe, Gorka Labaka, Eneko Agirre, and Kyunghyun Cho. 2018b. Unsupervised Neural Machine Translation. In *International Conference on Learning Representations*.

Dzmitry Bahdanau, Kyunghyun Cho, and Yoshua Bengio. 2015. Neural Machine Translation by Jointly Learning to Align and Translate. In *3rd International Conference on Learning Representations, ICLR 2015*.

Mona Baker. 1993. Corpus Linguistics and Translation Studies: Implications and Applications. *Text and technology: in honour of John Sinclair*, pages 233–252.

Colin Bannard and Chris Callison-Burch. 2005. Paraphrasing with Bilingual Parallel Corpora. In *Proceedings of the 43rd Annual Meeting on Association for Computational Linguistics*, pages 597–604.

Ondřej Bojar, Rajen Chatterjee, Christian Federmann, Yvette Graham, Barry Haddow, Shujian Huang, Matthias Huck, Philipp Koehn, Qun Liu, Varvara Logacheva, et al. 2017. Findings of the 2017 Conference on Machine Translation (WMT17). In *Proceedings of the Second Conference on Machine Translation*, pages 169–214.

Thorsten Brants, Ashok C Popat, Peng Xu, Franz J Och, and Jeffrey Dean. 2007. Large Language Models in Machine Translation. In *Proceedings of the 2007 Joint Conference on Empirical Methods in Natural Language Processing and Computational Natural Language Learning (EMNLP-CoNLL)*.

Nikhil Buduma and Nicholas Locascio. 2017. *Fundamentals of Deep Learning: Designing Next-Generation Machine Intelligence Algorithms*. "O'Reilly Media, Inc.".

Rajen Chatterjee, Matteo Negri, Raphael Rubino, and Marco Turchi. 2018. Findings of the WMT 2018 Shared Task on Automatic Post-Editing. In *Proceedings of the Third Conference on Machine Translation: Shared Task Papers*, pages 710–725.

Yong Cheng, Wei Xu, Zhongjun He, Wei He, Hua Wu, Maosong Sun, and Yang Liu. 2016. Semi-Supervised Learning for Neural Machine Translation. In *Proceedings of the 54th Annual Meeting of the Association for Computational Linguistics*, volume 1, pages 1965–1974.

Ryan Cotterell and Julia Kreutzer. 2018. Explaining and Generalizing Back-Translation through Wakesleep. *arXiv preprint arXiv:1806.04402*.

Tobias Domhan and Felix Hieber. 2017. Using Target-side Monolingual Data for Neural Machine Translation through Multi-task Learning. In *Proceedings of the 2017 Conference on Empirical Methods in Natural Language Processing*, pages 1500–1505.

John Dryden. 1685. *Sylvae [Translator's preface]*. A Scolar Press facsimile. Scolar Press.

Sergey Edunov, Myle Ott, Michael Auli, and David Grangier. 2018. Understanding Back-Translation at Scale. In *Proceedings of the 2018 Conference on Empirical Methods in Natural Language Processing (EMNLP)*, pages 489–500.

Marina Fomicheva et al. 2017. *The Role of Human Reference Translation in Machine Translation Evaluation*. Ph.D. thesis, Universitat Pompeu Fabra.

Jonas Gehring, Michael Auli, David Grangier, Denis Yarats, and Yann N. Dauphin. 2017. Convolutional Sequence to Sequence Learning. In *Proceedings of the 34th International Conference on Machine Learning - Volume 70*, pages 1243–1252.

Martin Gellerstam. 1986. Translationese in Swedish novels translated from English. *Translation Studies in Scandinavia*, pages 88–95.

Çağlar Gülçehre, Orhan Firat, Kelvin Xu, Kyunghyun Cho, Loic Barrault, Huei-Chi Lin, Fethi Bougares, Holger Schwenk, and Yoshua Bengio. 2015. On using Monolingual Corpora in Neural Machine Translation. *arXiv preprint arXiv:1503.03535*.

Çağlar Gülçehre, Orhan Firat, Kelvin Xu, Kyunghyun Cho, and Yoshua Bengio. 2017. On Integrating a Language Model into Neural Machine Translation. *Comput. Speech Lang.*, pages 137–148.

Di He, Yingce Xia, Tao Qin, Liwei Wang, Nenghai Yu, Tieyan Liu, and Wei-Ying Ma. 2016. Dual Learning for Machine Translation. In *Conference on Advances in Neural Information Processing Systems (NeurIPS)*.

Matthieu Hermet and Désilets Alain. 2009. Using First and Second Language Models to Correct Preposition Errors in Second Language Authoring. In *Proceedings of the Fourth Workshop on Innovative Use of NLP for Building Educational Applications*, pages 64–72.

Vu Cong Duy Hoang, Philipp Koehn, Gholamreza Haffari, and Trevor Cohn. 2018. Iterative Backtranslation for Neural Machine Translation. In *Proceedings of the 2nd Workshop on Neural Machine Translation and Generation*, volume 1, pages 18–24.

Maria Holmqvist, Sara Stymne, Jody Foo, and Lars Ahrenberg. 2009. Improving Alignment for SMT by Reordering and Augmenting the Training Corpus. In *Proceedings of the Fourth Workshop on Statistical Machine Translation*, pages 120–124. Association for Computational Linguistics.

Marcin Junczys-Dowmunt. 2018. Microsoft's Submission to the WMT2018 News Translation Task: How I Learned to Stop Worrying and Love the Data. In *Proceedings of the Third Conference on Machine Translation, Volume 2: Shared Task Papers*, pages 429–434. Association for Computational Linguistics.

Marcin Junczys-Dowmunt and Roman Grundkiewicz. 2016. Log-linear Combinations of Monolingual and Bilingual Neural Machine Translation Models for Automatic Post-Editing. In *Proceedings of the First Conference on Machine Translation: Volume 2, Shared Task Papers*, pages 751–758.

Marcin Junczys-Dowmunt and Roman Grundkiewicz. 2018. MS-UEdin Submission to the WMT2018 APE Shared Task: Dual-Source Transformer for Automatic Post-Editing. In *Proceedings of the Third Conference on Machine Translation: Shared Task Papers*, pages 822–826.

Moshe Koppel and Noam Ordan. 2011. Translationese and Its Dialects. In *Proceedings of the 49th Annual Meeting of the Association for Computational Linguistics: Human Language Technologies - Volume 1*, pages 1318–1326.

Guillaume Lample, Alexis Conneau, Ludovic Denoyer, and Marc'Aurelio Ranzato. 2018a. Unsupervised Machine Translation Using Monolingual Corpora Only. In *International Conference on Learning Representations*.

Guillaume Lample, Myle Ott, Alexis Conneau, Ludovic Denoyer, and Marc'Aurelio Ranzato. 2018b. Phrase-Based & Neural Unsupervised Machine Translation. In *Proceedings of the 2018 Conference on Empirical Methods in Natural Language Processing (EMNLP)*.

Gennadi Lembersky, Noam Ordan, and Shuly Wintner. 2012. Language Models for Machine Translation: Original vs. Translated Texts. *Computational Linguistics*, 38(4).

Nitin Madnani, Joel Tetreault, and Martin Chodorow. 2012. Exploring grammatical error correction with not-so-crummy machine translation. In *Proceedings of the Seventh Workshop on Building Educational Applications Using NLP*, pages 44–53. Association for Computational Linguistics.

Jonathan Mallinson, Rico Sennrich, and Mirella Lapata. 2017. Paraphrasing Revisited with Neural Machine Translation. In *Proceedings of the 15th Conference of the European Chapter of the Association for Computational Linguistics: Volume 1, Long Papers*, volume 1, pages 881–893.

Xing Niu, Michael Denkowski, and Marine Carpuat. 2018. Bi-Directional Neural Machine Translation with Synthetic Parallel Data. In *Proceedings of the 2nd Workshop on Neural Machine Translation and Generation*, pages 84–91.

Kishore Papineni, Salim Roukos, Todd Ward, and Wei-Jing Zhu. 2002. BLEU: a Method for Automatic Evaluation of Machine Translation. In *Proceedings of the 40th annual meeting on association for computational linguistics*, pages 311–318. Association for Computational Linguistics.

Jan-Thorsten Peter, Tamer Alkhouli, Hermann Ney, Matthias Huck, Fabienne Braune, Alexander Fraser, Aleš Tamchyna, Ondřej Bojar, Barry Haddow, Rico Sennrich, Frédéric Blain, Lucia Specia, Jan Niehues, Alex Waibel, Alexandre Allauzen, Lauriane Aufrant, Franck Burlot, elena knyazeva, Thomas Lavergne, François Yvon, Mārcis Pinnis, and Stella Frank. 2016. The QT21/HimL Combined Machine Translation System. In *Proceedings of the First Conference on Machine Translation (WMT16)*, pages 344–355.

Alberto Poncelas, Dimitar Shterionov, Andy Way, Gideon Maillette de Buy Wenniger, and Peyman Passban. 2018. Investigating Backtranslation in Neural Machine Translation. In *Proceedings of the*

21st Annual Conference of the European Association for Machine Translation, pages 249–258.

Martin Popel. 2018. CUNI Transformer Neural MT System for WMT18. In *Proceedings of the Third Conference on Machine Translation: Shared Task Papers*, pages 482–487.

Matt Post. 2018. A Call for Clarity in Reporting Bleu Scores. In *Proceedings of the Third Conference on Machine Translation: Research Papers*, pages 186–191.

Friedrich Schleiermacher. 1816. *Über die verschiedenen Methoden des Übersetzens*. Abhandlungen der Königlichen Akademie der Wissenschaften in Berlin. Walter de Gruyter GmbH.

Larry Selinker. 1972. Interlanguage. *International Review of Applied Linguistics*, pages 209–241.

Rico Sennrich, Barry Haddow, and Alexandra Birch. 2016a. Edinburgh Neural Machine Translation Systems for WMT 16. In *Proceedings of the First Conference on Machine Translation*, pages 371–376.

Rico Sennrich, Barry Haddow, and Alexandra Birch. 2016b. Improving Neural Machine Translation Models with Monolingual Data. In *Proceedings of the 54th Annual Meeting of the Association for Computational Linguistics (Volume 1: Long Papers)*, pages 86–96.

Peter Shaw, Jakob Uszkoreit, and Ashish Vaswani. 2018. Self-Attention with Relative Position Representations. In *Proceedings of the 2018 Conference of the North American Chapter of the Association for Computational Linguistics: Human Language Technologies*, pages 464–468.

Jonathan Shen, Patrick Nguyen, Yonghui Wu, Zhifeng Chen, Mia X. Chen, Ye Jia, Anjuli Kannan, Tara N. Sainath, and Yuan Cao et al. 2019. Lingvo: a Modular and Scalable Framework for Sequence-to-Sequence Modeling. *CoRR*, abs/1902.08295.

Felix Stahlberg, Adri de Gispert, and Bill Byrne. 2018. The University of Cambridge's Machine Translation Systems for WMT18. In *Proceedings of the Third Conference on Machine Translation, Volume 2: Shared Task Papers*, pages 508–516.

Sara Stymne. 2017. The Effect of Translationese on Tuning for Statistical Machine Translation. In *The 21st Nordic Conference on Computational Linguistics*, pages 241–246.

Gideon Toury. 1995. *Descriptive Translation Studies and Beyond*. Benjamins translation library. John Benjamins Publishing Company.

Ashish Vaswani, Noam Shazeer, Niki Parmar, Jakob Uszkoreit, Lion Jones, Aidan N Gomez, Łukasz Kaiser, and Illia Polosukhin. 2017. Attention Is All You Need. In *Advances in Neural Information Processing Systems*, pages 5998–6008.

Marina Warner. 2018. The Politics of Translation. *London Review of Books*, 40 no. 19:22.

Tian Wu, Zhongjun He, Enhong Chen, and Haifeng Wang. 2018. Improving Neural Machine Translation with Neural Sentence Rewriting. In *2018 International Conference on Asian Language Processing (IALP)*.

Yingce Xia, Tao Qin, Wei Chen, Jiang Bian, Nenghai Yu, and Tie-Yan Liu. 2017. Dual Supervised Learning. In *International Conference on Machine Learning (ICML)*.

Zhirui Zhang, Shujie Liu, Mu Li, Ming Zhou, and Enhong Chen. 2018. Joint Training for Neural Machine Translation Models with Monolingual Data. In *Thirty-Second AAAI Conference on Artificial Intelligence*.

Generalizing Back-Translation in Neural Machine Translation

Miguel Graça[1†]   **Yunsu Kim**[1]   **Julian Schamper**[1†]   **Shahram Khadivi**[2]   **Hermann Ney**[1]

[1]Human Language Technology and Pattern Recognition Group
RWTH Aachen University, Aachen, Germany
`{surname}@i6.informatik.rwth-aachen.de`
[2]eBay, Inc., Aachen, Germany
`{skhadivi}@ebay.com`

Abstract

Back-translation — data augmentation by translating target monolingual data — is a crucial component in modern neural machine translation (NMT). In this work, we reformulate back-translation in the scope of cross-entropy optimization of an NMT model, clarifying its underlying mathematical assumptions and approximations beyond its heuristic usage. Our formulation covers broader synthetic data generation schemes, including sampling from a target-to-source NMT model. With this formulation, we point out fundamental problems of the sampling-based approaches and propose to remedy them by (i) disabling label smoothing for the target-to-source model and (ii) sampling from a restricted search space. Our statements are investigated on the WMT 2018 German $\leftrightarrow$ English news translation task.

1   Introduction

Neural machine translation (NMT) (Bahdanau et al., 2014; Vaswani et al., 2017) systems make use of back-translation (Sennrich et al., 2016a) to leverage monolingual data during the training. Here an inverse, target-to-source, translation model generates synthetic source sentences, by translating a target monolingual corpus, which are then jointly used as bilingual data.

Sampling-based synthetic data generation schemes were recently shown to outperform beam search (Edunov et al., 2018; Imamura et al., 2018). However, the generated corpora are reported to stray away from the distribution of natural data (Edunov et al., 2018). In this work, we focus on investigating why sampling creates better training data by re-writing the loss criterion of an NMT model to include a model-based data generator.

By doing so, we obtain a deeper understanding of synthetic data generation methods, identifying their desirable properties and clarifying the practical approximations.

In addition, current state-of-the-art NMT models suffer from probability smearing issues (Ott et al., 2018) and are trained using label smoothing (Pereyra et al., 2017). These result in low-quality sampled sentences, which influence the synthetic corpora. We investigate considering only high-quality hypotheses by restricting the search space of the model via (i) ignoring words under a probability threshold during sampling and (ii) N-best list sampling.

We validate our claims in experiments on a controlled scenario derived from the WMT 2018 German $\leftrightarrow$ English translation task, which allows us to directly compare the properties of synthetic and natural corpora. Further, we present the proposed sampling techniques on the original WMT German $\leftrightarrow$ English task. The experiments show that our restricted sampling techniques work comparable or superior to other generation methods by imitating human-generated data better. In terms of translation quality, these do not result in consistent improvements over the typical beam search strategy.

2   Related Work

Sennrich et al. (2016a) introduce the back-translation technique for NMT and show that the quality of the back-translation model, and therefore resulting pseudo-corpus, has a positive effect on the quality of the subsequent source-to-target model. These findings are further investigated in (Hoang et al., 2018; Burlot and Yvon, 2018) where the authors confirm work effect. In our work, we expand upon this concept by arguing that the quality of the resulting model not only depends on the

---

† Now at DeepL GmbH.

Proceedings of the Fourth Conference on Machine Translation (WMT), Volume 1: Research Papers, pages 45–52
Florence, Italy, August 1-2, 2019. ©2019 Association for Computational Linguistics

data fitness of the back-translation model but also on how sentences are generated from it.

Cotterell and Kreutzer (2018) frame back-translation as a variational process, with the space of source sentences as the latent space. Their approach argues that the distribution of the synthetic data generator and the true translation probability should match. Thus it is invaluable to clarify and investigate the sampling distributions that current state-of-the-art data generation techniques utilize. A simple property is that a target sentence must be allowed to be aligned to multiple source sentences during the training phase. Several efforts (Hoang et al., 2018; Edunov et al., 2018; Imamura et al., 2018) confirm that this is in fact beneficial. Here, we unify these findings by re-writing the optimization criterion of NMT models to depend on a data generator, which we define for beam search, sampling and N-best list sampling approaches.

3　How Back-Translation Fits in NMT

In NMT, one is interested in translating a source sentence $f_1^J = f_1, \ldots, f_j, \ldots, f_J$ into a target sentence $e_1^I = e_1, \ldots, e_i, \ldots, e_I$. For this purpose, the translation process is modelled via a neural model $p_\theta(e_i | f_1^J, e_1^{i-1})$ with parameters θ.

The optimal optimization criterion of an NMT model requires access to the true joint distribution of source and target sentence pairs $Pr(f_1^J, e_1^I)$. This is approximated by the empirical distribution $\hat{p}(f_1^J, e_1^I)$ derived from a bilingual data-set $(f_{1,s}^{J_s}, e_{1,s}^{I_s})_{s=1}^S$. The model parameters are trained to minimize the cross-entropy, normalized over the number of target tokens, over the same.

$$L(\theta) = - \sum_{(f_1^J, e_1^I)} Pr(f_1^J, e_1^I) \cdot \frac{1}{I} \log p_\theta(e_1^I | f_1^J) \tag{1}$$

$$= - \sum_{(f_1^J, e_1^I)} \hat{p}(f_1^J, e_1^I) \cdot \frac{1}{I} \log p_\theta(e_1^I | f_1^J) \tag{2}$$

$$= -\frac{1}{S} \sum_{s=1}^{S} \frac{1}{I_s} \log p_\theta(e_{1,s}^{I_s} | f_{1,s}^{J_s}) \tag{3}$$

Target monolingual data can be included by generating a pseudo-parallel source corpus via, e.g. back-translation or sampling-based methods. In this section, we describe such generators as a component of the optimization criterion of NMT models and discuss approximations made in practice.

3.1　Derivation of the Generation Criterion

Eq. 1 is the starting point of our derivation in Eqs. 4-6. $Pr(f_1^J, e_1^I)$ can be decomposed into the true language probability $Pr(e_1^I)$ and true translation probability $Pr(f_1^J | e_1^I)$. These two probabilities highlight the assumptions in the scenario of back-translation: we have access to an empirical target distribution $\hat{p}(e_1^I)$ with which $Pr(e_1^I)$ is approximated, derived from the monolingual corpus $(e_{1,s}^{I_s})_{s=1}^S$. However, one lacks access to $\hat{p}(f_1^J | e_1^I)$. Generating synthetic data is essentially the approximation of the true probability of $Pr(f_1^J | e_1^I)$. It can be described as a sampling distribution[1] $q(f_1^J | e_1^I; p)$ parameterized by the target-to-source model p.

$$L(\theta) = - \sum_{(f_1^J, e_1^I)} Pr(f_1^J, e_1^I) \cdot \frac{1}{I} \log p_\theta(e_1^I | f_1^J) \tag{4}$$

$$= - \sum_{e_1^I} Pr(e_1^I) \cdot \frac{1}{I} \sum_{f_1^J} Pr(f_1^J | e_1^I) \cdot \log p_\theta(e_1^I | f_1^J) \tag{5}$$

$$= - \sum_{e_1^I} \hat{p}(e_1^I) \cdot \frac{1}{I} \sum_{f_1^J} q(f_1^J | e_1^I; p) \cdot \log p_\theta(e_1^I | f_1^J) \tag{6}$$

This derivation highlights an apparent condition that the generation procedure $q(f_1^J | e_1^I; p)$ should result in a distribution of source sentences similar to the true data distribution $Pr(f_1^J | e_1^I)$. Cotterell and Kreutzer (2018) show a similar derivation hinting towards an iterative wake-sleep variational scheme (Hinton et al., 1995), which reaches similar conclusions.

Following this, we formulate two issues with the back-translation approach: (i) the choice of generation procedure q and (ii) the adequacy of the target-to-source model p. The search method q is responsible not only for controlling the output of source sentences but also to offset the deficiencies of the target-to-source model p.

An implementation for q is, for example, beam search where q is a *deterministic* sampling procedure, which returns the highest scoring sentence according to the search criterion:

$$q_{\text{beam}}(f_1^J | e_1^I; p) =$$
$$\begin{cases} 1, & f_1^J = \underset{\hat{J}, f_1^{\hat{J}}}{\mathrm{argmax}} \left\{ \frac{1}{\hat{J}} \log p(f_1^{\hat{J}} | e_1^I) \right\} \\ 0, & \text{otherwise} \end{cases} \tag{7}$$

---

[1] The properties of a probability distribution hold for $q(f_1^J | e_1^I; p)$.

Sampling as described by Edunov et al. (2018) would be simply the equality

$$q_{\text{sample}}(f_1^J | e_1^I; p) = p(f_1^J | e_1^I). \qquad (8)$$

3.2 Approximations

Applications of back-translation and its variants largely follows the initial approach presented in (Sennrich et al., 2016a). Each target authentic sentence is aligned to a single synthetic source sentence. This new dataset is then used as if it were bilingual. This section is dedicated to the clarification of the effect of such a strategy in the optimization criterion, especially with non-deterministic sampling approaches (Edunov et al., 2018; Imamura et al., 2018).

Firstly, the sum over all possible source sentences in Eq. 6 is approximated by a restricted search space of N sentences, with $N = 1$ being a common choice. Yet, the cost of *generating* the data and *training* on the same scales linearly with N and it is unattractive to choose higher values.

Secondly, the pseudo-corpora are static across training, i.e. the synthetic sentences do not change across training epochs, which appears to cancel out the benefits of sampling-based methods. Correcting this behaviour requires an on-the-fly sentence generation, which increases the complexity of the implementation and slows down training considerably. Back-translation is not affected by this approximation since the target-to-source model always generates the same translation.

The approximations are shown in Eq. 9 with a fixed pseudo-parallel corpus where $e_{1,s}^{I_s}$ is aligned to N source sentences $(f_{1,s,n}^{J_s,n})_{n=1}^N$.

$$L(\theta) \approx -\sum_{s=1}^{S} \frac{1}{N \cdot I_s} \sum_{n=1}^{N} \log p_\theta\left(e_{1,s}^{I_s} | f_{1,s,n}^{J_s,n}\right) \quad (9)$$

We hypothesize that these conditions become less problematic when large amounts of monolingual data are present due to the law of large numbers, which states that repeated occurrences of the same sentence e_1^I will lead to a representative distribution of source sentences f_1^J according to $q(f_1^J | e_1^I; p)$. In other words, given a high number of representative target samples, Eq. 9 matches Eq. 6 with $N = 1$. This shifts the focus of the problem to find an appropriate search method q and generator p.

4 Improving Synthetic Data

In this section, we discuss how the known generation methods $q(f_1^J | e_1^I; p)$ fail in approximating $Pr(f_1^J | e_1^I)$ due to modelling issues of model p and consider how the generation approach q can be adapted to compensate p.

We base our remaining work on the approximations presented in Section 3.2 and consider $N = 1$ synthetic sentences. The reasoning for this is twofold: (i) it is the most attractive scenario in terms of computational costs and (ii) the approximations lose their influence with large target monolingual corpora.

4.1 Issues in Translation Modelling

With sampling-based approaches, one does not only care about whether high-quality sentences get assigned a high probability, but also that low-quality sentences are assigned a low probability.

Label smoothing (LS) (Pereyra et al., 2017) is a common component of state-of-the-art NMT systems (Ott et al., 2018). This teaches the model to (partially) fit a uniform word distribution, causing unrestricted sampling to periodically sample from the same. Even without LS, NMT models tend to smear their probability to low-quality hypotheses (Ott et al., 2018).

To showcase the extent of this effect, we provide the average cumulative probabilities of top-N words for NMT models, see Section 5.2, trained with and without label smoothing in Figure 1. The distributions are created on the development corpus. We observe that training a model with label smoothing causes a re-allocation of roughly 7% probability mass to all except the top-100 words. This re-allocation is not problematic during beam search, since this strategy only looks at the top-scoring candidates. However, when considering sampling for data generation, there is a high likelihood that one will sample from the space of low probability words, creating non-parallel outputs, see Table 4.

4.2 Restricting the Search Space

Changing the search approach q is less arduous than changing the model p since it does not involve re-training the model. Restricting the search space to high-probability sentences avoids the issues highlighted in Section 4.1 and provides a middle-ground between unrestricted sampling and beam search.

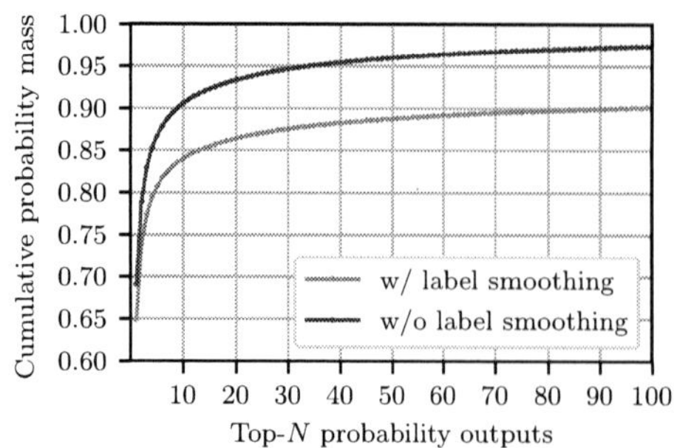

Figure 1: Cumulative probabilities of the top-N word candidates as estimated on newstest2015 English $\rightarrow$ German with and without label smoothing. See section 5.2 for descriptions of the models.

Edunov et al. (2018) consider top-k sampling to avoid the aforementioned problem, however, there is no guarantee that the candidates are confident predictions. We propose two alternative methods: (i) restrict the sampling outputs to words with a minimum probability and (ii) weighted sampling from the N-best candidates.

4.2.1 Restricted Sampling

The first approach follows sampling directly from the model $p(\cdot|e_1^I, f_1^{j-1})$ at each position j, but only taking words with at least $\tau \in [0, 0.5)$ probability into account. Afterwards, another softmax activation[2] is performed only over these words by masking all the remaining ones with large negative values. If no words have over τ probability, then the maximum probability word is chosen. Note that a large τ gets closer to greedy search ($\tau \geq 0.5$) and a lower value gets near to unrestricted sampling.

$$q(f|e_1^I, f_1^{j-1}; p) = \qquad (10)$$
$$\begin{cases} \text{softmax}\big(p(f|e_1^I, f_1^{j-1}), C\big), & |C| > 0 \\ 1, & |C| = 0 \wedge \\ & f = \underset{f'}{\text{argmax}}\Big\{p(f'|e_1^I, f_1^{j-1})\Big\} \\ 0, & \text{otherwise} \end{cases}$$

with $C \subseteq V_f$ being the subset of words of the source vocabulary V_f with at least τ probability:

$$C = \big\{f \mid p(f|e_1^I, f_1^{j-1}) \geq \tau\big\} \qquad (11)$$

and $\text{softmax}\big(p(f|e_1^I, f_1^{j-1}), C\big)$ being a soft-max normalization restricted to the elements in C.

---

[2]Alternatively an L1-normalization would be sufficient.

4.2.2 N-best List Sampling

The second approach involves generating a list of N-best candidates, normalizing the output scores with a soft-max operation, as in Section 4.2.1, and finally sampling a hypothesis.

The score of a translation is abbreviated by $s(f_1^J|e_1^I) = \frac{1}{J} \log p(f_1^J|e_1^I)$.

$$q_{\text{nbest}}(f_1^J|e_1^I; p) = \qquad (12)$$
$$\begin{cases} \text{softmax}\big(s(f_1^J|e_1^I), C\big), & f_1^J \in C \\ 0, & \text{otherwise} \end{cases}$$

with $C \subseteq \mathbb{D}_{src}$ being the set of N-best translations found by the target-to-source model and $\mathbb{D}_{src}$ being the set of all source sentences:

$$C = \underset{\mathcal{D} \subset \mathbb{D}_{src}: |\mathcal{D}| = N}{\text{argmax}} \Big\{ \sum_{f_1^J \in \mathcal{D}} s(f_1^J|e_1^I) \Big\}. \qquad (13)$$

5 Experiments

5.1 Setup

This section makes use of the WMT 2018 German $\leftrightarrow$ English [3] news translation task, consisting of 5.9M bilingual sentences. The German and English monolingual data is subsampled from the deduplicated NewsCrawl2017 corpus. In total 4M sentences are used for German and English monolingual data. All data is tokenized, true-cased and then preprocessed with joint byte pair encoding (Sennrich et al., 2016b)[4].

We train Base Transformer (Vaswani et al., 2017) models using the Sockeye toolkit (Hieber et al., 2017). Optimization is done with Adam (Kingma and Ba, 2014) with a learning rate of 3e-4, multiplied with 0.7 after every third 20k-update checkpoint without improvements in development set perplexity. In Sections 5.2 and 5.3, word batch sizes of 16k and 4k are used respectively. Inference uses a beam size of 5 and applies hypothesis length normalization.

Case-sensitive BLEU (Papineni et al., 2002) is computed using the `mteval_13a.pl` script from Moses (Koehn et al., 2007). Model selection is performed based on the BLEU performance on newstest2015. All experiments were performed using the workflow manager Sisyphus (Peter et al., 2018). We report the statistical significance of

---

[3]http://www.statmt.org/wmt18/translation-task.html

[4]50k merge operations and a vocabulary threshold of 50 are used.

48

	test2015	test2017	test2018
beam search	30.9*	31.9*	**40.1**
sampling	30.4*	31.0*	37.9*
w/o LS	30.4*	31.3*	37.9*
$\tau = 10\%$	**31.1***	**32.1***	39.8
50-best sampling	**31.1***	31.9*	39.8
reference	**32.6**	**33.5**	40.0

Table 1: BLEU$^{[\%]}$ results for the controlled scenario. * denotes a p-value of < 0.01 w.r.t. the reference.

| | Entropy | PPL | |
	En $\to$ De	Train	test2015
beam search	2.60	2.74	5.77
sampling	3.13	9.07	5.55
w/o LS	**2.93**	**5.17**	**5.31**
$\tau = 10\%$	2.66	3.34	5.61
50-best sampling	2.62	2.84	5.70
reference	**2.91**	**5.18**	**4.50**

Table 2: IBM-1 model entropy and perplexity (PPL) on the training and development set for the controlled scenario using different synthetic generation methods.

our results with MultEval (Clark et al., 2011). A low p-value indicates that the performance gap between two systems is likely to hold given a different sample of a random process, e.g. an initialization seed.

5.2 Controlled Scenario

To compare the performance of each generation method to natural sentences, we shuffle and split the German $\to$ English bilingual data into 1M bilingual sentences and 4.9M monolingual sentences. This gives us a reference translation for each sentence and eliminates domain adaptation effects. The generator model is trained on the smaller corpus until convergence on BLEU, roughly 100k updates. The final source-to-target model is trained from scratch on the concatenated synthetic and natural corpora until convergence on BLEU, roughly 250k updates for all variants.

Table 1 showcases the translation quality of the models trained on different kinds of synthetic corpora. Contrary to the observations in Edunov et al. (2018), unrestricted sampling does not outperform beam search and once the search space is restricted all methods perform similarly well.

To further investigate this, we look at other relevant statistics of a generated corpus and the performance of the subsequent models in Table 2. These are the perplexities (PPL) of the model on the training and development data and the entropy of a target-to-source IBM-1 model (Brown et al., 1993) trained with GIZA++ (Och and Ney, 2003). The training set PPL varies strongly with each generation method since each produces hypotheses of differing quality. All methods with a restricted search space have a larger translation entropy and smaller training PPL than natural data. This is due to the sentences being less noisy and also the translation options being less varied. Unrestricted sam-

pling seems to overshoot the statistics of natural data, attaining higher entropy values.

However, once LS is removed, the best PPL on the development set is reached and the remaining statistics match the natural data very closely. Nevertheless, the performance in BLEU lags behind the methods that consider high-quality hypotheses as reported in Table 1. Looking further into the models, we notice that when trained on corpora with more variability, i.e. larger translation entropy, the probability distributions are flatter. We explain the better dev perplexities with unrestricted sampling with the same reason for which label smoothing is helpful: it makes the model less biased towards more common events (Ott et al., 2018). This uncertainty is, however, not beneficial for translation performance.

5.3 Real-world Scenario

Previously, we applied different synthetic data generation methods to a controlled scenario for the purpose of investigation. We extend the experiments to the original WMT 2018 German $\leftrightarrow$ English task and showcase the results in Table 3. In contrast to the experiments of Section 5.2, the distribution of the monolingual data now differs from the bilingual data. The models are trained on the bilingual data for 1M updates and then fine-tuned for further 1M updates on the concatenated bilingual and synthetic corpora.

The restricted sampling techniques perform comparable to or better than the other synthetic data generation methods in all cases. Especially on English $\to$ German, unrestricted sampling only produces statistical significant improvements over beam search when LS is replaced. Furthermore, restricting the search space via 50-best list sam-

	De $\rightarrow$ En		En $\rightarrow$ De	
	test2017	test2018	test2017	test2018
beam search	35.7	**43.6**	28.2	41.3
sampling	35.8	42.3*	28.6	41.5
w/o LS	35.9	42.5*	**29.1***	41.7
$\tau = 10\%$	35.9	43.0*	28.7*	41.6
50-best samp.	**36.0**	**43.6**	28.6*	**41.8***

Table 3: WMT 2018 German $\leftrightarrow$ English $\textsc{Bleu}^{[\%]}$ values comparing different synthetic data generation methods.
* denotes a p-value of < 0.01 w.r.t. beam search.

pling improves significantly in both test sets.

We observe that on German $\rightarrow$ English newstest2018 particularly, there is a large drop in performance when using unrestricted sampling. This is slightly alleviated by applying a minimum probability threshold of $\tau = 10\%$, but there is still a gap to be closed. This behaviour is investigated in the following section.

5.3.1 Scalability

A benefit of non-deterministic generation methods is the scalability in contrast to beam search. Under the assumption of a good fitting translation model, as argued in Section 3, sampling does appear to be the best option.

We compare different monolingual corpus sizes for the German $\rightarrow$ English task in Figure 2 on three different test sets. Particularly, newstest2018 shows the exact opposite behaviour from the remaining test sets: the amount of data generated via beam search improves the resulting model, whereas sampling improves the system by a small margin. Normal sampling has a general tendency to perform better with more data, but it saturates in two test sets (newstest2015 and newstest2018). Restricted sampling appears to be the most consistent approach, always outperforming unrestricted sampling and also always scaling with a larger set of monolingual data.

These observations are strongly linked to the properties of current state-of-the-art models, see Section 4.1 and experimental setup via e.g. the domain of the bilingual, monolingual and test data. Therefore, the high performance scaling with beam search in newstest2018 might be due to its *relatedness* to the training data as measured by the high $\textsc{Bleu}$ values attained in inference.

5.4 Synthetic Source Examples

To highlight the issues present in unrestricted sampling, we compare the outputs of different generation methods in Table 4. The unrestricted sampling output hypothesizes a second sentence which is not related at all to the input sentence but generates a much longer sequence. The restricted sampling methods and the model trained without label smoothing provide an accurate translation of the input sentence. Compared to the beam search hypothesis, they have a reasonable variation which is indeed closer to the human-translated reference.

6 Conclusion

In this work, we link the optimization criterion of an NMT model with a synthetic data generator defined for both beam search and additional sampling-based methods. By doing so, we identify that the search method plays an important role, as it is responsible for offsetting the shortcomings of the generator model. Specifically, label smoothing and probability smearing issues cause sampling-based methods to generate unnatural sentences.

We analyze the performance of our techniques on a closed- and open-domain of the WMT 2018 German $\leftrightarrow$ English news translation task. We provide qualitative and quantitative evidence of the detrimental behaviours and show that these can be influenced by re-training the generator model without label smoothing or by restricting the search space to not consider low-probability outputs. In terms of translation quality, sampling from 50-best lists outperforms beam search, albeit at a higher computational cost. Restricted sampling or the disabling of label smoothing for the generator model are shown to be cost-effective ways of improving upon the unrestricted sampling approach of Edunov et al. (2018).

Acknowledgments

This work has received funding from the European Research Council (ERC) (under the European Union's Horizon 2020 research and innovation programme, grant agreement No 694537, project "SEQCLAS"), the Deutsche Forschungsgemeinschaft (DFG; grant agreement NE 572/8-1,

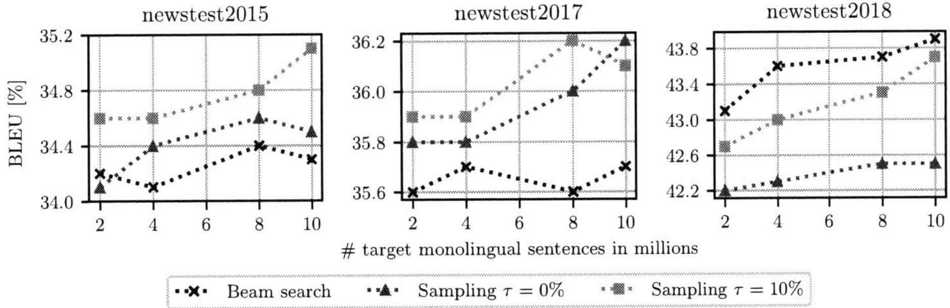

Figure 2: WMT 2018 German $\rightarrow$ English $\text{BLEU}^{[\%]}$ values comparing different synthetic data generation methods with a differing size of synthetic corpus.

source	it is seen as a long sag@@ a full of surprises .
beam search	es wird als eine lange Geschichte voller Überraschungen angesehen .
sampling	es wird als eine lange S@@ aga voller Überraschungen angesehen . injury , Skepsis , Feuer) , Duschen verursach@@ ter Körper , Pal@@ ä@@ ste , Gol@@ fen , Flu@@ r und Mu@@ ffen , Diesel@@ - Total Bab@@ ylon , der durch@@ s Wasser und Wasser@@ kraft fliet .
w/o label smoothing	es wurde als eine lange Geschichte voller Überraschungen gesehen .
$\tau = 10\%$	es wird als lange S@@ age voller Überraschungen angesehen .
50-best sampling	es wird als eine lange S@@ age voller Überraschungen gesehen .
reference	er wird als eine lange S@@ aga voller Überraschungen angesehen .

Table 4: Random example generated by different methods for the controlled scenario of WMT 2018 German $\rightarrow$ English. @@ denotes the subword token delimiter.

project "CoreTec"), and eBay Inc. The GPU cluster used for the experiments was partially funded by DFG Grant INST 222/1168-1. The work reflects only the authors' views and none of the funding agencies is responsible for any use that may be made of the information it contains.

References

Dzmitry Bahdanau, Kyunghyun Cho, and Yoshua Bengio. 2014. Neural machine translation by jointly learning to align and translate. *arXiv preprint arXiv:1409.0473*. Version 4.

Peter F Brown, Vincent J Della Pietra, Stephen A Della Pietra, and Robert L Mercer. 1993. The mathematics of statistical machine translation: Parameter estimation. *Computational linguistics*, 19(2):263–311.

Franck Burlot and François Yvon. 2018. Using monolingual data in neural machine translation: a systematic study. In *Proceedings of the Third Conference on Machine Translation (WMT 2018)*, pages 144–155.

Jonathan H Clark, Chris Dyer, Alon Lavie, and Noah A Smith. 2011. Better hypothesis testing for statistical machine translation: Controlling for optimizer instability. In *Proceedings of the 49th Annual Meeting of the Association for Computational Linguistics (ACL 2011)*, pages 176–181.

Ryan Cotterell and Julia Kreutzer. 2018. Explaining and generalizing back-translation through wake-sleep. *arXiv preprint arXiv:1806.04402*. Version 1.

Sergey Edunov, Myle Ott, Michael Auli, and David Grangier. 2018. Understanding back-translation at scale. *arXiv preprint arXiv:1808.09381*. Version 2.

Felix Hieber, Tobias Domhan, Michael Denkowski, David Vilar, Artem Sokolov, Ann Clifton, and Matt Post. 2017. Sockeye: A toolkit for neural machine translation. *arXiv preprint arXiv:1712.05690*. Version 2.

Geoffrey E Hinton, Peter Dayan, Brendan J Frey, and Radford M Neal. 1995. The" wake-sleep" algorithm for unsupervised neural networks. *Science*, 268(5214):1158–1161.

Vu Cong Duy Hoang, Philipp Koehn, Gholamreza Haffari, and Trevor Cohn. 2018. Iterative back-translation for neural machine translation. In *Proceedings of the 2nd Workshop on Neural Machine Translation and Generation (WNMT 2018)*, pages 18–24.

Kenji Imamura, Atsushi Fujita, and Eiichiro Sumita. 2018. Enhancement of encoder and attention using target monolingual corpora in neural machine translation. In *Proceedings of the 2nd Workshop on Neural Machine Translation and Generation (WNMT 2018)*, pages 55–63.

Diederik P Kingma and Jimmy Ba. 2014. Adam: A method for stochastic optimization. *arXiv preprint arXiv:1412.6980*. Version 9.

Philipp Koehn, Hieu Hoang, Alexandra Birch, Chris Callison-Burch, Marcello Federico, Nicola Bertoldi, Brooke Cowan, Wade Shen, Christine Moran, Richard Zens, et al. 2007. Moses: Open source toolkit for statistical machine translation. In *Proceedings of the 45th Annual Meeting of the Association for Computational Linguistics (ACL 2007)*, pages 177–180.

Franz Josef Och and Hermann Ney. 2003. A systematic comparison of various statistical alignment models. *Computational linguistics*, pages 19–51.

Myle Ott, Michael Auli, David Granger, and Marc'Aurelio Ranzato. 2018. Analyzing uncertainty in neural machine translation. *arXiv preprint arXiv:1803.00047*. Version 4.

Kishore Papineni, Salim Roukos, Todd Ward, and Wei-Jing Zhu. 2002. Bleu: a method for automatic evaluation of machine translation. In *Proceedings of the 40th Annual Meeting on Association for Computational Linguistics (ACL 2002)*, pages 311–318.

Gabriel Pereyra, George Tucker, Jan Chorowski, Łukasz Kaiser, and Geoffrey Hinton. 2017. Regularizing neural networks by penalizing confident output distributions. *arXiv preprint arXiv:1701.06548*. Version 1.

Jan-Thorsten Peter, Eugen Beck, and Hermann Ney. 2018. Sisyphus, a workflow manager designed for machine translation and automatic speech recognition. In *Proceedings of the 2018 Conference on Empirical Methods in Natural Language Processing (EMNLP 2018)*, pages 84–89.

Rico Sennrich, Barry Haddow, and Alexandra Birch. 2016a. Improving neural machine translation models with monolingual data. In *Proceedings of the 54th Annual Meeting of the Association for Computational Linguistics (ACL 2016)*, pages 86–96.

Rico Sennrich, Barry Haddow, and Alexandra Birch. 2016b. Neural machine translation of rare words with subword units. In *Proceedings of the 54th Annual Meeting of the Association for Computational Linguistics (ACL 2016)*, pages 1715–1725.

Ashish Vaswani, Noam Shazeer, Niki Parmar, Jakob Uszkoreit, Llion Jones, Aidan N Gomez, Łukasz Kaiser, and Illia Polosukhin. 2017. Attention is all you need. In *Advances in Neural Information Processing Systems (NIPS 2017)*, pages 6000–6010.

Tagged Back-Translation

Isaac Caswell, Ciprian Chelba, David Grangier
Google Research
{icaswell, ciprianchelba, grangier}@google.com

Abstract

Recent work in Neural Machine Translation (NMT) has shown significant quality gains from noised-beam decoding during back-translation, a method to generate synthetic parallel data. We show that the main role of such synthetic noise is not to diversify the source side, as previously suggested, but simply to indicate to the model that the given source is synthetic. We propose a simpler alternative to noising techniques, consisting of tagging back-translated source sentences with an extra token. Our results on WMT outperform noised back-translation in English-Romanian and match performance on English-German, re-defining state-of-the-art in the former.

1 Introduction

Neural Machine Translation (NMT) has made considerable progress in recent years (Bahdanau et al., 2015; Gehring et al., 2017; Vaswani et al., 2017). Traditional NMT has relied solely on parallel sentence pairs for training data, which can be an expensive and scarce resource. This motivates the use of monolingual data, usually more abundant (Lambert et al., 2011). Approaches using monolingual data for machine translation include language model fusion for both phrase-based (Brants et al., 2007; Koehn, 2009) and neural MT (Gülçehre et al., 2015, 2017), back-translation (Sennrich et al., 2016; Poncelas et al., 2018), unsupervised machine translation (Lample et al., 2018a; Artetxe et al., 2018), dual learning (Cheng et al., 2016; Di He and Ma, 2016; Xia et al., 2017), and multi-task learning (Domhan and Hieber, 2017).

We focus on back-translation (BT), which, despite its simplicity, has thus far been the most effective technique (Sennrich et al., 2017; Ha et al., 2017; García-Martínez et al., 2017). Back-translation entails training an intermediate target-to-source model on genuine bitext, and using this model to translate a large monolingual corpus from the target into the source language. This allows training a source-to-target model on a mixture of genuine parallel data and synthetic pairs from back-translation.

We build upon Edunov et al. (2018) and Imamura et al. (2018), who investigate BT at the scale of hundreds of millions of sentences. Their work studies different decoding/generation methods for back-translation: in addition to regular beam search, they consider sampling and adding noise to the one-best hypothesis produced by beam search. They show that sampled BT and noised-beam BT significantly outperform standard BT, and attribute this success to increased source-side diversity (sections 5.2 and 4.4).

Our work investigates noised-beam BT (NoisedBT) and questions the role noise is playing. Rather than increasing source diversity, our work instead suggests that the performance gains come simply from signaling to the model that the source side is back-translated, allowing it to treat the synthetic parallel data differently than the natural bitext. We hypothesize that BT introduces both helpful signal (strong target-language signal and weak cross-lingual signal) and harmful signal (amplifying the biases of machine translation). Indicating to the model whether a given training sentence is back-translated should allow the model to separate the helpful and harmful signal.

To support this hypothesis, we first demonstrate that the permutation and word-dropping noise used by Edunov et al. (2018) do not improve or significantly degrade NMT accuracy, corroborating that noise might act as an indicator that the source is back-translated, without much loss in mutual information between the source and target. We then train models on WMT English-German (EnDe) without BT

Proceedings of the Fourth Conference on Machine Translation (WMT), Volume 1: Research Papers, pages 53–63
Florence, Italy, August 1-2, 2019. ©2019 Association for Computational Linguistics

noise, and instead explicitly tag the synthetic data with a reserved token. We call this technique "Tagged Back-Translation" (TaggedBT). These models achieve equal to slightly higher performance than the noised variants. We repeat these experiments with WMT English-Romanian (EnRo), where NoisedBT underperforms standard BT and TaggedBT improves over both techniques. We demonstrate that TaggedBT also allows for effective iterative back-translation with EnRo, a technique which saw quality losses when applied with standard back-translation.

To further our understanding of TaggedBT, we investigate the biases encoded in models by comparing the entropy of their attention matrices, and look at the attention weight on the tag. We conclude by investigating the effects of the back-translation tag at decoding time.

2   Related Work

This section describes prior work exploiting target-side monolingual data and discusses related work tagging NMT training data.

2.1   Leveraging Monolingual Data for NMT

Monolingual data can provide valuable information to improve translation quality. Various methods for using target-side LMs have proven effective for NMT (He et al., 2016; Gülçehre et al., 2017), but have tended to be less successful than back-translation – for example, Gülçehre et al. (2017) report under +0.5 BLEU over their baseline on EnDe newstest14, whereas Edunov et al. (2018) report over +4.0 BLEU on the same test set. Furthermore, there is no straighforward way to incorporate source-side monolingual data into a neural system with a LM.

Back-translation was originally introduced for phrase-based systems (Bertoldi and Federico, 2009; Bojar and Tamchyna, 2011), but flourished in NMT after work by Sennrich et al. (2016). Several approaches have looked into iterative forward- and BT experiments (using source-side monolingual data), including Cotterell and Kreutzer (2018), Vu Cong Duy Hoang and Cohn (2018), and Niu et al. (2018). Recently, iterative back-translation in both directions has been devised has a way to address unsupervised machine translation (Lample et al., 2018b; Artetxe et al., 2018).

Recent work has focused on the importance of diversity and complexity in synthetic training data. Fadaee and Monz (2018) find that BT benefits difficult-to-translate words the most, and select from the back-translated corpus by oversampling words with high prediction loss. Imamura et al. (2018) argue that in order for BT to enhance the encoder, it must have a more diverse source side, and sample several back-translated source sentences for each monolingual target sentence. Our work follows most closely Edunov et al. (2018), who investigate alternative decoding schemes for BT. Like Imamura et al. (2018), they argue that BT through beam or greedy decoding leads to an overly regular domain on the source side, which poorly represents the diverse distribution of natural text.

Beyond the scope of this work, we briefly mention alternative techniques leveraging monolingual data, like forward translation (Ueffing et al., 2007; Kim and Rush, 2016), or source copying (Currey et al., 2017).

2.2   Training Data Tagging for NMT

Tags have been used for various purposes in NMT. Tags on the source sentence can indicate the target language in multi-lingual models (Johnson et al., 2016). Yamagishi et al. (2016) use tags in a similar fashion to control the formality of a translation from English to Japanese. Kuczmarski and Johnson (2018) use tags to control gender in translation. Most relevant to our work, Kobus et al. (2016) use tags to mark source sentence domain in a multi-domain setting.

3   Experimental Setup

This section presents our datasets, evaluation protocols and model architectures. It also describes our back-translation procedure, as well as noising and tagging strategies.

3.1   Data

We perform our experiments on WMT18 EnDe bitext, WMT16 EnRo bitext, and WMT15 EnFr bitext respectively. We use WMT Newscrawl for monolingual data (2007-2017 for De, 2016 for Ro, 2007-2013 for En, and 2007-2014 for Fr). For bitext, we filter out empty sentences and sentences longer than 250 subwords. We remove pairs whose whitespace-tokenized length ratio is greater than 2. This results in about 5.0M pairs for EnDe, and 0.6M pairs for EnRo. We do not filter the EnFr bitext, resulting in 41M sentence pairs.

For monolingual data, we deduplicate and filter sentences with more than 70 tokens or 500 characters. Furthermore, after back-translation, we remove any sentence pairs where the back-translated source is longer than 75 tokens or 550 characters. This results in 216.5M sentences for EnDe, 2.2M for EnRo, 149.9M for RoEn, and 39M for EnFr. For monolingual data, all tokens are defined by whitespace tokenization, not wordpieces.

The DeEn model used to generate BT data has 28.6 SacreBLEU on newstest12, the RoEn model used for BT has a test SacreBLEU of 31.9 (see Table 4.b), and the FrEn model used to generate the BT data has 39.2 SacreBLEU on newstest14.

3.2 Evaluation

We rely on BLEU score (Papineni et al., 2002) as our evaluation metric.

While well established, any slight difference in post-processing and BLEU computation can have a dramatic impact on output values (Post, 2018). For example, Lample and Conneau (2019) report 33.3 BLEU on EnRo using unsupervised NMT, which at first seems comparable to our reported 33.4 SacreBLEU from iterative TaggedBT. However, when we use their preprocessing scripts and evaluation protocol, our system achieves 39.2 BLEU on the same data, which is close to 6 points higher than the same model evaluated by SacreBLEU.

We therefore report strictly SacreBLEU[1], using the reference implementation from Post (2018), which aims to standardize BLEU evaluation.

3.3 Architecture

We use the transformer-base and transformer-big architectures (Vaswani et al., 2017) implemented in *lingvo* (Shen et al., 2019). Transformer-base is used for the bitext noising experiments and the EnRo experiments, whereas the transformer-big is used for the EnDe tasks with BT. Both use a vocabulary of 32k subword units. As an alternative to the checkpoint averaging used in Edunov et al. (2018), we train with exponentially weighted moving average (EMA) decay with weight decay parameter $\alpha = 0.999$ (Buduma and Locascio, 2017).

Transformer-base models are trained on 16 GPUs with synchronous gradient updates and per-gpu-batch-size of 4,096 tokens, for an effective

batch size of 64k tokens/step. Training lasts 400k steps, passing over 24B tokens. For the final EnDe TaggedBT model, we train transformer-big similarly but on 128 GPUs, for an effective batch size of 512k tokens/step. A training run of 300M steps therefore sees about 150B tokens. We pick checkpoints with newstest2012 for EnDe and newsdev2016 for EnRo.

3.4 Noising

We focused on noised beam BT, the most effective noising approach according to Edunov et al. (2018). Before training, we noised the decoded data (Lample et al., 2018a) by applying 10% word-dropout, 10% word blanking, and a 3-constrained permutation (a permutation such that no token moves further than 3 tokens from its original position). We refer to data generated this way as NoisedBT. Additionally, we experiment using only the 3-constrained permutation and no word dropout/blanking, which we abbreviate as P3BT.

3.5 Tagging

We tag our BT training data by prepending a reserved token to the input sequence, which is then treated in the same way as any other token. We also experiment with both noising and tagging together, which we call Tagged Noised Back-Translation, or TaggedNoisedBT. This consists simply of prepending the <BT> tag to each noised training example.

An example training sentence for each of these set-ups can be seen in Table 1. We do not tag the bitext, and always train on a mix of back-translated data and (untagged) bitext unless explicitly stated otherwise.

Noise type	Example sentence
[no noise]	Raise the child, love the child.
P3BT	child Raise the, love child the.
NoisedBT	Raise child ___ love child, the.
TaggedBT	<BT> Raise the child, love the child.
TaggedNoisedBT	<BT> Raise, the child the ___ love.

Table 1: Examples of the five noising settings examined in this paper

4 Results

This section studies the impact of training data noise on translation quality, and then presents our results with TaggedBT on EnDe and EnRo.

---

[1] BLEU + case.mixed + lang.LANGUAGE_PAIR + num-refs.1 + smooth.exp + test.SET + tok.13a + version.1.2.15

4.1 Noising Parallel Bitext

We first show that noising EnDe bitext sources does not seriously impact the translation quality of the transformer-base baseline. For each sentence pair in the corpus, we flip a coin and noise the source sentence with probability p. We then train a model from scratch on this partially noised dataset. Table 2 shows results for various values of p. Specifically, it presents the somewhat unexpected finding that even when noising 100% of the source bitext (so the model has never seen well-formed English), BLEU on well-formed test data only drops by 2.5.

This result prompts the following line of reasoning about the role of noise in BT: (i) By itself, noising does not add meaningful signal (or else it would improve performance); (ii) It also does not damage the signal much; (iii) In the context of back-translation, the noise could therefore signal whether a sentence were back-translated, without significantly degrading performance.

% noised	SacreBLEU	
	Newstest '12	Newstest '17
0%	22.4	28.1
20%	22.4	27.9
80%	21.5	27.0
100%	21.2	25.6

Table 2: SacreBLEU degradation as a function of the proportion of bitext data that is noised.

4.2 Tagged Back-Translation for EnDe

We compare the results of training on a mixture of bitext and a random sample of 24M back-translated sentences in Table 3.a, for the various set-ups of BT described in sections 3.4 and 3.5. Like Edunov et al. (2018), we confirm that BT improves over bitext alone, and noised BT improves over standard BT by about the same margin. All methods of marking the source text as back-translated (NoisedBT, P3BT, TaggedBT, and TaggedNoisedBT) perform about equally, with TaggedBT having the highest average BLEU by a small margin. Tagging and noising together (TaggedNoisedBT) does not improve over either tagging or noising alone, supporting the conclusion that tagging and noising are not orthogonal signals but rather different means to the same end.

Table 3.b verifies our result at scale applying TaggedBT on the full BT dataset (216.5M sentences), upsampling the bitext so that each batch contains an expected 20% of bitext. As in the smaller scenario, TaggedBT matches or slightly out-performs NoisedBT, with an advantage on seven test-sets and a disadvantage on one. We also compare our results to the best-performing model from Edunov et al. (2018). Our model is on par with or slightly superior to their result[2], out-performing it on four test sets and underperforming it on two, with the largest advantage on Newstest2018 (+1.4 BLEU).

As a supplementary experiment, we consider training only on BT data, with no bitext. We compare this to training only on NoisedBT data. If noising in fact increases the quality or diversity of the data, one would expect the NoisedBT data to yield higher performance than training on unaltered BT data, when in fact it has about 1 BLEU lower performance (Table 3.a, "BT alone" and "NoisedBT alone").

We also compare NoisedBT versus Tagged-NoisedBT in a set-up where the bitext itself is noised. In this scenario, the noise can no longer be used by the model as an implicit tag to differentiate between bitext and synthetic BT data, so we expect the TaggedNoisedBT variant to perform better than NoisedBT by a similar margin to NoisedBT's improvement over BT in the unnoised-bitext setting. The last sub-section of Table 3.a confirms this.

4.3 Tagged Back-Translation for EnRo

We repeat these experiments for WMT EnRo (Table 4). This is a much lower-resource task than EnDe, and thus can benefit more from monolingual data. In this case, NoisedBT is actually harmful, lagging standard BT by -0.6 BLEU. TaggedBT closes this gap and passes standard BT by +0.4 BLEU, for a total gain of +1.0 BLEU over NoisedBT.

4.4 Tagged Back-Translation for EnFr

We performed a minimal set of experiments on WMT EnFr, which are summarized in Table 5. This is a much higher-resource language pair than either EnRo or EnDe, but Edunov et al. (2018) demonstrate that noised BT (using sampling) can still help in this set-up. In this case, we see that BT alone hurts performance compared to the strong bitext baseline, but NoisedBT indeed surpasses the bitext model. TaggedBT out-performs all other

---

[2]SacreBLEU for the WMT-18 model at `github.com/pytorch/fairseq`

a. Results on 24M BT Set

Model	AVG 13-18	2010	2011	2012	2013	2014	2015	2016	2017	2018
Bitext	32.05	24.8	22.6	23.2	26.8	28.5	31.1	34.7	29.1	42.1
BT	33.12	24.7	22.6	23.5	26.8	30.8	30.9	36.1	30.6	43.5
NoisedBT	34.70	26.2	**23.7**	**24.7**	**28.5**	31.3	33.1	37.7	**31.7**	**45.9**
P3BT	34.57	26.1	23.6	24.5	28.1	31.8	33.0	37.4	31.5	45.6
TaggedBT	**34.83**	**26.4**	23.6	24.5	28.1	**32.1**	**33.4**	**37.8**	**31.7**	**45.9**
TaggedNoisedBT	34.52	26.3	23.4	24.6	27.9	31.4	33.1	37.4	**31.7**	45.6
BT alone	31.20	23.5	21.2	22.7	25.2	29.3	29.4	33.7	29.1	40.5
NoisedBT alone	30.28	23.2	21.0	22.1	24.6	28.4	28.2	33.0	28.1	39.4
Noised(BT + Bitext)	32.07	24.2	22.1	23.5	26.2	29.7	30.1	35.1	29.4	41.9
+ Tag on BT	33.53	25.5	22.8	24.5	27.6	30.3	31.9	36.9	30.4	44.1

b. Results on 216M BT Set

Model	AVG 13-18	2010	2011	2012	2013	2014	2015	2016	2017	2018
Edunov et al. (2018)	35.28			25.0	**29.0**	**33.8**	34.4	37.5	**32.4**	44.6
NoisedBT	35.17	**26.7**	24.0	**25.2**	28.6	32.6	33.9	38.0	32.2	45.7
TaggedBT	**35.42**	26.5	**24.2**	**25.2**	28.7	32.8	**34.5**	**38.1**	**32.4**	**46.0**

Table 3: SacreBLEU on Newstest EnDe for different types of noise, with back-translated data either sampled down to 24M or using the full set of 216M sentence pairs.

a. Forward models (EnRo)

Model	dev	test
Gehring et al. (2017)		*29.9*
Sennrich 2016 (BT)	*29.3*	*28.1*
bitext	26.5	28.3
BT	31.6	32.6
NoisedBT	29.9	32.0
TaggedBT	30.5	33.0
It.-3 BT	31.3	32.8
It.-3 NoisedBT	31.2	32.6
It.-3 TaggedBT	31.4	**33.4**

b. Reverse models (RoEn)

Model	dev	test
bitext	32.9	31.9
It.-2 BT	39.5	**37.3**

Table 4: Comparing SacreBLEU scores for different flavors of BT for WMT16 EnRo. Previous works' scores are reported in italics as they use `detok.multi-bleu` instead of SacreBLEU, so are not guaranteed to be comparable. In this case, however, we do see identical BLEU on our systems when we score them with `detok.multi-bleu`, so we believe it to be a fair comparison.

methods, beating NoisedBT by an average of +0.3 BLEU over all test sets.

It is worth noting that our numbers are lower than those reported by Edunov et al. (2018) on the years they report (36.1, 43.8, and 40.9 on 2013, 2014, and 2015 respectively). We did not investigate this result. We suspect that this is an error/inoptimlaity in our set-up, as we did not optimize these models, and ran only one experiment for each of the four set-ups. Alternately, sampling could outperform noising in the large-data regime.

4.5 Iterative Tagged Back-Translation

We further investigate the effects of TaggedBT by performing one round of iterative back-translation (Cotterell and Kreutzer, 2018; Vu Cong Duy Hoang and Cohn, 2018; Niu et al., 2018), and find another difference between the different varieties of BT: NoisedBT and TaggedBT allow the model to bootstrap improvements from an improved reverse model, whereas standard BT does not. This is consistent with our argument that data tagging allows the model to extract information out of each data set more effectively.

For the purposes of this paper we call a model trained with standard back-translation an **Iteration-1 BT model**, where the back-translations were generated by a model trained only on bitext. We inductively define the **Iteration-k BT model** as that model which is trained on BT data generated by an **Iteration-(k-1) BT** model, for $k > 1$. Unless otherwise specified, any BT model mentioned in this paper is an Iteration-1 BT model.

We perform these experiments on the English-Romanian dataset, which is smaller and thus better suited for this computationally expensive process. We used the (Iteration-1) TaggedBT model to generate the RoEn back-translated training data. Using this we trained a superior RoEn model, mixing 80% BT data with 20% bitext. Using this Iteration-2 RoEn model, we generated new EnRo BT data, which we used to train the Iteration-3 EnRo models. SacreBLEU scores for all these models are displayed in Table 4.

Model	Avg	2008	2009	2010	2011	2012	2013	2014	2015
Bitext	32.8	26.3	28.8	32.0	32.9	30.1	33.5	40.6	38.4
BT	29.2	22.2	27.3	28.8	29.3	27.9	30.7	32.6	34.8
NoisedBT	33.8	26.8	29.9	33.4	**33.9**	**31.3**	34.3	42.3	38.8
TaggedBT	**34.1**	**27.0**	**30.0**	33.6	33.9	31.2	**34.4**	**42.7**	**39.8**

Table 5: Results on WMT15 EnFr, with bitext, BT, NoisedBT, and TaggedBT.

We find that the iteration-3 BT models improve over their Iteration-1 counterparts only for NoisedBT (+1.0 BLEU, dev+test avg) and TaggedBT (+0.7 BLEU, dev+test avg), whereas the Iteration-3 BT model shows no improvement over its Iteration-1 counterpart (-0.1 BLEU, dev+test avg). In other words, both techniques that (explicitly or implicitly) tag synthetic data benefit from iterative BT. We speculate that this separation of the synthetic and natural domains allows the model to bootstrap more effectively from the increasing quality of the back-translated data while not being damaged by its quality issues, whereas the simple BT model cannot make this distinction, and is equally "confused" by the biases in higher or lower-quality BT data.

An identical experiment with EnDe did not see either gains or losses in BLEU from iteration-3 TaggedBT. This is likely because there is less room to bootstrap with the larger-capacity model. This said, we do not wish to read too deeply into these results, as the effect size is not large, and neither is the number of experiments. A more thorough suite of experiments is warranted before any strong conclusions can be made on the implications of tagging on iterative BT.

5 Analysis

In an attempt to gain further insight into TaggedBT as it compares with standard BT or NoisedBT, we examine attention matrices in the presence of the back translation tag and measure the impact of the tag at decoding time.

5.1 Attention Entropy and Sink-Ratio

To understand how the model treats the tag and what biases it learns from the data, we investigate the entropy of the attention probability distribution, as well as the attention captured by the tag.

We examine decoder attention (at the top layer) on the first source token. We define Attention Sink Ratio for index j (ASR_j) as the averaged attention over the jth token, normalized by uniform attention, i.e.

$$\text{ASR}_j(x, \hat{y}) = \frac{1}{|\hat{y}|} \sum_{i=1}^{|\hat{y}|} \frac{\alpha_{ij}}{\tilde{\alpha}}$$

where α_{ij} is the attention value for target token i in hypothesis $\hat{y}$ over source token j and $\tilde{\alpha} = \frac{1}{|x|}$ corresponds to uniform attention. We examine ASR on text that has been noised and/or tagged (depending on the model), to understand how BT sentences are treated during training. For the tagged variants, there is heavy attention on the tag when it is present (Table 6), indicating that the model relies on the information signalled by the tag.

Our second analysis probes word-for-word translation bias through the average source-token entropy of the attention probability model when decoding natural text. Table 6 reports the average length-normalized Shannon entropy:

$$\tilde{\text{H}}(x, \hat{y}) = -\frac{1}{|\hat{y}|} \sum_{i=1}^{|\hat{y}|} \frac{1}{\log |x|} \sum_{j=1}^{|x|} \alpha_{ij} \log(\alpha_{ij})$$

The entropy of the attention probabilities from the model trained on BT data is the clear outlier. This low entropy corresponds to a concentrated attention matrix, which we observed to be concentrated on the diagonal (See Figure 1a and 1d). This could indicate the presence of word-by-word translation, a consequence of the harmful part of the signal from back-translated data. The entropy on parallel data from the NoisedBT model is much higher, corresponding to more diffuse attention, which we see in Figure 1b and 1e. In other words, the word-for-word translation biases in BT data, that were incorporated into the BT model, have been manually undone by the noise, so the model's understanding of how to decode parallel text is not corrupted. We see that TaggedBT leads to a similarly high entropy, indicating the model has learnt this without needing to manually "break" the literal-translation bias. As a sanity check, we see that the entropy of the P3BT model's attention is also high, but is lower than that of the NoisedBT model, because P3 noise is less destructive. The one sur-

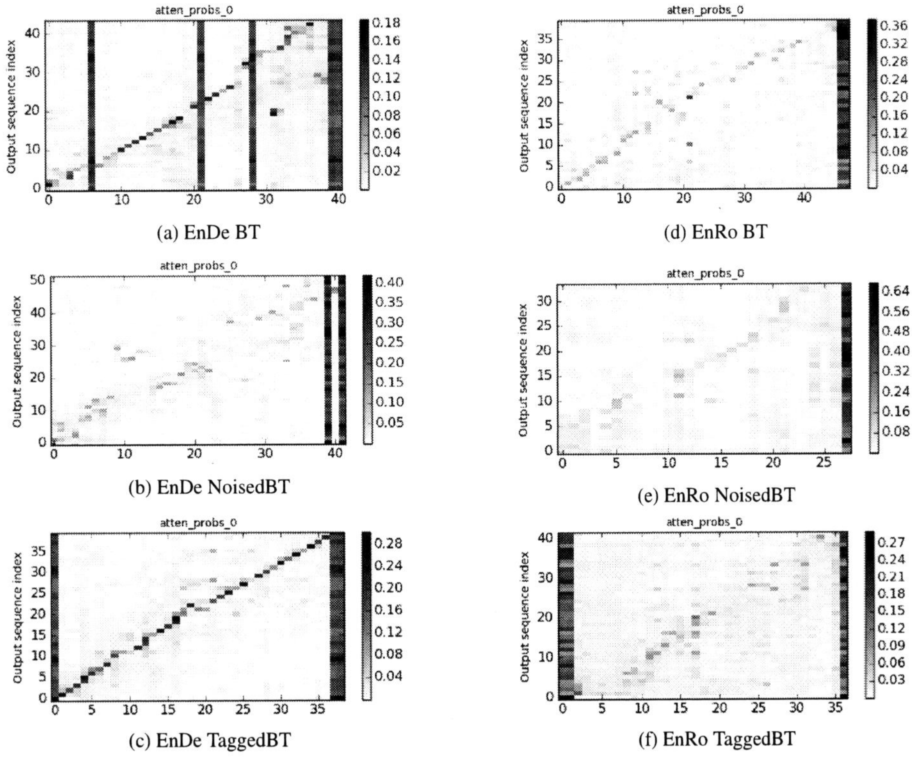

(a) EnDe BT   (d) EnRo BT

(b) EnDe NoisedBT   (e) EnRo NoisedBT

(c) EnDe TaggedBT   (f) EnRo TaggedBT

Figure 1: Comparison of attention maps at the first encoder layer for a random training example for BT (row 1), NoisedBT (row 2), and TaggedBT (row 3), for both EnDe (col 1) and EnRo (col 2). Note the heavy attention on the tag (position 0 in row 3), and the diffuse attention map learned by the NoiseBT models. These are the models from Table 3.a

prising entry on this table is probably the low entropy of the TaggedNoisedBT. Our best explanation is that TaggedNoisedBT puts disproportionately high attention on the sentence-end token, with 1.4x the $ASR_{|x|}$ that TaggedBT has, naturally leading to lower entropy.

Model	ASR_0	$ASR_{|x|}$	$\tilde{H}$
Bitext baseline	0.31	10.21	0.504
BT	0.28	10.98	**0.455**
P3BT	0.37	7.66	0.558
NoisedBT	1.01	3.96	0.619
TaggedBT	**5.31**	5.31	0.597
TaggedNoisedBT	**7.33**	7.33	0.491

Table 6: Attention sink ratio on the first and last token and entropy (at decoder layer 5) for the models in Table 3.a, averaged over all sentences in newstest14. For ASR, data is treated as if it were BT (noised and/or tagged, resp.), whereas for entropy the natural text is used. Outliers discussed in the text are bolded.

5.2 Decoding with and without a tag

In this section we look at what happens when we decode with a model on newstest data as if it were back-translated. This means that for the TaggedBT model we tag the true source, and for the NoisedBT model, we noise the true source. These "as-if-BT" decodings contrast with "standard decode", or decoding with the true source. An example sentence from newstest2015 is shown in Table 8, decoded by both models both in the standard fashion and in the "as-if-BT" fashion. The BLEU scores of each decoding method are presented in Table 7.

The noised decode – decoding newstest sentences with the NoisedBT model after noising the source – yields poor performance. This is unsurprising given the severity of the noise model used (recall Table 1). The tagged decode, however, yields only somewhat lower performance than the standard decode on the same model (-2.9BLEU on average). There are no clear reasons for this qual-

Model	Decode type	AVG 13-17	2010	2011	2012	2013	2014	2015	2016	2017
TaggedBT	standard	**33.24**	26.5	**24.2**	**25.2**	**28.7**	**32.8**	**34.5**	**38.1**	**32.4**
	as BT (tagged)	30.30	24.3	22.2	23.4	26.6	30.0	30.5	34.2	30.2
NoisedBT	standard	33.06	**26.7**	24.0	**25.2**	28.6	32.6	33.9	38.0	32.2
	as BT (noised)	10.66	8.1	6.5	7.5	8.2	11.1	10.0	12.7	11.3

Table 7: Comparing standard decoding with decoding as if the input were back-translated data, meaning that it is tagged (for the TaggedBT model) or noised (for the NoisedBT model) .

Model	Decode type	Example
TaggedBT	standard	Wie der Reverend Martin Luther King Jr. vor fünfzig Jahren sagte:
	as-if-BT (tagged)	Wie sagte der Reverend Martin Luther King jr. Vor fünfzig Jahren:
NoisedBT	standard	Wie der Reverend Martin Luther King Jr. vor fünfzig Jahren sagte:
	as-if-BT (noised)	Als Luther King Reverend ___ Jr. vor fünfzig Jahren:
Source		As the Reverend Martin Luther King Jr. said fifty years ago:
Reference		Wie Pastor Martin Luther King Jr. vor fünfzig Jahren sagte:

Table 8: Example decodes from newstest2015 for decoding in standard and "as-if-BT" varieties. Here, NoisedBT and TaggedBT produce equivalent outputs with standard decoding; TaggedBT produces less natural output with tagged input; and NoisedBT produces a low-quality output with noised input.

ity drop – the model correctly omits the tag in the outputs, but simply produces slightly lower quality hypotheses. The only noticeable difference in decoding outputs between the two systems is that the tagged decoding produces about double the quantity of English outputs (2.7% vs. 1.2%, over newstest2010-newstest2017, using a language ID classifier).

That the tagged-decode BLEU is still quite reasonable tells us that the model has not simply learned to ignore the source sentence when it encounters the input tag, suggesting that the $p(y|\text{BT}(x))$ signal is still useful to the model, as Sennrich et al. (2016) also demonstrated. The tag might then be functioning as a domain tag, causing the model to emulate the domain of the BT data – including both the desirable target-side news domain and the MT biases inherent in BT data.

To poke at the intuition that the quality drop comes in part from emulating the NMT biases in the synthetic training data, we probe a particular shortcoming of NMT: copy rate. We quantify the copy rate with the unigram overlap between source and target as a percentage of tokens in the target side, and compare those statistics to the bitext and the back-translated data (Table 9). We notice that the increase in unigram overlap with the tagged decode corresponds to the increased copy rate for the back-translated data (reaching the same value of 11%), supporting the hypothesis that the tag helps the model separate the domain of the parallel versus the back-translated data. Under this lens, quality gains from TaggedBT/NoisedBT could be re-framed as transfer learning from a

multi-task set-up, where one task is to translate simpler "translationese" (Gellerstam, 1986; Freitag et al., 2019) source text, and the other is to translate true bitext.

Data	src-tgt unigram overlap
TaggedBT (standard decode)	8.9%
TaggedBT (tagged decode)	10.7%
Bitext	5.9%
BT Data	11.4 %

Table 9: Source-target overlap for both back-translated data with decoding newstest as if it were bitext or BT data. Model decodes are averaged over newstest2010-newstest2017.

6 Negative Results

In addition to tagged back-translation, we tried several tagging-related experiments that did not work as well. We experimented with tagged forward-translation (TaggedFT), and found that the tag made no substantial difference, often lagging behind untagged forward-translation (FT) by a small margin (~ 0.2 BLEU). For EnDe, (Tagged)FT underperformed the bitext baseline; for EnRo, (Tagged)FT performed about the same as BT. Combining BT and FT had additive effects, yielding results slightly higher than iteration-3 TaggedBT (Table 4), at 33.9 SacreBLEU on test; but tagging did not help in this set-up. We furthermore experimented with year-specific tags on the BT data, using a different tag for each of the ten years of newscrawl. The model trained on these data performed identically to the normal TaggedBT model. Using this model we replicated the "as-if-bt" experiments from Table 8 using year-specific tags, and although there was a slight correlation between year tag and that year's dataset, the standard-decode still resulted in the highest BLEU.

7 Conclusion

In this work we develop TaggedBT, a novel technique for using back-translation in the context of NMT, which improves over the current state-of-the-art method of Noised Back-Translation, while also being simpler and more robust. We demonstrate that while Noised Back-Translation and standard Back-Translation are more or less effective depending on the task (low-resource, mid-resource, iterative BT), TaggedBT performs well on all tasks.

On WMT16 EnRo, TaggedBT improves on vanilla BT by 0.4 BLEU. Our best BLEU score of 33.4 BLEU, obtained using Iterative TaggedBT, shows a gain of +3.5 BLEU over the highest previously published result on this test-set that we are aware of. We furthermore match or out-perform the highest published results we are aware of on WMT EnDe that use only back-translation, with higher or equal BLEU on five of seven test sets.

In addition, we conclude that noising in the context of back-translation acts merely as an indicator to the model that the source is back-translated, allowing the model to treat it as a different domain and separate the helpful signal from the harmful signal. We support this hypothesis with experimental results showing that heuristic noising techniques like those discussed here, although they produce text that may seem like a nigh unintelligible mangling to humans, have a relatively small impact on the cross-lingual signal. Our analysis of attention and tagged decoding provides further supporting evidence for these conclusions.

8 Future Work

A natural extension of this work is to investigate a more fine-grained application of tags to both natural and synthetic data, for both back-translation and forward-translation, using quality and domain tags as well as synth-data tags. Similarly, tagging could be investigated as an alternative to data selection, as in van der Wees et al. (2017); Axelrod et al. (2011), or curriculum learning approaches like fine-tuning on in-domain data (Thompson et al., 2018; Hassan Sajjad and Nadir

Durrani and Fahim Dalvi and Yonatan Belinkov and Stephan Vogel, 2017; Freitag and Al-Onaizan, 2016). Finally, the token-tagging method should be contrasted with more sophisticated versions of tagging, like concatenating a trainable domain embedding with all token embeddings, as in Kobus et al. (2016).

9 Acknowledgements

Thank you to Markus Freitag, Melvin Johnson and Wei Wang for advising and discussions about these ideas; thank you to Keith Stevens, Mia Chen, and Wei Wang for technical help and bug fixing; thank you to Sergey Edunov for a fast and thorough answer to our question about his paper; and of course to the various people who have given comments and suggestions throughout the process, including Bowen Liang, Naveen Arivazhagan, Macduff Hughes, and George Foster.

References

Mikel Artetxe, Gorka Labaka, and Eneko Agirre. 2018. Unsupervised Statistical Machine Translation. In *Proceedings of the 2018 Conference on Empirical Methods in Natural Language Processing*, pages 3632–3642.

Amittai Axelrod, Xiaodong He, and Jianfeng Gao. 2011. Domain adaptation via pseudo in-domain data selection. In *Proceedings of the 2011 Conference on Empirical Methods in Natural Language Processing*, pages 355–362.

Dzmitry Bahdanau, Kyunghyun Cho, and Yoshua Bengio. 2015. Neural Machine Translation by Jointly Learning to Align and Translate. In *3rd International Conference on Learning Representations, ICLR 2015*.

Nicola Bertoldi and Marcello Federico. 2009. Domain adaptation for statistical machine translation with monolingual resources. In *Proceedings of the fourth workshop on statistical machine translation*, pages 182–189. Association for Computational Linguistics.

Ondřej Bojar and Aleš Tamchyna. 2011. Improving translation model by monolingual data. In *Proceedings of the Sixth Workshop on Statistical Machine Translation*, pages 330–336. Association for Computational Linguistics.

Thorsten Brants, Ashok C Popat, Peng Xu, Franz J Och, and Jeffrey Dean. 2007. Large Language Models in Machine Translation. In *Proceedings of the 2007 Joint Conference on Empirical Methods in Natural Language Processing and Computational Natural Language Learning (EMNLP-CoNLL)*.

Nikhil Buduma and Nicholas Locascio. 2017. *Fundamentals of deep learning: Designing next-generation machine intelligence algorithms.* "O'Reilly Media, Inc.".

Yong Cheng, Wei Xu, Zhongjun He, Wei He, Hua Wu, Maosong Sun, and Yang Liu. 2016. Semi-Supervised Learning for Neural Machine Translation. In *Proceedings of the 54th Annual Meeting of the Association for Computational Linguistics*, volume 1, pages 1965–1974.

Ryan Cotterell and Julia Kreutzer. 2018. Explaining and Generalizing Back-Translation through Wakesleep. *arXiv preprint arXiv:1806.04402.*

Anna Currey, Antonio Valerio Miceli Barone, and Kenneth Heafield. 2017. Copied monolingual data improves low-resource neural machine translation. In *Proceedings of the Second Conference on Machine Translation*, pages 148–156.

Tao Qin Liwei Wang Nenghai Yu Tieyan Liu Di He, Yingce Xia and Wei-Ying Ma. 2016. Dual Learning for Machine Translation. In *Conference on Advances in Neural Information Processing Systems (NeurIPS).*

Tobias Domhan and Felix Hieber. 2017. Using Target-side Monolingual Data for Neural Machine Translation through Multi-task Learning. In *Proceedings of the 2017 Conference on Empirical Methods in Natural Language Processing*, pages 1500–1505.

Sergey Edunov, Myle Ott, Michael Auli, and David Grangier. 2018. Understanding Back-Translation at Scale. In *Proceedings of the 2018 Conference on Empirical Methods in Natural Language Processing (EMNLP)*, pages 489–500.

Marzieh Fadaee and Christof Monz. 2018. Back-Translation Sampling by Targeting Difficult Words in Neural Machine Translation. *CoRR*, abs/1808.09006.

Markus Freitag and Yaser Al-Onaizan. 2016. Fast Domain Adaptation for Neural Machine Translation. *CoRR*, abs/1612.06897.

Markus Freitag, Isaac Caswell, and Scott Roy. 2019. Text Repair Model for Neural Machine Translation. *CoRR*, abs/1904.04790.

Mercedes García-Martínez, Özan Çağlayan, Walid Aransa, Adrien Bardet, Fethi Bougares, and Loïc Barrault. 2017. LIUM Machine Translation Systems for WMT17 News Translation Task. *CoRR*, abs/1707.04499.

Jonas Gehring, Michael Auli, David Grangier, Denis Yarats, and Yann N. Dauphin. 2017. Convolutional Sequence to Sequence Learning. In *Proceedings of the 34th International Conference on Machine Learning - Volume 70*, pages 1243–1252.

Martin Gellerstam. 1986. Translationese in Swedish novels translated from English. *Translation Studies in Scandinavia*, pages 88–95.

Çağlar Gülçehre, Orhan Firat, Kelvin Xu, Kyunghyun Cho, Loic Barrault, Huei-Chi Lin, Fethi Bougares, Holger Schwenk, and Yoshua Bengio. 2015. On using Monolingual Corpora in Neural Machine Translation. *arXiv preprint arXiv:1503.03535.*

Çağlar Gülçehre, Orhan Firat, Kelvin Xu, Kyunghyun Cho, and Yoshua Bengio. 2017. On Integrating a Language Model into Neural Machine Translation. *Comput. Speech Lang.*, pages 137–148.

Thanh-Le Ha, Jan Niehues, and Alexander H. Waibel. 2017. Effective Strategies in Zero-Shot Neural Machine Translation. *CoRR*, abs/1711.07893.

Hassan Sajjad and Nadir Durrani and Fahim Dalvi and Yonatan Belinkov and Stephan Vogel. 2017. Neural machine translation training in a multi-domain scenario. *arXiv preprint arXiv:1708.08712v2.*

Wei He, Zhongjun He, Hua Wu, and Haifeng Wang. 2016. Improved neural machine translation with SMT features. In *Thirtieth AAAI conference on artificial intelligence.*

Kenji Imamura, Atsushi Fujita, and Eiichiro Sumita. 2018. Enhancement of Encoder and Attention Using Target Monolingual Corpora in Neural Machine Translation. In *Proceedings of the 2nd Workshop on Neural Machine Translation and Generation*, volume 1, pages 55–63.

Melvin Johnson, Mike Schuster, Quoc V. Le, Maxim Krikun, Yonghui Wu, Zhifeng Chen, Nikhil Thorat, Fernanda B. Vi'egas, Martin Wattenberg, Greg Corrado, Macduff Hughes, and Jeffrey Dean. 2016. Google's Multilingual Neural Machine Translation System: Enabling Zero-Shot Translation. *CoRR*, abs/1611.04558.

Yoon Kim and Alexander M. Rush. 2016. Sequence-Level Knowledge Distillation. In *Proceedings of the 2016 Conference on Empirical Methods in Natural Language Processing*, pages 1317–1327, Austin, Texas. Association for Computational Linguistics.

Catherine Kobus, Josep Maria Crego, and Jean Senellart. 2016. Domain Control for Neural Machine Translation. *CoRR*, abs/1612.06140.

Philipp Koehn. 2009. *Statistical machine translation.* Cambridge University Press.

James Kuczmarski and Melvin Johnson. 2018. Gender-aware natural language translation. *Technical Disclosure Commons.*

Patrik Lambert, Holger Schwenk, Christophe Servan, and Sadaf Abdul-Rauf. 2011. Investigations on translation model adaptation using monolingual data. In *Proceedings of the Sixth Workshop on Statistical Machine Translation*, pages 284–293. Association for Computational Linguistics.

Guillaume Lample and Alexis Conneau. 2019. Cross-lingual Language Model Pretraining. *arXiv preprint arXiv:1901.07291*.

Guillaume Lample, Alexis Conneau, Ludovic Denoyer, and Marc'Aurelio Ranzato. 2018a. Unsupervised Machine Translation Using Monolingual Corpora Only. In *International Conference on Learning Representations*.

Guillaume Lample, Myle Ott, Alexis Conneau, Ludovic Denoyer, and Marc'Aurelio Ranzato. 2018b. Phrase-Based & Neural Unsupervised Machine Translation. In *Proceedings of the 2018 Conference on Empirical Methods in Natural Language Processing (EMNLP)*.

Xing Niu, Michael Denkowski, and Marine Carpuat. 2018. Bi-Directional Neural Machine Translation with Synthetic Parallel Data. *ACL 2018*, page 84.

Kishore Papineni, Salim Roukos, Todd Ward, and Wei-Jing Zhu. 2002. BLEU: a Method for Automatic Evaluation of Machine Translation. In *Proceedings of the 40th annual meeting on association for computational linguistics*, pages 311–318. Association for Computational Linguistics.

Alberto Poncelas, Dimitar Shterionov, Andy Way, Gideon Maillette de Buy Wenniger, and Peyman Passban. 2018. Investigating Backtranslation in Neural Machine Translation. In *Proceedings of the 21st Annual Conference of the European Association for Machine Translation*, pages 249–258.

Matt Post. 2018. A Call for Clarity in Reporting Bleu Scores. *arXiv preprint arXiv:1804.08771*.

Rico Sennrich, Alexandra Birch, Anna Currey, Ulrich Germann, Barry Haddow, Kenneth Heafield, Antonio Valerio Miceli Barone, and Philip Williams. 2017. The University of Edinburgh's Neural MT Systems for WMT17. *CoRR*, abs/1708.00726.

Rico Sennrich, Barry Haddow, and Alexandra Birch. 2016. Improving Neural Machine Translation Models with Monolingual Data. In *Proceedings of the 54th Annual Meeting of the Association for Computational Linguistics (Volume 1: Long Papers)*, pages 86–96.

Jonathan Shen, Patrick Nguyen, Yonghui Wu, Zhifeng Chen, Mia X. Chen, Ye Jia, Anjuli Kannan, Tara N. Sainath, and Yuan Cao et al. 2019. Lingvo: a Modular and Scalable Framework for Sequence-to-Sequence Modeling. *CoRR*, abs/1902.08295.

Brian Thompson, Huda Khayrallah, Antonios Anastasopoulos, Arya D. McCarthy, Kevin Duh, Rebecca Marvin, Paul McNamee, Jeremy Gwinnup, Tim Anderson, and Philipp Koehn. 2018. Freezing Subnetworks to Analyze Domain Adaptation in Neural Machine Translation. In *Proceedings of the Third Conference on Machine Translation: Research Papers*, pages 124–132. Association for Computational Linguistics.

Nicola Ueffing, Gholamreza Haffari, and Anoop Sarkar. 2007. Semi-supervised model adaptation for statistical machine translation. *Machine Translation*, 21(2):77–94.

Ashish Vaswani, Noam Shazeer, Niki Parmar, Jakob Uszkoreit, Llion Jones, Aidan N Gomez, Łukasz Kaiser, and Illia Polosukhin. 2017. Attention Is All You Need. In *Advances in Neural Information Processing Systems*, pages 5998–6008.

Gholamreza Haffari Vu Cong Duy Hoang, Philipp Koehn and Trevor Cohn. 2018. Iterative Backtranslation for Neural Machine Translation. In *Proceedings of the 2nd Workshop on Neural Machine Translation and Generation*, volume 1, pages 18–24.

Marlies van der Wees, Arianna Bisazza, and Christof Monz. 2017. Dynamic Data Selection for Neural Machine Transaltion. In *Proceedings of the 2017 Conference on Empirical Methods in Natural Language Processing*, pages 1400–1410.

Yingce Xia, Tao Qin, Wei Chen, Jiang Bian, Nenghai Yu, and Tie-Yan Liu. 2017. Dual Supervised Learning. In *International Conference on Machine Learning (ICML)*.

Hayahide Yamagishi, Shin Kanouchi, Takayuki Sato, and Mamoru Komachi. 2016. Controlling the voice of a sentence in Japanese-to-English neural machine translation. In *Proceedings of the 3rd Workshop on Asian Translation (WAT2016)*, pages 203–210.

Hierarchical Document Encoder for Parallel Corpus Mining

Mandy Guo, Yinfei Yang, Keith Stevens, Daniel Cer, Heming Ge,
Yun-Hsuan Sung, Brian Strope, Ray Kurzweil

Google AI
1600 Amphitheatre Parkway
Mountain View, CA, USA
{xyguo, yinfeiy, kstevens, cer, hemingge, yhsung, raykurzweil}@google.com

Abstract

We explore using multilingual document embeddings for nearest neighbor mining of parallel data. Three document-level representations are investigated: (i) document embeddings generated by simply averaging multilingual sentence embeddings; (ii) a neural bag-of-words (BoW) document encoding model; (iii) a hierarchical multilingual document encoder (HiDE) that builds on our sentence-level model. The results show document embeddings derived from sentence-level averaging are surprisingly effective for clean datasets, but suggest models trained hierarchically at the document-level are more effective on noisy data. Analysis experiments demonstrate our hierarchical models are very robust to variations in the underlying sentence embedding quality. Using document embeddings trained with HiDE achieves state-of-the-art performance on United Nations (UN) parallel document mining, 94.9% P@1[1] for en-fr and 97.3% P@1 for en-es.

1 Introduction

Obtaining a high-quality parallel training corpus is one of the most critical issues in machine translation. Previous work on parallel document mining using large distributed systems has proven effective (Uszkoreit et al., 2010; Antonova and Misyurev, 2011), but these systems are often heavily engineered and computationally intensive. Recent work on parallel data mining has focused on sentence-level embeddings (Guo et al., 2018; Artetxe and Schwenk, 2018; Yang et al., 2019). However, these sentence embedding methods have had limited success when applied to document-level mining tasks (Guo et al., 2018). A recent study from Yang et al. (2019) shows that document embeddings obtained from averaging sentence embeddings can achieve state-of-the-art performance in document retrieval on the United Nation (UN) corpus. This simple averaging approach, however, heavily relies on high quality sentence embeddings and the cleanliness of documents in the application domain.

In our work, we explore using three variants of document-level embeddings for parallel document mining: (i) simple averaging of embeddings from a multilingual sentence embedding model (Yang et al., 2019); (ii) trained document-level embeddings based on document unigrams; (iii) a simple hierarchical document encoder (HiDE) trained on documents pairs using the output of our sentence-level model.

The results show document embeddings are able to achieve strong performance on parallel document mining. On a test set mined from the web, all models achieve strong retrieval performance, the best being 91.4% P@1 for en-fr and 81.8% for en-es from the hierarchical document models. On the United Nations (UN) document mining task (Ziemski et al., 2016), our best model achieves 96.7% P@1 for en-fr and 97.3% P@1 for en-es, a 3%+ absolute improvement over the prior state-of-the-art (Guo et al., 2018; Uszkoreit et al., 2010). We also evaluate on a noisier version of the UN task where we do not have the ground truth sentence alignments from the original corpus. An off-the-shelf sentence splitter is used to split the document into sentences.[2] The results shows that the HiDE model is robust to the noisy sentence segmentations, while the averaging of sentence embeddings approach is more sensitive. We further perform analysis on the robustness of our models based on different quality sentence-level embeddings, and show that the

---

[1]We use evaluation metrics precision at N, here P@1 means precision at 1

[2]To introduce noise in sentence alignment, which is often seen in the real applications, in the parallel documents

Proceedings of the Fourth Conference on Machine Translation (WMT), Volume 1: Research Papers, pages 64–72
Florence, Italy, August 1-2, 2019. ©2019 Association for Computational Linguistics

HiDE model performs well even when the under-lying sentence-level model is relatively weak.

We summarize our contributions as follows:

- We introduce and explore different approaches for using document embeddings in parallel document mining.

- We adapt the previous work on hierarchical networks to introduce a simple hierarchical document encoder trained on document pairs for this task.

- Empirical results show our best document embedding model leads to state-of-the-art results on the document-level bitext retrieval task on two different datasets. The proposed hierarchical models are very robust to variations in sentence splitting and the underlying sentence embedding quality.

2 Related Work

Parallel document mining has been extensively studied. One standard approach is to identify bitexts using metadata, such as document titles (Yang and Li, 2002), publication dates (Munteanu and Marcu, 2005, 2006), or document structure (Chen and Nie, 2000; Resnik and Smith, 2003; Shi et al., 2006). However, the metadata related to the documents can often be sparse or unreliable (Uszkoreit et al., 2010). More recent research has focused on embedding-based approaches, where texts are mapped to an embedding space to calculate their similarity distance and determine whether they are parallel (Grégoire and Langlais, 2017; Hassan et al., 2018; Schwenk, 2018). Guo et al. (2018) has studied document-level mining from sentence embeddings using a hyperparameter tuned similarity function, but had limited success compared to the heavily engineered system proposed by Uszkoreit et al. (2010).

An extensive amount of work has also been done on learning document embeddings. Le and Mikolov (2014); Li et al. (2015); Dai et al. (2015) explored Paragraph Vector with various lengths (sentence, paragraph, document) trained on next word/n-gram prediction given context sampled from the paragraph. The work from Roy et al. (2016); Chen (2017); Wu et al. (2018) obtained document embeddings from word-level embeddings. More recent work has been focused on learning document embeddings through hierarchical training. The work from Yang et al. (2016);

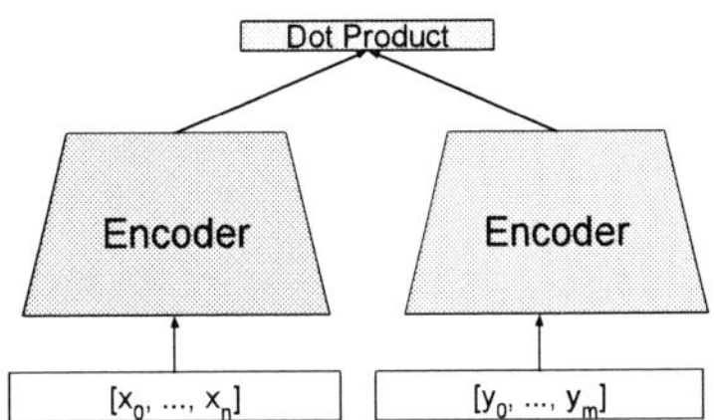

Figure 1: Dual encoder for parallel corpus mining, where (x, y) represents translation pairs.

Miculicich et al. (2018) approached Document Classification and Neural Machine Translation using Hierarchical Attention Networks, and Wang et al. (2017) proposed using a hierarchy of Recurrent Neural Networks (RNNs) to summarize the cross-sentence context. However, the amount of work applying document embeddings to the translation pair mining task has been limited.

Yang et al. (2019) recently showed strong parallel document retrieval results using document embeddings obtained by averaging sentence embeddings. Our paper extends this work to explore different variants of document-level embeddings for parallel document mining, including using an end-to-end hierarchical encoder model.

3 Model

This section introduces our document embedding models and training procedure.

3.1 Translation Candidate Ranking Task using a Dual Encoder

All models use the dual encoder architecture in Figure 1, allowing candidate translation pairs to be scored using an efficient dot-product operation. The embeddings that feed the dot-product are trained by modeling parallel corpus mining as a translation ranking task (Guo et al., 2018). Given translation pair (x, y), we learn to rank true translation y over other candidates, $\mathcal{Y}$. We use batch negatives, with sentence y_i of the pair (x_i, y_i) serving as a random negative for all source x_j in a training batch such that $j \neq i$. Following Artetxe and Schwenk (2018), a shared multilingual encoder is used to map both x and y to their embedding space representations x' and y'. Within a batch, all pairwise dot-products can be computed using a single matrix multiplication. We train using additive margin softmax (Yang et al., 2019), subtracting a margin term m from the dot-product scores for true translation pairs. For batch size K

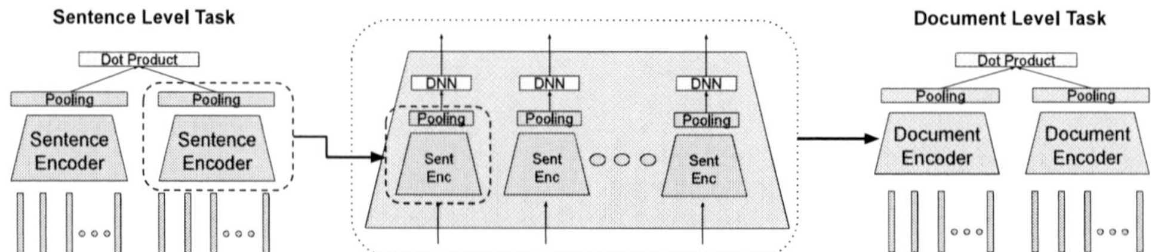

Figure 2: Illustration of the DNN $\rightarrow$ pooling version of the Hierarchical Document Encoder (HiDE). Each sentence is processed by our Transformer based encoding model with the final sentence-level embedding being produced by pooling across the last layer's positional heads. Document-level embeddings are composed by pooling across the sentence-level embeddings after each sentence embedding has been adapted by additional feed-forward layers.

and margin m, the log-likelihood loss function is given by Eq. 1.

$$\mathcal{J} = -\frac{1}{K}\sum_{i=1}^{K} \log \frac{e^{x'_i \cdot y'^{\top}_i - m}}{e^{x'_i \cdot y'^{\top}_i - m} + \sum_{k=1}^{K} e^{x'_k, k\neq i \cdot y'^{\top}_k}} \tag{1}$$

Models are trained with a bidirectional ranking objective (Yang et al., 2019). Given source and target pair (x, y), forward translation ranking, $\mathcal{J}_{forward}$, maximizes $p(y|x)$, while backward translation ranking, $\mathcal{J}_{backward}$, maximizes $p(x|y)$. Bidirectional loss $\mathcal{J}$ sums the two directional losses:

$$\mathcal{J} = \mathcal{J}_{forward} + \mathcal{J}_{backward} \tag{2}$$

3.1.1 Sentence-Level Embeddings

Sentence embeddings are produced by a Transformer model (Vaswani et al., 2017) with pooling over the last block.[3] Semantically similar hard negatives are included to augment batch negatives (Guo et al., 2018; Chidambaram et al., 2018; Yang et al., 2019). We denote document embeddings derived from averaged sentence embeddings as **Sentence-Avg**.

3.1.2 Bag-of-words Document Embeddings

Our bag-of-words (BoW) document embeddings, **Document BoW**, are constructed by feeding document unigrams into a deep averaging network (DAN) (Iyyer et al., 2015) trained on the parallel document ranking task.[4]

3.2 Hierarchical Document Encoder (HiDE)

As illustrated in Figure 2, our hierarchical model is also trained on the parallel document ranking task, but taking as input embeddings from our sentence-level model. For **HiDE$_{\mathbf{DNN\rightarrow pooling}}$**, sentence embeddings are adapted to the document-level task by applying a feed-forward DNN to each sentence embedding. Average pooling aggregates the adapted sentence representations into the final fixed-length document embedding. We contrast performance with a variant of the model, **HiDE$_{\mathbf{pooling\rightarrow DNN}}$**, that performs average pooling first followed by a feed-forward DNN to adapt the representation to document-level mining.

4 Experiments

This section describes our training data, model configurations, and retrieval results for our embedding models: Sentence-Avg, Document BoW, HiDE$_{DNN\rightarrow pooling}$, and HiDE$_{pooling\rightarrow DNN}$.

4.1 Data

We focus on two language pairs: English-French (en-fr) and English-Spanish (en-es). Two corpora are used for training and evaluation.

The first corpus is obtained from web (**WebData**) using a parallel document mining system and automatic sentence alignments, both following an approach similar to Uszkoreit et al. (2010). Parallel documents number 13M for en-fr and 6M for en-es, with 400M sentence pairs for each language pair. We split this corpus into training (80%), development (10%), and test set (10%).

We also evaluate the trained models on a second corpus, the United Nations (**UN**) Parallel Corpus (Ziemski et al., 2016), as an out-of-domain test set. The UN corpus contains a fully aligned sub-

---

[3]For pooling, we concatenate the combination of min, max and attentional pooling.

[4]The model uses feed-forward hidden layers of size 320, 320, 500, and 500.

Corpus	Document Pairs
	English - French
WebData	(s_1) Specs Toshiba Coverside FL not categorized (4407839940), (s_2) Search by brand, (s_3) Icecat: syndicator of product information via global Open catalog with more than 4578703 data-sheets & 19844 brands – Register (free) (s_1) Fiche produit Toshiba Coverside FL non classé (4407839940), (s_2) Partenaires en ligne, (s_3) Edit my products
Clean UN	(s_1) 1 July 2011, (s_2) Original: English, (s_3) Tenth meeting, (s_4) Cartagena, Colombia, 17 - 21 October 2011, (s_5) Item 4 of the provisional agenda (s_1) 1er juillet 2011, (s_2) Original : anglais, (s_3) Dixième réunion, (s_4) Cartagena (Colombie), 17-21 octobre 2011, (s_5) Point 4 de l'ordre du jour provisoire*
Noisy UN	(s_1) 6–7 May 1999 Non-governmental organizations New York, 14 to 18 December 1998 Corrigendum 1., (s_2) Paragraph 1, draft decision I, under "Special consultative status" 2., (s_3) Paragraph 48 Add Japan to the list of States Members of the United Nations represented by observers. (s_1) 6 et 7 mai 1999 Organisations non gouvernementales New York, 14-18 décembre 1998 Rectificatif Paragraphe 1, projet de décision I, sous la rubrique "Statut consultatif spécial" Paragraphe 48 Ajouter le Japon à la liste des États Membres de l'Organisation des Nations Unies représentés par des observateurs.
	English - Spanish
WebData	(s_1) Alcudia travel Guide & Map - android apps on Google play, (s_2) Travel & Local, (s_3) Alcudia travel Guide & Map, (s_4) Maps, GPS Navigation Travel & Local, (s_5) Offers in-app purchases" (s_1) Beirut Travel Guide & map - aplicaciones Android en Google play, (s_2) Todavía más ", (s_3) Seleccin de los editores, (s_4) Libros de texto, (s_5) Comprar tarjeta de regalo
Clean UN	(s_1) [Original: English], (s_2) Monthly report to the United Nations on the operations of the Kosovo Force, (s_3) 1. Over the reporting period (1-28 February 2003) there were just over 26,600 troops of the Kosovo Force (KFOR) in theatre. (s_1) [Original: inglés], (s_2) Informe mensual de las Naciones Unidas sobre las operaciones de la Fuerza Internacional de Seguridad en Kosovo, (s_3) En el período sobre el que se informa (1 a 28 de febrero 2003) había en el teatro de operaciones algo más de 26.600 efectivos de la Fuerza Internacional de Seguridad en Kosovo (KFOR).
Noisy UN	(s_1) (Original: English) Monthly report to the United Nations on the operations of the Kosovo Force 1., (s_2) Over the reporting period (1-28 February 2003) there were just over 26,600 troops of the Kosovo Force (KFOR) in theatre. (s_1) (Original: inglés) Informe mensual de las Naciones Unidas sobre las operaciones de la Fuerza Internacional de Seguridad en Kosovo En el período sobre el que se informa (1 a 28 de febrero 2003) había en el teatro de operaciones algo más de 26.600 efectivos de la Fuerza Internacional de Seguridad en Kosovo (KFOR).

Table 1: Example document snippets from the WebData, original UN corpus, UN corpus with noisy sentence segmentation. We only show the starting sentences for each document, the original documents can go very long. Symbol (s_n) means sentence n in the document to show sentence segmentation.

corpus of ∼86k document pairs for the six official UN languages.[5] As this corpus is small, it is only used for evaluation.

The sentence segmentation in the fully aligned subcorpus is particularly good due to the process used to construct the dataset. While automatic sentence splitting is performed using the Eserix spltter, documents are only included in the fully aligned subcorpus if sentences are consistently aligned across all six languages. This implicitly filters documents with noisy sentence segmentations. Exceptions are errors in the sentence segmentation that are systematically replicated across the documents in all six languages.

We create a noisier version of the UN dataset that makes use of an robust off-the-shelf sentence splitter, but which necessarily introduces noise compare to sentences that were split by consensus across all six languages within the original UN dataset. Models are evaluated on this noisy UN corpus, as any real application of our models will almost certainly need to contend with noisy automatic sentence splits.

Table 1 shows examples from each dataset. The WebData dataset is very noisy and contains a large amount of template-like queries from web. In this dataset, sentence alignments can be also very noisy, and sometimes sentences are not direct translations of each other. The original UN

---

[5] Arabic, Chinese, English, French, Russian, and Spanish.

is translated sentence by sentence by human annotators, so it is perfectly aligned at the sentence-level with ground truth translations. The noisy UN, however, could have incorrect sentence-level mappings, but these could still be correct translations on the document-level. The sentence splitter used to generate the noisy UN dataset could also perform differently in different languages for the parallel content, resulting in mismatches at the sentence-level. As seen in the Noisy UN examples shown in Table 1, the English text is split into 3 sentences, while the corresponding French or Spanish texts are only split into 1 sentence.

4.2 Configuration

Our sentence-level encoder follows a similar setup as Yang et al. (2019). The sentence encoder has a shared 200k token multilingual vocabulary with 10K OOV buckets. Vocabulary items and OOV buckets map to 320 dim. word embeddings. For each token, we also extract character n-grams ($n = [3, 6]$) hashed to 200k buckets mapped to 320 dim. character embeddings. Word and character n-gram representations are summed together to produce the final input token representation. Updates to the word and character embeddings are scaled by a gradient multiplier of 25 (Chidambaram et al., 2018). The encoder uses 3 transformer blocks with hidden size of 512, filter size of 2048, and 8 attention heads. Additive margin softmax uses $m = 0.3$. We train for 40M steps for both language pairs using an SGD optimizer with batch size K=100 and learning rate 0.003.

During document-level training, sentence embeddings are fixed due to the computational cost of dynamically encoding all of the sentences in a document. Sentence embeddings are adapted using a four-layer DNN model with residual connections and hidden sizes 320, 320, 500, and 500. The first three layers use ReLU activations with the final layer using Tanh. Document embeddings are trained with an SGD optimizer, batch size $K = 200$, learning rate 0.0001, and additive margin softmax $m = 0.5$ for en-fr, and $m = 0.6$ for en-es. We train for 5M steps for en-fr and 2M steps for en-es. Light hyperparameter tuning uses our development set from WebData.

4.3 Mining Translations and Evaluation

Translation candidates are mined with approximate nearest neighbor (ANN) (Vanderkam et al., 2013) search over our multilingual embeddings (Guo et al., 2018; Artetxe and Schwenk, 2018).[6] The evaluation metric is precision at N (P@N), which evaluates if the true translation is in the top N candidates returned by the model.

4.3.1 Results on WebData Test Set

Table 2 presents document embedding P@N retrieval performance using our WebData test set, for N = 1, 3, 10. The evaluation uses 1M candidate documents for en-fr and 0.6M for en-es. We obtain the best performance from our hierarchical models, HiDE$_*$. Adapting the sentence embeddings prior to pooling, HiDE$_{\text{DNN}\rightarrow\text{pooling}}$ performs better than attempting to adapt the representation after pooling, HiDE$_{\text{pooling}\rightarrow\text{DNN}}$. Document BoW embeddings outperform Sentence-Avg, showing training a simple model for document-level representations (DAN) outperforms pooling of sentence embeddings from a complex model (Transformer).

4.3.2 Results on UN Corpus

Table 3 shows document matching P@1 for our models on both the original UN dataset sentence segmentation and on the noisier sentence segmentation. P@1 is evaluated using all of the UN documents in a target language as translation candidates. The prior state-of-the-art is Uszkoreit et al. (2010).[7] Using both the official and noisy sentence segmentations, HiDE$_{\text{DNN}\rightarrow\text{pooling}}$ outperforms Uszkoreit et al. (2010), a heavily engineered system that incorporates both MT and monolingual duplicated document detection.

Guo et al. (2018) uses sentence-to-sentence alignments to heuristically identify document pairs. Alignments were computed using sentence embeddings generated over the UN corpus annotated sentence splits. With corpus annotated splits, Sentence-Avg performs better than Guo et al. (2018). Furthermore, even with noisy sentence splits HiDE$_*$ outperforms Guo et al. (2018).

The performance of all our document embeddings methods that build on sentence-level representations is remarkably strong when we use the sentence boundaries annotated in the UN corpus. Surprisingly, Sentence-Avg performed poorly on the WebData test data but is very competitive with both variants of HiDE when using the original UN corpus sentence splits.[8] However, on the UN

---

[6]Prior work only used ANN over sentence embeddings.

[7]Uszkoreit et al. (2010) was applied to the UN dataset by Guo et al. (2018).

[8]We use similar sentence-level encoder setup as Yang

Document Embedding	en-fr (1M)			en-es (0.6M)		
	P@1	P@3	P@10	P@1	P@3	P@10
HiDE$_{\text{DNN}\rightarrow\text{pooling}}$	**91.40**	**94.13**	**95.67**	**81.83**	**87.85**	**91.45**
HiDE$_{\text{pooling}\rightarrow\text{DNN}}$	90.63	93.50	95.11	78.84	85.04	88.88
Document BoW	83.83	90.47	94.18	78.09	85.04	91.03
Sentence-Avg	78.07	83.53	87.06	67.49	74.22	79.01

Table 2: Precision at N (P@N) of target document retrieval on the WebData test set. Models attempt to select the true translation target for a source document from the entire corpus (1 million parallel documents for en-fr, and 0.6 million for en-es).

Model	en-fr	en-es
UN Corpus Sentence Segmentation		
HiDE$_{\text{DNN}\rightarrow\text{pooling}}$	96.6	**97.3**
HiDE$_{\text{pooling}\rightarrow\text{DNN}}$	96.5	96.1
Sentence-Avg	**96.7**	**97.3**
Noisy Sentence Segmentation		
HiDE$_{\text{DNN}\rightarrow\text{pooling}}$	**94.9**	**96.0**
HiDE$_{\text{pooling}\rightarrow\text{DNN}}$	91.0	94.4
Sentence-Avg	86.8	95.7
No sentence splitting		
Document BoW	74.3	71.9
Prior work		
Uszkoreit et al. (2010)	93.4	94.4
Guo et al. (2018)	89.0	90.4

Table 3: Document matching on the UN corpus evaluated using P@1. For methods that require sentence splitting, we report results using both the UN sentence annotations and an off-the-shelf sentence splitter.

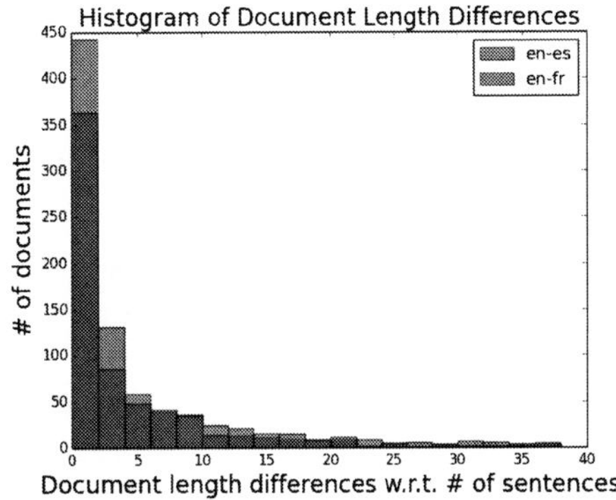

Figure 3: Histogram of document length differences w.r.t. # of sentences in each parallel document pair.

data with noisy sentence splits, HiDE$_*$ once again significantly outperforms Sentence-Avg. Averaging sentence embeddings appears to be a strong baseline for clean datasets, but the hierarchical model helps when composing document embeddings from noisier input representations.[9] Similar to the WebData test set, on the noisy UN data, HiDE$_{\text{DNN}\rightarrow\text{pooling}}$ outperforms HiDE$_{\text{pooling}\rightarrow\text{DNN}}$. We note that while Document BoW performed well on the in-domain test set, it performs poorly on the UN data. Preliminary analysis suggests this is due in part to differences in length between the WebData and UN documents.

We also observe that the performance of Sentence-Avg model dropped significantly in en-fr when transitioning from the Clean UN to the Noisy UN, but in en-es, the performance drop is much less. We compute the histogram of the document length differences in each document pair w.r.t. the # of sentences in each document on the noisy UN corpus. As shown in figure 3, the en-es dataset indeed has better agreement on the sentence split comparing with en-fr, which indicates the Sentence-Avg model is sensitive to the sentence segmentation quality of the parallel document pairs.

5 Analysis

In this section, we first analyze the errors produced by the document embedding models. We then explore how the performance of sentence-level models affect the performance of document-level models that incorporate sentence-embeddings.

5.1 Errors

We first look at the false positive examples retrieved by HiDE$_{\text{DNN}\rightarrow\text{pooling}}$ model on en-es Web-Doc development set. We observe that the actual error results often have similar sentence structure and meaning comparing to the expected result.

Table 4 list two typical example snippets for

---

et al. (2019), we are able to obtain matching results on the original UN corpus

[9]We note that in practice parallel document mining will tend to operate over noisy datasets.

Example 1		
Source	Audio-technica mb 3k b-stock - Thomann ireland, Dynamic Microphones finder, 40 €– 60, 60 €– 100, 100 €– 120, 120 €– 160, 160 €– 200, 200 €– 280, 280 €– 460, in stock items	
Expected Result	Beyerdynamic tg-x58 b-stock - Thomann españa, Micrófonos dinámicos de voz encontrar ..., Gama de precios, 40 €– 60, 60 €– 100, 100 €– 120, 120 €– 160, 160 €– 200, 200 €– 280, 280 €– 460, Reajustar todos los filtros	
Actual Result	Audio-technica atm63 u - Thomann españa, Micrófonos dinámicos de voz encontrar ..., Gama de precios, 40 €– 60, 60 €– 100, 100 €– 120, 120 €– 160, 160 €– 200, 200 €– 280, 280 €– 400, Reajustar todos los filtros	
Example 2		
Source	Casual man suit photo - android apps on google play, Casual man suit photo, Casual shirt Photo suit is photography application to make your face in nice fashionable man suit., This is so easy and free to make your photo into nice looking suit without any hard work and it's all free.	
Expected Result	Casual fotos - aplicaciones de android en Google play, Todavía más ", Selección de nuestros expertos, Libros de texto, Comprar tarjeta regalo, Mi lista de deseos, Mi actividad de Play, Guía para padres, Arte y Diseño, Bibliotecas y demos, Casa y hogar	
Actual Result	Traje de la foto de la camisa formal de los hombre - aplicaciones de android en Google play, Todavía más ", Selección de nuestros expertos, Libros de texto, Comprar tarjeta regalo, Mi lista de deseos, Mi actividad de Play, Guía para padres, Arte y Diseño, Bibliotecas y demos, Casa y hogar	

Table 4: Example document snippets of source, expected result, and actual result retrieved by HiDE$_{DNN \rightarrow pooling}$ model on the en-es development sets.

HiDE$_{DNN \rightarrow pooling}$. In the first example, our model matches the translation of "Audio-technica" to "Audio-technica" instead of "Beyerdynamic". We observe that in multiple cases, HiDE model is able to retrieve a more accurate translation pair than the labeled expected result. As shown in Table 1, the WebData automatically mined from the web is noisy and may contains non-translation pairs. This results indicates the proposed model is robust to the training data noise. The second example shows another typical error where the documents are template-like. The actual results retrieved by HiDE$_{DNN \rightarrow pooling}$ still largely match the expected text.

We also look at the actual results retrieved from Sentence-Avg model. The Sentence-Avg model also suffers from the template-like documents (e.g. Example 2 in Table 4) similar to the HiDE$_{DNN \rightarrow pooling}$ model. Other than that, though some correctly translated words can be found, the retrieved error documents differ much more in sentence structure and meaning from the expected results. For example, the expected and actual results can both be documents about the same subject, but from entirely different perspectives. We also found that some of the WebData target documents are in English instead of Spanish. In these cases, the Sentence-Avg model is more likely to retrieve a document in the same language as the source document instead of retrieving a translated document.

5.2 HiDE performance on Coarse Sentence-level Models

We further explore how the performance of sentence-level models affect the performance of document-level models that incorporate sentence-embeddings. We use different encoder configurations to produce sentence embeddings of varying quality as expressed by P@1 results for sentence-level retrieval on the UN dataset.[10] Table 5 shows the P@1 of target document retrieval on both the WebData test set and the noisy UN corpus for HiDE$_{DNN \rightarrow pooling}$ and Sentence-Avg. While sentence encoding quality does impact document-level performance, the HiDE model is surprisingly robust once the sentence encoder reaches around 66% P@1, whereas the Sentence-Avg model requires much higher quality sentence-level embeddings (around 85% for en-fr, and 80% for en-es). The robustness of HiDE model provides a means for obtaining high-quality document embeddings without high-quality sentence embeddings, and thus provides the option to trade-off sentence-level embedding quality for speed and memory performance.

6 Conclusion

In this paper, we explore parallel document mining using several document embedding methods.

---

[10]Model sentence-level model performance was varied by generating models with hyperparameters selected to degrade performance (e.g., fewer training sets, no margin softmax).

Languages	P@1 at Sentence Level	P@1 on WebDoc test		P@1 on Noisy UN	
		HiDE$_{\text{DNN}\to\text{pooling}}$	Sentence-Avg	HiDE$_{\text{DNN}\to\text{pooling}}$	Sentence-Avg
en-fr	48.9	66.6	0.6	70.3	4.4
	66.9	89.2	54.3	92.6	63.9
	81.3	90.5	72.9	92.1	76.9
	86.1	91.3	78.1	94.9	86.9
en-es	54.9	59.0	1.2	81.3	4.7
	67.0	79.1	54.2	93.2	82.9
	80.6	79.8	60.1	91.2	88.9
	89.0	81.9	67.4	96.0	95.7

Table 5: P@1 of target document retrieval on WebData test set and noisy UN corpus for HiDE$_{\text{DNN}\to\text{pooling}}$ and Sentence-Avg models with different sentence-level P@1 performance . The sentence-level peroformance is measured on the sentence-level UN retrieval task from the entire corpus (11.3 million sentence candidates).

Mining using document embeddings achieves a new state-of-the-art perfomance on the UN parallel document mining task (en-fr, en-es). Document embeddings computed by simply averaging sentence embeddings provide a very strong baseline for clean datasets, while hierarchical embedding models perform best on noisier data. Finally, we show document embeddings based on aggregations of sentence embeddings are surprisingly robust to variations in sentence embedding quality, particularly for our hierarchical models.

Acknowledgements

We are grateful to the anonymous reviewers and our teammates in Deacartes and Google Translate for their valuable discussions, especially Chris Tar, Gustavo Adolfo Hernandez Abrego, and Wolfgang Macherey.

References

Alexandra Antonova and Alexey Misyurev. 2011. Building a web-based parallel corpus and filtering out machine-translated text. In *Proceedings of the 4th Workshop on Building and Using Comparable Corpora: Comparable Corpora and the Web*, pages 136–144. Association for Computational Linguistics.

Mikel Artetxe and Holger Schwenk. 2018. Margin-based parallel corpus mining with multilingual sentence embeddings. *CoRR*, abs/1811.01136.

Jiang Chen and Jian-Yun Nie. 2000. Parallel web text mining for cross-language ir. In *Content-Based Multimedia Information Access-Volume 1*, pages 62–77. Centre de Hautes Etudes Internationale D'Informatique Documentaire.

Minmin Chen. 2017. Efficient vector representation for documents through corruption. *5th International Conference on Learning Representations*.

Muthuraman Chidambaram, Yinfei Yang, Daniel Cer, Steve Yuan, Yun-Hsuan Sung, Brian Strope, and Ray Kurzweil. 2018. Learning cross-lingual sentence representations via a multi-task dual-encoder model. *CoRR*, abs/1810.12836.

Andrew M. Dai, Christopher Olah, and Quoc V. Le. 2015. Document embedding with paragraph vectors. *CoRR*, abs/1507.07998.

Francis Grégoire and Philippe Langlais. 2017. A deep neural network approach to parallel sentence extraction. *arXiv preprint arXiv:1709.09783*.

Mandy Guo, Qinlan Shen, Yinfei Yang, Heming Ge, Daniel Cer, Gustavo Hernandez Abrego, Keith Stevens, Noah Constant, Yun-hsuan Sung, Brian Strope, and Ray Kurzweil. 2018. Effective parallel corpus mining using bilingual sentence embeddings. In *Proceedings of the Third Conference on Machine Translation: Research Papers*, pages 165–176. Association for Computational Linguistics.

Hany Hassan, Anthony Aue, Chang Chen, Vishal Chowdhary, Jonathan Clark, Christian Federmann, Xuedong Huang, Marcin Junczys-Dowmunt, William Lewis, Mu Li, et al. 2018. Achieving human parity on automatic chinese to english news translation. *arXiv preprint arXiv:1803.05567*.

Mohit Iyyer, Varun Manjunatha, Jordan Boyd-Graber, and Hal Daumé III. 2015. Deep unordered composition rivals syntactic methods for text classification. In *Proceedings of the 53rd Annual Meeting of the Association for Computational Linguistics and the 7th International Joint Conference on Natural Language Processing (Volume 1: Long Papers)*, pages 1681–1691, Beijing, China. Association for Computational Linguistics.

Quoc Le and Tomas Mikolov. 2014. Distributed representations of sentences and documents. In *Proceedings of the 31st International Conference on International Conference on Machine Learning - Volume 32*, ICML'14, pages II–1188–II–1196. JMLR.org.

Bofang Li, Tao Liu, Xiaoyong Du, Deyuan Zhang, and Zhe Zhao. 2015. Learning document embeddings by predicting n-grams for sentiment classification of long movie reviews. *CoRR*, abs/1512.08183.

Lesly Miculicich, Dhananjay Ram, Nikolaos Pappas, and James Henderson. 2018. Document-level neural machine translation with hierarchical attention networks. In *Proceedings of the 2018 Conference on Empirical Methods in Natural Language Processing*, pages 2947–2954, Brussels, Belgium. Association for Computational Linguistics.

Dragos Stefan Munteanu and Daniel Marcu. 2005. Improving machine translation performance by exploiting non-parallel corpora. *Computational Linguistics*, 31(4):477–504.

Dragos Stefan Munteanu and Daniel Marcu. 2006. Extracting parallel sub-sentential fragments from non-parallel corpora. In *Proceedings of the 21st International Conference on Computational Linguistics and the 44th Annual Meeting of the Association for Computational Linguistics*, pages 81–88. Association for Computational Linguistics.

Philip Resnik and Noah A. Smith. 2003. The web as a parallel corpus. *Comput. Linguist.*, 29(3):349–380.

Dwaipayan Roy, Debasis Ganguly, Mandar Mitra, and Gareth J. F. Jones. 2016. Representing documents and queries as sets of word embedded vectors for information retrieval. *CoRR*, abs/1606.07869.

Holger Schwenk. 2018. Filtering and mining parallel data in a joint multilingual space. In *Proceedings of the 56th Annual Meeting of the Association for Computational Linguistics (Volume 2: Short Papers)*, pages 228–234, Melbourne, Australia. Association for Computational Linguistics.

Lei Shi, Cheng Niu, Ming Zhou, and Jianfeng Gao. 2006. A dom tree alignment model for mining parallel data from the web. In *Proceedings of the 21st International Conference on Computational Linguistics and the 44th Annual Meeting of the Association for Computational Linguistics*, pages 489–496. Association for Computational Linguistics.

Jakob Uszkoreit, Jay M. Ponte, Ashok C. Popat, and Moshe Dubiner. 2010. Large scale parallel document mining for machine translation. In *Proceedings of the 23rd International Conference on Computational Linguistics*, COLING '10, pages 1101–1109, Stroudsburg, PA, USA. Association for Computational Linguistics.

Dan Vanderkam, Rob Schonberger, Henry Rowley, and Sanjiv Kumar. 2013. Nearest neighbor search in google correlate. Technical report, Google.

Ashish Vaswani, Noam Shazeer, Niki Parmar, Jakob Uszkoreit, Llion Jones, Aidan N Gomez, Ł ukasz Kaiser, and Illia Polosukhin. 2017. Attention is all you need. In I. Guyon, U. V. Luxburg, S. Bengio, H. Wallach, R. Fergus, S. Vishwanathan, and R. Garnett, editors, *Advances in Neural Information Processing Systems 30*, pages 5998–6008. Curran Associates, Inc.

Longyue Wang, Zhaopeng Tu, Andy Way, and Qun Liu. 2017. Exploiting cross-sentence context for neural machine translation. In *Proceedings of the 2017 Conference on Empirical Methods in Natural Language Processing*, pages 2826–2831, Copenhagen, Denmark. Association for Computational Linguistics.

Lingfei Wu, Ian En-Hsu Yen, Kun Xu, Fangli Xu, Avinash Balakrishnan, Pin-Yu Chen, Pradeep Ravikumar, and Michael J. Witbrock. 2018. Word mover's embedding: From word2vec to document embedding. In *Proceedings of the 2018 Conference on Empirical Methods in Natural Language Processing*, pages 4524–4534. Association for Computational Linguistics.

Christopher C Yang and Kar Wing Li. 2002. Mining english/chinese parallel documents from the world wide web. In *Proceedings of the 11th International World Wide Web Conference, Honolulu, USA*.

Yinfei Yang, Gustavo Hernández Ábrego, Steve Yuan, Mandy Guo, Qinlan Shen, Daniel Cer, Yun-Hsuan Sung, Brian Strope, and Ray Kurzweil. 2019. Improving multilingual sentence embedding using bi-directional dual encoder with additive margin softmax. *CoRR*, abs/1902.08564.

Zichao Yang, Diyi Yang, Chris Dyer, Xiaodong He, Alex Smola, and Eduard Hovy. 2016. Hierarchical attention networks for document classification. In *Proceedings of the 2016 Conference of the North American Chapter of the Association for Computational Linguistics: Human Language Technologies*, pages 1480–1489, San Diego, California. Association for Computational Linguistics.

Michal Ziemski, Marcin Junczys-Dowmunt, and Bruno Pouliquen. 2016. The united nations parallel corpus v1. 0. In *Proceedings of the Tenth International Conference on Language Resources and Evaluation*, LREC '16. European Language Resources Association.

The Effect of Translationese in Machine Translation Test Sets

Mike Zhang
Information Science Programme
University of Groningen
The Netherlands
`j.j.zhang.1@student.rug.nl`

Antonio Toral
Center for Language and Cognition
University of Groningen
The Netherlands
`a.toral.ruiz@rug.nl`

Abstract

The effect of translationese has been studied in the field of machine translation (MT), mostly with respect to training data. We study in depth the effect of translationese on test data, using the test sets from the last three editions of WMT's news shared task, containing 17 translation directions. We show evidence that (i) the use of translationese in test sets results in inflated human evaluation scores for MT systems; (ii) in some cases system rankings do change and (iii) the impact translationese has on a translation direction is inversely correlated to the translation quality attainable by state-of-the-art MT systems for that direction.

1 Introduction

Translated texts in a human language exhibit unique characteristics that set them apart from texts originally written in that language. It is common then to refer to translated texts with the term *translationese*. The characteristics of translationese can be grouped along the so-called universal features of translation or translation universals (Baker, 1993), namely simplification, normalisation and explicitation. In addition to these three, interference is recognised as a fundamental law of translation (Toury, 2012): "phenomena pertaining to the make-up of the source text tend to be transferred to the target text". In a nutshell, compared to original texts, translations tend to be simpler, more standardised, and more explicit and they retain some characteristics that pertain to the source language.

The effect of translationese has been studied in machine translation (MT), mainly with respect to the training data, during the last decade. Previous work has found that an MT system performs better when trained on parallel data whose source side is original and whose target side is translationese,

rather than the opposite (Kurokawa et al., 2009; Lembersky, 2013).

A recent paper has studied the effect of translationese on test sets (Toral et al., 2018), in the context of assessing the claim of human parity made on Chinese-to-English WMT's 2017 test set (Hassan et al., 2018). The source side of this test set, as it is common in WMT (Bojar et al., 2016, 2017, 2018), was half original and half translationese. It was found out that the translationese part was artificially easier to translate, which resulted in inflated scores for MT systems.

Noting that this finding was based on one test set for a single translation direction, we explore this topic in more depth, studying the effect of translationese in all the language pairs of the news shared task of WMT 2016 to 2018. Our research questions (RQs) are the following:

- RQ1. Does the use of translationese in the source side of MT test sets unfairly favour MT systems in general or is this just an artifact of the Chinese-to-English test set from WMT 2017?

- RQ2. If the answer to RQ1 is yes, does this effect of translationese have an impact on WMT's system rankings? In other words, would removing the part of the test set whose source side is translationese result in any change in the rankings?

- RQ3. If the answer to RQ1 is yes, would some language pairs be more affected than others? E.g. based on the level of the relatedness between the two languages involved.

The remainder of the paper will be organized as follows. Section 2 provides an overview of previous work about the effect of translationese in MT. Next, Section 3 describes the data sets used in

Proceedings of the Fourth Conference on Machine Translation (WMT), Volume 1: Research Papers, pages 73–81
Florence, Italy, August 1-2, 2019. ©2019 Association for Computational Linguistics

our research. This is followed by Section 4, Section 5 and Section 6, where we conduct the experiments for RQ1, RQ2 and RQ3, respectively. Finally, Section 7 outlines our conclusions and lines of future work.

2 Related Work

There is previous research in the field of MT that has looked at the impact of translationese, mostly on training data, but there are works that have focused also on tuning and testing data sets.

The pioneering work on this topic by Kurokawa et al. (2009) showed that French-to-English statistical MT systems trained on human translations from French to English (original source and translationese target, henceforth referred to as O→T) outperformed systems trained on human translations in the opposite direction (i.e. translationese source and original target, henceforth referred to as T→O). These findings were corroborated by Lembersky (2013), who also adapted phrase tables to translationese, which resulted in further improvements. Lembersky et al. (2012) focused on the monolingual data used to train the language model of a statistical MT system and found that using translated texts led to better translation quality than relying on original texts.

Stymne (2017) investigated the effect of translationese on tuning for statistical MT, using data from the WMT 2008–2013 (Bojar et al., 2013) for three language pairs. The results using O→T and T→O tuning texts were compared; the former led to a better length ratio and a better translation, in terms of automatic evaluation metrics.

Finally, Toral et al. (2018) investigated the effect of translationese on the Chinese→English (ZH→EN) test set from WMT's 2017 news shared task. They hypothesized that the sentences originally written in EN are easier to translate than those originally written in ZH, due to the simplification principle of translationese, namely that translated sentences tend to be simpler than their original counterparts (Laviosa-Braithwaite, 1998). Two additional universal principles of translation, explicitation and normalisation, would also indicate that a ZH text originally written in EN would be easier to translate. In fact, they looked at a human translation and the translation by an MT system (Hassan et al., 2018) and observed that the human translation outperforms the MT system when the input text is written in the original language

(ZH), but the difference between the two is not significant when the original language is translationese (ZH input originally written EN). Therefore, they concluded that the use of translationese as the source language in test sets distorts the results in favour of MT systems.

3 Data Sets

We use the test data from WMT16, WMT17, and WMT18 news translation tasks (*newstest2016, newstest2017, and newstest2018*) exclusively, because they provide results using the *direct assessment* (DA) score (Graham et al., 2013, 2014, 2017), which is the metric we will use in our experiments. DA is a crowd-sourced human evaluation metric to determine MT quality. To elaborate, after participants submit their translations produced by their MT systems, a human evaluation campaign is run. This is to assess the translation quality of the systems, and to rank them accordingly. Human evaluation scores are provided via crowdsourcing and/or by participants, using Appraise (Federmann, 2012). Human assessors are asked to rate a given candidate translation by how adequately it expresses the meaning of the corresponding reference translation, thus avoiding the use of the source texts and therefore not requiring bilingual speakers. The rating is done on an analogue scale, which corresponds to an absolute 0-100 scale.

To prevent differences in scoring strategies of distinct human assessors, the human assessment scores for translations are standardized according to each individual human assessor's overall mean and standard deviation score, which is indicated as the z-score in WMT finding papers. Average standardized scores for individual segments belonging to a given system are then computed, before the final overall DA score for that system is computed as the average of its standardized segment scores.

Finally, systems are ranked to produce the shared task results. There is of course the possibility that some systems score similarly in the shared task. If that is the case, those systems are clustered together. Specifically, clusters are determined by grouping systems together, and comparing the scores they obtained. According to the Wilcoxon rank-sum test, if systems do not significantly outperform others, they are in the same cluster, the opposite is the case if they do outperform each other (Bojar et al., 2016, 2017, 2018).

Language Direction	WMT16			WMT17			WMT18		
	# sys.	# seg.	# assess.	# sys.	# seg.	# assess.	# sys.	# seg.	# assess.
Chinese→English				16	32,016	38,736	14	55,734	32,919
English→Chinese				11	22,011	16,253	14	55,734	32,411
Czech→English	12	30,000	16,800	4	12,020	21,992	5	14,915	12,209
English→Czech				14	42,070	32,564	5	14,915	10,080
Estonian→English							14	28,000	28,868
English→Estonian							14	28,000	15,800
Finnish→English	9	63,040	30,080	6	18,012	27,545	9	27,000	18,868
English→Finnish				12	36,024	8,289	12	36,000	9,995
German→English	10	68,800	33,760	11	33,044	36,189	16	47,968	48,469
English→German				16	48,064	10,229	16	47,968	13,754
Latvian→English				9	18,009	30,321			
English→Latvian				17	34,017	6,882			
Romanian→English	7	27,920	16,000						
Russian→English	10	64,960	37,040	9	27,009	24,837	8	24,000	17,711
English→Russian				9	27,009	25,798	9	27,000	27,977
Turkish→English	9	48,640	18,400	10	30,070	25,853	6	18,000	29,784
English→Turkish				8	24,056	2,219	8	24,000	3,644

Table 1: Datasets used in this study (DA scores from WMT16–18 news translation task). Columns contain (from left to right) the number of submitted systems (# sys.), total number of segments prior to quality control (# seg.), and total number of assessments human assessors carried out (# assess.)

Table 1 provides an overview of the number of systems, segments, and assessments in the previously mentioned editions of WMT for all available language directions. These are the datasets that we use in this work.

4 Effect of Translationese on Direct Assessment Scores

The test sets used by Bojar et al. (2016, 2017, 2018) are bilingual, thus having two sides: source text and reference translation. The source is written in the language that is to be translated from (original language), while the reference is written in the language into which the source text is to be translated (target language). In all the test sets used in our experiments English is one of the two languages involved, being either the source or the target.

Taking as an example of WMT test set the one for Chinese-to-English from 2017, this contains 2,001 sentence pairs. Out of these, 1,000 sentences were originally written in Chinese and translated by a human translator into English, hence the target text is translationese. The other half consists of 1,001 sentences that were originally written in English and translated by a human translator into Chinese, hence the source text is translationese in this subset. A graphical depiction of this can be found in Figure 1. The advantage of this procedure is that the same test set can be used for the English-to-Chinese direction, thus reducing the costs involved in creating test sets in half.

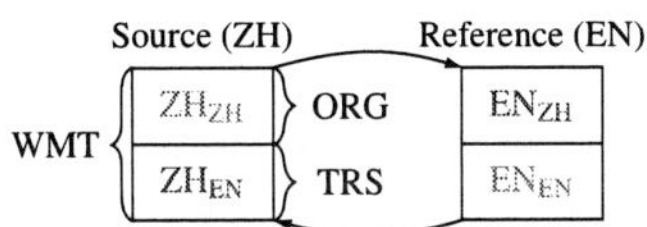

Figure 1: Example of a WMT test set for English (EN) → Chinese (ZH) translation direction, where English is translated into Chinese, and Chinese into English. Indicated as a subscript is which the original language was, red means original language and blue translationese.

Source and reference files contain documents, each of which is provided with a label indicating in which language it was originally written. In our experiments we compute the DA scores for each test set (i) on the whole test set, which corresponds to the results reported in WMT, (ii) on the subset for which the source text was originally written in the source language (referred to as ORG in our experiments) and (iii) on the remaining subset, for which the source text was originally written in the target language, and is thus translationese (referred to as TRS in our experiments).

Table 2 shows the absolute difference in DA score for the ORG and TRS subsets, taking the

Language Direction	WMT16			WMT17			WMT18		
	WMT	ORG	TRS	WMT	ORG	TRS	WMT	ORG	TRS
Chinese→English				73.2	-1.5	+3.9	78.8	-1.3	+2.0
English→Chinese				73.2	-4.1	+5.0	80.7	-4.0	+2.3
Czech→English	75.4	-5.8	+5.7	74.6	-4.3	+4.2	71.8	-1.6	+1.6
English→Czech				62.0	-5.8	+7.4	67.2	-6.6	+7.2
Estonian→English							73.3	-4.0	+4.0
English→Estonian							64.9	-4.1	+3.9
Finnish→English	66.9	-3.2	+3.0	73.8	-2.1	+2.2	75.2	-2.4	+2.3
English→Finnish				59.6	-5.1	+5.6	64.7	-7.7	+8.0
German→English	75.8	-4.1	+4.1	78.2	-2.4	+2.2	79.9	-3.8	+4.3
English→German				72.9	-5.1	+4.4	85.5	-1.9	+1.9
Latvian→English				76.2	-0.4	+0.6			
English→Latvian				54.4	-11.2	+11.7			
Romanian→English	73.9	-0.4	+0.5						
Russian→English	74.2	-1.2	+1.8	82.0	-0.7	+0.6	81.0	-0.1	0.0
English→Russian				75.4	-5.8	+5.8	72.0	-7.4	+7.4
Turkish→English	57.1	-1.6	+1.6	68.8	-3.8	+3.9	74.3	-3.2	+3.9
English→Turkish				53.4	-13.4	+11.8	66.3	-4.1	+5.5

Table 2: DA scores for the best MT system for each translation direction of WMT's 2016–2018 news translation shared task. Columns ORG and TRS show the absolute difference of the DA scores in those subsets compared to the whole test set (WMT).

whole test set (WMT) as starting point for the comparison. We observe a clear and common trend: using original input results in a lower DA score, while using translationese input increases the DA score. This trend is consistent for all the 17 translation directions considered and for all the 3 years of WMT studied, thus providing enough evidence to answer RQ1: the use of translationese as input of test sets results in higher DA scores for MT systems.

5 Effect of Translationese on Rankings

We compute Kendall's τ to give an overview of to what degree rankings change for each translation direction. The τ coefficient is obtained by comparing WMT rankings to the resulting rankings if only the ORG subset is used as input. Since systems can share the same cluster, and thus the same ranking, we compute Kendall's τ both with and without ties. With ties, all systems in the same cluster are considered to occupy the same rank, hence the correlation with ties is sensitive only to changes that go beyond clusters. E.g. if a system moves from the second cluster to the first one. In contrast, without ties all the ranking changes are considered, even if a system changes position but remains within the same cluster.

Table 3 shows the Kendall's τ correlations for all translation directions between the rankings on the whole test set (WMT) and on the ORG subset. We do see that some of the translation directions have a τ coefficient of 1, which means that the agreement between the two rankings is perfect, i.e. the rankings in WMT and ORG are exactly the same. However, we observe that there were few systems submitted to such translation directions (e.g. $\tau = 1$ for Romanian→English in 2017, for which 7 systems were submitted, see Table 1). Apart from those, other language directions show that there are at least slight rank changes between the WMT rankings and ORG rankings. Looking at the low ranked translation directions, we observe that some are close to a τ coefficient of 0, especially in correlations without ties, such as German→English in WMT 2017 ($\tau = 0.345$). This means that some rankings have only a weak correlation.

Probably related to the differences in DA scores between WMT and ORG (RQ1), we also find that systems' rankings change for most language pairs when comparing WMT and ORG rankings. We see that there is no perfect correlation between rankings, apart from a few language directions for which only a few systems were submitted. This

Language Direction	With Ties			Mean		Without Ties			Language Direction
	WMT16	WMT17	WMT18			WMT16	WMT17	WMT18	
Romanian → English†	1.000*	-	-	1.000	1.000	1.000*	-	-	Romanian → English †
Turkish → English	0.983*	0.948*	1.000*	0.977	1.000	1.000*	1.000*	1.000*	Czech → English
Finnish → English	0.943*	0.966*	1.000*	0.970	0.978	-	-	0.978*	English → Estonian †
Czech → English	0.929*	1.000*	0.949*	0.959	0.956	-	-	0.956*	Estonian → English †
German → English	0.979*	0.939*	0.906*	0.941	0.944	-	0.944*	-	Latvian → English †
English → Czech	-	0.904*	0.949*	0.927	0.929	-	0.929*	0.929*	English → Turkish
Latvian → English†	-	0.921*	-	0.921	0.917	-	0.889*	0.944*	English → Russian
English → Finnish	-	0.868*	0.968*	0.918	0.898	-	0.927*	0.868*	English → Chinese
English → Russian	-	0.873*	0.935*	0.904	0.882	-	0.882*	-	English → Latvian †
Chinese → English	-	0.923*	0.882*	0.903	0.869	0.733*	0.944*	0.929*	Russian → English
English → German	-	0.863*	0.856*	0.860	0.852	1.000*	1.000*	0.556*	Finnish → English
English → Estonian†	-	-	0.845*	0.845	0.848	0.833*	0.911*	0.800*	Turkish → English
Estonian → English†	-	-	0.830*	0.830	0.784	-	0.633*	0.934*	Chinese → English
English → Chinese	-	0.847*	0.789*	0.818	0.726	-	0.451*	1.000*	English → Czech
English → Turkish	-	0.890*	0.734*	0.812	0.713	0.911*	0.345	0.883*	German → English
Russian → English	0.557	0.845*	0.890*	0.764	0.675	-	0.817*	0.533*	English → German
English → Latvian †	-	0.718*	-	0.718	0.637	-	0.970*	0.303	English → Finnish

Table 3: Kendall's τ coefficient for each translation direction and year. The coefficient is obtained by comparing WMT's ranking with the ranking if only original language is used as input (subset ORG), with and without ties. A (*) indicates the significance level at p-level p≤0.05. Furthermore, language directions are sorted by the computed mean Kendall's τ. A † indicates that the mean is computed over one year.

Chinese→English

	#	SYSTEM	RAW.WMT	Z.WMT	#	↑↓	SYSTEM	RAW.ORG	Z.ORG	#	↑↓	SYSTEM	RAW.TRS	Z.TRS
wmt17	1	SogouKnowing-nmt	73.2	0.209	1	2↑	xmunmt	71.7	0.167	1	1↑	uedin-nmt	77.1	0.316
		uedin-nmt	73.8	0.208		1↓	SogouKnowing-nmt	71.9	0.161		1↓	SogouKnowing-nmt	74.4	0.257
		xmunmt	72.3	0.184		1↓	uedin-nmt	70.5	0.101	3	2↑	online-A	73.6	0.208
	4	online-B	69.9	0.113		—	online-B	68.7	0.081		1↓	xmunmt	72.9	0.202
		online-A	70.4	0.109		1↑	NRC	69.1	0.064	5	1↓	online-B	71.1	0.145
		NRC	69.8	0.079	6	1↓	online-A	67.4	0.012		1↑	jhu-nmt	70.0	0.110
	7	jhu-nmt	67.9	0.023	7	—	jhu-nmt	65.8	-0.062		1↓	NRC	70.4	0.093
	8	afrl-mitll-opennmt	66.9	-0.016		1↑	CASICT-cons	65.4	-0.087		—	afrl-mitll-opennmt	69.2	0.063
		CASICT-cons	67.1	-0.026		1↓	afrl-mitll-opennmt	64.5	-0.095		—	CASICT-cons	68.9	0.036
		ROCMT	65.4	-0.058		—	ROCMT	63.4	-0.108		—	ROCMT	67.4	-0.006
	11	Oregon-State-Uni-S	64.3	-0.107		—	Oregon-State-Uni-S	62.7	-0.162		—	Oregon-State-Uni-S	65.9	-0.054
	12	PROMT-SMT	61.7	-0.209	12	3↑	online-F	60.0	-0.261	12	—	PROMT-SMT	64.0	-0.137
		NMT-Ave-Multi-Cs	61.2	-0.265		1↓	PROMT-SMT	59.4	-0.282		—	NMT-Ave-Multi-Cs	63.3	-0.193
		UU-HNMT	60.0	-0.276		—	UU-HNMT	58.8	-0.301	14	2↑	online-G	61.1	-0.245
		online-F	59.6	-0.279		2↓	NMT-Ave-Multi-Cs	59.2	-0.337		1↓	UU-HNMT	61.1	-0.251
		online-G	59.3	-0.305		—	online-G	57.4	-0.363		1↓	online-F	59.2	-0.296
wmt18	1	NiuTrans	78.8	0.140	1	—	NiuTrans	77.5	0.091	1	8↑	UMD	80.8	0.239
		online-B	77.7	0.111		—	online-B	77.4	0.089		6↑	NICT	80.5	0.232
		UCAM	77.9	0.109		2↑	Tencent-ensemble	77.0	0.067		2↓	NiuTrans	81.1	0.222
		Unisound-A	78.0	0.108		1↓	UCAM	76.3	0.048		—	Unisound-A	80.9	0.222
		Tencent-ensemble	77.5	0.099		1↓	Unisound-A	76.4	0.041		2↑	Li-Muze	80.7	0.214
		Unisound-B	77.5	0.094		—	Unisound-B	75.8	0.029		3↓	UCAM	80.5	0.211
		Li-Muze	77.9	0.091		—	Li-Muze	76.2	0.016		1↓	Unisound-B	80.5	0.206
		NICT	77.0	0.089		—	NICT	75.0	0.004		3↑	uedin	79.6	0.180
		UMD	76.7	0.078		—	UMD	74.3	-0.021		4↓	Tencent-ensemble	78.1	0.149
	10	online-Y	75.0	-0.005		—	online-Y	73.8	-0.047		8↓	online-B	78.1	0.147
		uedin	74.5	-0.017	11	—	uedin	71.5	-0.137	11	1↑	online-A	77.1	0.068
	12	online-A	73.6	-0.061		—	online-A	71.4	-0.140		2↓	online-Y	76.8	0.061
	13	online-G	65.9	-0.327	13	1↑	online-F	65.2	-0.353	13	—	online-G	67.8	-0.262
	14	online-F	64.4	-0.377		1↓	online-G	64.9	-0.364	14	—	online-F	63.1	-0.417

Table 4: Results of the Chinese→English language direction with WMT, ORG, and TRS input. Systems are ordered by standardized mean DA score. If a system does not contain a rank, this means that it shares the same cluster as the system above it. Clusters are obtained according to Wilcoxon rank-sum test at p-level p ≤ 0.05. Indicated in the [↑↓] column are the changes in absolute ranking (i.e. how many positions a system goes up or down).

indicates that the rankings do change to a certain degree. Computing Kendall's τ with ties results in higher correlation coefficients than without ties, implying that systems do shift, but tend to stay in the same cluster they occupied in the WMT ranking. In some editions of WMT, the rankings for certain language pairs change considerably. The biggest change in terms of ranking takes place for PROMT's rule-based system RU→EN for WMT16. This system advances four positions in the ranking when only original source text is considered, going from rank 5 to rank 1 (although tied with several other systems). It is worth noting that while the DA score for the majority of systems decreases when using original source text, the opposite happens for PROMT's system.

Thus far we have looked at a single result per translation direction and year, based on the best system in Table 2, and on the correlation between systems in Table 3. Now we zoom in on a translation direction: Chinese→English. Table 4 shows how DA scores change between the whole test set (WMT) and the subsets ORG and TRS, both in terms of raw and standarized scores. In addition, the table depicts how many positions a system goes up or down in the ranking.

In the table we observe consistently that the DA score for ORG input is lower than that for WMT, while that for TRS is higher than that for WMT. It is also worth noting that most top scoring systems change in rankings, and that system clusters shift. Due to limited space we provide equivalent tables to Table 4 for the remaining 16 translation directions as an appendix.

6 Effect of Translationese on Different Language Pairs

We aim to find out not only whether translationese has an effect on test sets (RQ1 and RQ2), but also to study whether some language pairs are more affected than others (RQ3). Two hypotheses in this regard are as follows: (i) the degree of translationese's impact has to do with the translation quality attainable for a translation direction, as represented by the DA score of the best MT system submitted; (ii) the degree of translationese's impact has to do with how related are the two languages involved.

In order to test the second hypothesis, the degree of similarity between languages has to be quantified. We make use of the lang2vec tool (Lit-

tell et al., 2017) using the URIEL Typological Database (Littell et al., 2016) to compute the similarity between pairs of languages. Similar to the approach of Berzak et al. (2017), all the 103 available morphosyntactic features in URIEL are obtained; these are derived from the World Atlas of Language Structures (WALS) (Dryer and Haspelmath, 2013), Syntactic Structures of the Worlds Languages (SSWL) (Collins and Kayne, 2009) and Ethnologue (Lewis et al., 2009). Missing feature values are filled with a prediction from a k-nearest neighbors classifier. We also extract URIEL's 3,718 language family features derived from Glottolog (Hammarström et al., 2019). Each of these features represents membership in a branch of Glottolog's world language tree. Truncating features with the same value for all the languages present in our study, 87 features remain, consisting of 60 syntactic features and 27 family tree features. We then measure the level of relatedness between two languages using the linguistic similarity (LS) by Berzak et al. (2017) (Equation 1), i.e. the cosine similarity between the URIEL feature vectors for two languages v_y and v'_y.

$$LS_{y,y'} = \frac{v_y \cdot v_{y'}}{\|v_y\| \, \|v_{y'}\|} \tag{1}$$

Together with the LS for a language direction, we take the best system of the most recent year in our data set, WMT18, for that language direction. The motivation behind is that a top performing system from the most recent campaign should be representative of the current state-of-the-art in machine translation for the translation direction it was submitted to.

To look into the effect of translationese across different language pairs, we present two approaches, following the hypotheses put forward at the beginning of this section: (i) compare the DA score of the best system for each translation direction on subset ORG to the relative or absolute difference in DA score for that system between subset ORG and the whole set (WMT); (ii) compare the LS of the two languages in each translation direction to the relative or absolute difference in DA scores for the best system between subset ORG and the whole set (WMT);

Figure 2 shows the Pearson correlation and 95% confidence region of the DA score of the best scoring system for each language direction on subset ORG against the absolute and relative difference

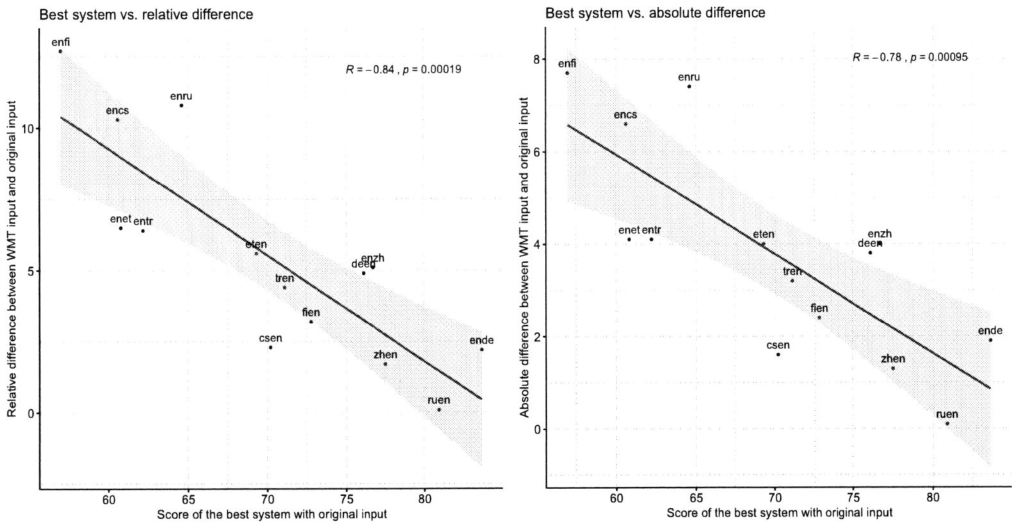

Figure 2: Pearson correlation between the DA scores of the best system for each translation direction at WMT18 and the relative (left) and absolute (right) difference in DA score (%) of comparing WMT input and ORG input. The languages are abbreviated into ISO 639-1 codes (Byrum, 1999).

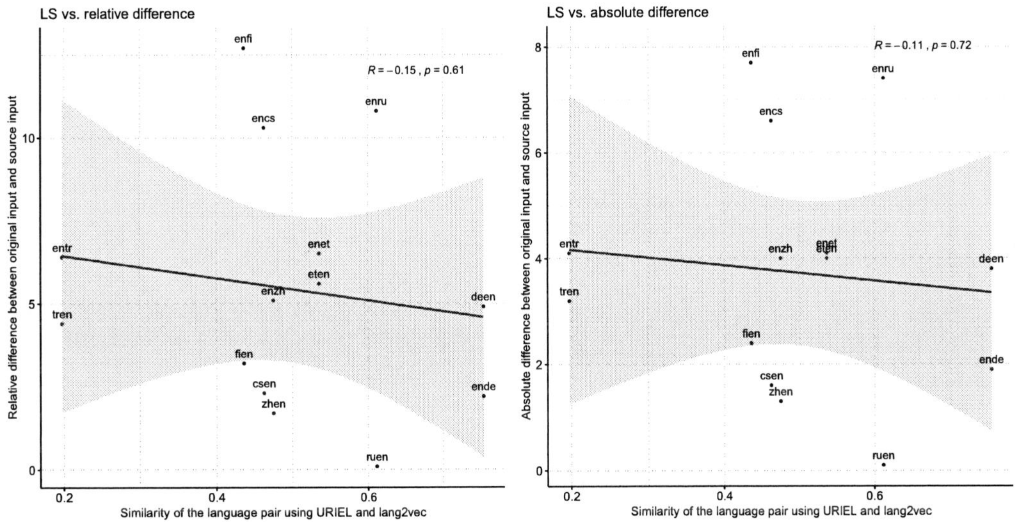

Figure 3: Pearson correlation between Linguistic Similarity for each language direction and the relative (left) and absolute (right) difference (%) in DA score of comparing WMT input and ORG input. The languages are abbreviated into ISO 639-1 codes (Byrum, 1999).

of the DA scores of those systems between WMT input and ORG input. We observe an interesting trend; higher scoring systems tend to have lower differences in score, which indicates that translationese has less effect. Considering either relative or absolute differences, the correlations are in both cases significant and strong ($p < 0.001$, $|R| > 0.75$).

Figure 3 shows the Pearson correlation and 95% confidence region of the LS of a language pair (English compared to another language in our data sets) against the absolute and relative difference of the DA scores of the best system for each translation direction between WMT input and ORG input. Here, we see a less obvious trend, and in fact both correlations are very weak and non-significant. However, just as in the previous figure we can see that most of the out-of-English systems tend to have a higher relative and absolute difference than systems that translate into English.

On a side note, we created different feature combinations from the earlier mentioned features for LS. Apart from syntactic and family tree features, phonological features are also present in URIEL. However, other combinations did not seem to alter the LS difference score, compared to using the mentioned features in the experimental setup.

7 Conclusion and Future Work

This paper has looked in depth at the effect of translationese in bidirectional test sets, commonly used in machine translation shared tasks, by conducting a series of experiments on data sets for 17 translation directions in the three last editions of the news shared task from WMT. Specifically, we have recomputed the direct assessment (DA) scores separately for the whole test set (WMT), and for the subsets whose source side contains original language (ORG) and translationese (TRS). Results show that using original language input lowers the DA scores, and translationese input increases the scores (RQ1), and perhaps more importantly, system rankings do change (RQ2). We have also investigated the degree to which these rankings change, by measuring the correlation between the rankings with a non-parametric correlation metric that supports ties (Kendall's τ). Results show that systems do change in absolute ranking, but tend to stay more in the same cluster as they were before.

Last, we looked at whether the effect of translationese correlates with certain characteristics of translation directions. We did not find a correlation between the effect of translationese and the level of relatedness of the two languages involved but we did find a correlation between the effect of translationese and the translation quality attainable for translation directions (RQ3). In other words, human evaluation for better performing systems would seem to be less affected by translationese. Related, we observe that translation directions that contain an under-resourced language tend to obtain low DA scores. Hence, we could say that the effect of translationese tends to be high specially when an under-resourced language is present, which could distort (inflate) the expectations in terms of translation quality for these languages.

As for future work, we plan to focus on studying what the characteristics of translationese are. I.e. what are the traits that set apart the language used in original test sets from translationese test sets.

All the code and data used in our experiments are available on GitHub[1].

References

Mona Baker. 1993. Corpus linguistics and translation studies: Implications and applications. *Text and technology: In honour of John Sinclair*, 233:250.

Yevgeni Berzak, Chie Nakamura, Suzanne Flynn, and Boris Katz. 2017. Predicting native language from gaze. *arXiv preprint arXiv:1704.07398*.

Ondřej Bojar, Rajen Chatterjee, Christian Federmann, Yvette Graham, Barry Haddow, Shujian Huang, Matthias Huck, Philipp Koehn, Qun Liu, Varvara Logacheva, et al. 2017. Findings of the 2017 conference on machine translation (wmt17). In *Proceedings of the Second Conference on Machine Translation*, pages 169–214.

Ondřej Bojar, Rajen Chatterjee, Christian Federmann, Yvette Graham, Barry Haddow, Matthias Huck, Antonio Jimeno Yepes, Philipp Koehn, Varvara Logacheva, Christof Monz, et al. 2016. Findings of the 2016 conference on machine translation. In *Proceedings of the First Conference on Machine Translation: Volume 2, Shared Task Papers*, volume 2, pages 131–198.

Ondřej Bojar, Mark Fishel, Christian Federmann, Yvette Graham, Barry Haddow, Matthias Huck, Philipp Koehn, Christof Monz, et al. 2018. Findings of the 2018 conference on machine translation (wmt18). In *Proceedings of the Third Conference on Machine Translation*, pages 272–303.

Ondřej Bojar, Christian Buck, Chris Callison-Burch, Christian Federmann, Barry Haddow, Philipp Koehn, Christof Monz, Matt Post, Radu Soricut, and Lucia Specia. 2013. Findings of the 2013 Workshop on Statistical Machine Translation. In *Proceedings of the Eighth Workshop on Statistical Machine Translation*, pages 1–44, Sofia, Bulgaria. Association for Computational Linguistics.

John D Byrum. 1999. Iso 639-1 and iso 639-2: International standards for language codes. iso 15924: International standard for names of scripts. In *Proceedings of the 65th International Federation of Library Associations and Institutions (IFLA) Council and General Conference, Bangkok, Thailand*. ERIC.

Chris Collins and Richard Kayne. 2009. Syntactic structures of the worlds languages.

---

[1] https://github.com/jjzha/translationese

Matthew S. Dryer and Martin Haspelmath. 2013. Wals online. max planck institute for evolutionary anthropology, leipzig.

Christian Federmann. 2012. Appraise: an open-source toolkit for manual evaluation of mt output. *The Prague Bulletin of Mathematical Linguistics*, 98:25–35.

Yvette Graham, Timothy Baldwin, Alistair Moffat, and Justin Zobel. 2013. Continuous measurement scales in human evaluation of machine translation. In *Proceedings of the 7th Linguistic Annotation Workshop and Interoperability with Discourse*, pages 33–41.

Yvette Graham, Timothy Baldwin, Alistair Moffat, and Justin Zobel. 2014. Is machine translation getting better over time? In *Proceedings of the 14th Conference of the European Chapter of the Association for Computational Linguistics*, pages 443–451.

Yvette Graham, Timothy Baldwin, Alistair Moffat, and Justin Zobel. 2017. Can machine translation systems be evaluated by the crowd alone. *Natural Language Engineering*, 23(1):3–30.

Harald Hammarström, Robert Forkel, and Martin Haspelmath. 2019. Glottolog 3.4. jena: Max planck institute for the science of human history. *Online v.: http://glottolog. org.*

Hany Hassan, Anthony Aue, Chang Chen, Vishal Chowdhary, Jonathan Clark, Christian Federmann, Xuedong Huang, Marcin Junczys-Dowmunt, William Lewis, Mu Li, et al. 2018. Achieving human parity on automatic chinese to english news translation. *arXiv preprint arXiv:1803.05567.*

David Kurokawa, Cyril Goutte, Pierre Isabelle, et al. 2009. Automatic detection of translated text and its impact on machine translation. *Proceedings of MT-Summit XII*, pages 81–88.

Sara Laviosa-Braithwaite. 1998. Universals of translation. *Routledge Encyclopedia of Translation Studies. London: Routledge*, pages 288–291.

Gennadi Lembersky. 2013. *The Effect of Translationese on Statistical Machine Translation*. University of Haifa, Faculty of Social Sciences, Department of Computer Science.

Gennadi Lembersky, Noam Ordan, and Shuly Wintner. 2012. Language models for machine translation: Original vs. translated texts. *Computational Linguistics*, 38(4):799–825.

M. Paul Lewis, Gary F. Simons, and Charles D. Fennig. 2009. Ethnologue: languages of the world, dallas: Sil international. *Online version: http://www. ethnologue. com.*

Patrick Littell, David R Mortensen, and Lori Levin. 2016. Uriel typological database. *Pittsburgh: CMU.*

Patrick Littell, David R Mortensen, Ke Lin, Katherine Kairis, Carlisle Turner, and Lori Levin. 2017. Uriel and lang2vec: Representing languages as typological, geographical, and phylogenetic vectors. In *Proceedings of the 15th Conference of the European Chapter of the Association for Computational Linguistics: Volume 2, Short Papers*, pages 8–14.

Sara Stymne. 2017. The effect of translationese on tuning for statistical machine translation. In *The 21st Nordic Conference on Computational Linguistics*, pages 241–246.

Antonio Toral, Sheila Castilho, Ke Hu, and Andy Way. 2018. Attaining the unattainable? reassessing claims of human parity in neural machine translation. *arXiv preprint arXiv:1808.10432.*

Gideon Toury. 2012. *Descriptive translation studies and beyond: Revised edition*, volume 100. John Benjamins Publishing.

Customizing Neural Machine Translation for Subtitling

Evgeny Matusov[*], **Patrick Wilken**[*], **Panayota Georgakopoulou**[*]
AppTek
Aachen, Germany
ematusov@apptek.com pwilken@apptek.com yota@athenaconsultancy.eu

Abstract

In this work, we customized a neural machine translation system for translation of subtitles in the domain of entertainment. The neural translation model was adapted to the subtitling content and style and extended by a simple, yet effective technique for utilizing intersentence context for short sentences such as dialog turns. The main contribution of the paper is a novel subtitle segmentation algorithm that predicts the end of a subtitle line given the previous word-level context using a recurrent neural network learned from human segmentation decisions. This model is combined with subtitle length and duration constraints established in the subtitling industry. We conducted a thorough human evaluation with two post-editors (English-to-Spanish translation of a documentary and a sitcom). It showed a notable productivity increase of up to 37% as compared to translating from scratch and significant reductions in human translation edit rate in comparison with the post-editing of the baseline non-adapted system without a learned segmentation model.

1 Introduction

In recent years, significant progress was observed in neural machine translation (NMT), with its quality increasing dramatically as compared to the previous generation of statistical phrase-based MT systems. However, user acceptance in the subtitling community has so far been rare. The reason for this, in our opinion, is that the state-of-the-art off-the-shelf NMT systems do not address the issues and challenges of the subtitling process in full.

In this paper, we present a customized NMT system for subtitling, with focus on the entertainment domain. From the user perspective, we show how the quality of translation and subtitle segmentation can improve in such a way that significantly reduced post-editing is required. We believe that such customized systems would lead to greater user acceptance in the subtitling industry and would contribute to the wider adoption of NMT technology with the subsequent benefits the latter brings in terms of productivity gain and time efficiency in subtitling workflows.

The paper is structured as follows. We start with the review of related research in Section 2. Section 3 describes the details of our baseline NMT system and how it compares to NMT systems from previous research. Section 4 presents the details of the changes to the MT system that were necessary to boost its performance on the subtitling tasks for entertainment domain, with a focus on Latin American Spanish as the target language. In Section 5, we present a novel algorithm for automatic subtitle segmentation that is combined with rule-based constraints which are necessary for correct subtitle representation on the screen. Finally, Section 6 describes the automatic and human evaluation of the proposed system, including post-editing experiments and feedback from professional translators.

2 Related Work

Evaluation of post-editing time and efficiency gain was presented by Etchegoyhen et al. (2014) on multiple language pairs and with many post-editors. However, that work only evaluated statistical MT systems, whereas here we evaluate a neural MT system. Also, the aspect of subtitle segmentation was not explicitly considered there; it was not clear what segmentation was used, if at all. Interesting findings on evaluation of statisti-

---

[*]equal contribution

Proceedings of the Fourth Conference on Machine Translation (WMT), Volume 1: Research Papers, pages 82–93
Florence, Italy, August 1-2, 2019. ©2019 Association for Computational Linguistics

cal MT for subtitling in production can be found in the work of Volk et al. (2010), who perform an extensive subjective error analysis of the MT output. Aspects of customizing MT, again statistical, using existing subtitle collections are discussed in (Müller and Volk, 2013).

There is little work on subtitle segmentation, and to the best of our knowledge, no research which targets segmentation of MT output. The work by Álvarez et al. (2017) uses conditional random fields and support vector machines to predict segment boundaries, whereas in this paper we rely on recurrent neural networks. That algorithm is evaluated in terms of monolingual post-editing effort in the work of Álvarez Muniain et al. (2016). Lison and Meena (2016) predict dialog turns in subtitles, which is related to subtitle segmentation, but was beyond the scope of our work. The latest research of Song et al. (2019) deals with predicting sentence-final punctuation within non-punctuated subtitles using a long-short-term memory network (LSTM); that model, and also the punctuation prediction LSTM of Tilk and Alumäe (2015) is related to what we use in our work, but we deal with subtitle segmentation that is more complex and less well-defined than prediction of punctuation, as we show in Section 5.

3 Baseline NMT Architecture

We trained our NMT models using an open-source toolkit (Zeyer et al., 2018) that is based on TensorFlow (Abadi et al., 2015). We trained an attention-based RNN model similar to Bahdanau et al. (2015) with additive attention.

The attention model projects both the source and the target words into a 620-dimensional embedding space. The bidirectional encoder consists of 4 layers, each of which uses LSTM cells with 1000 units. We used a unidirectional decoder with the same number of units. In the initial (sub)epochs, we employed a layer-wise pretraining scheme that resulted in better convergence and faster overall training speed (Zeyer et al., 2018). We also enhanced the computation of attention weights using fertility feedback similar to Tu et al. (2016); Bahar et al. (2017).

The training data was preprocessed using Sentencepiece (Kudo and Richardson, 2018), with 20K and 30K subword units estimated separately for English and Spanish, respectively, without any other tokenization. In training, all our models

relied on the Adam optimizer (Kingma and Ba, 2015) with a learning rate of 0.001. We applied a learning rate scheduling according to the Newbob scheme based on the perplexity on the validation set for a few consecutive evaluation checkpoints. We also employed label smoothing of 0.1 (Pereyra et al., 2017). The dropout rate ranged from 0.1 to 0.3.

Our baseline general-domain NMT system is a competitive single system that obtains the case-sensitive BLEU score of 34.4% on the WMT newstest 2013 En-Es set[1].

4 NMT Adaptation

4.1 Domain and style adaptation

Film content covers a large variety of genres, thus it is not easy to characterize the domain of these type of data. However, subtitles typically have shorter sentences than general texts (e.g. news articles), and brief utterances abound in many films. To create a customized system for subtitles, we used the OpenSubtitles parallel data[2], downloaded from the OPUS collection (Lison and Tiedemann, 2016), as the main training corpus. The corpus was filtered by running FastText based language identification (Joulin et al., 2016) and other heuristics (e.g. based on source/target lengths and length ratios in tokens and characters). In addition, we used other conversational corpora, such as GlobalVoices, transcribed TED talks and in-house crawled English-Spanish transcripts of the EU TV as parallel training data. We also added Europarl and News Commentary data to the main training corpus as sources of clean and well-aligned sentence pairs.

Neural MT systems often have problems translating rare words. To mitigate this problem, we developed a novel data augmentation technique. First, we computed word frequency statistics for the main training corpus described above. Then, we defined auxiliary out-of-domain training data from which we wanted to extract only specific sentence pairs. These data included all other publicly available training data, including ParaCrawl, CommonCrawl, EUbookshop, JRC-Acquis, EMEA, and other corpora from the OPUS collection. We computed word frequencies for each of these auxiliary corpora individually. Next,

---

[1] The BLEU score of a top online MT provider on this set was 35.0% as of July 2018.

[2] http://www.opensubtitles.org/

for each sentence pair in each auxiliary corpus we checked that:

- either the source or the target sentence has at least one word that is *rare* in the main corpus, and

- neither the source sentence, nor the target sentence includes any word that is out-of-vocabulary for the main training corpus and at the same time is *rare* in the auxiliary corpus.

We defined a word to be *rare* if its frequency is less than 50. Finally, we limited the total number of running words we add (counted on the source side) to 100M per auxiliary corpus. This was done to avoid oversampling from large, but noisy corpora such as CommonCrawl.

In practice, for the En-Es training data, 145M words of auxiliary data were added, which is ca. 17% of the auxiliary training data that was available. Overall, we used ca. 39M lines of parallel training data for training, with 447M running words on the English and 453M running words on the Spanish side.

Additional domain adaptation may include fine-tuning of the trained model with a reduced learning rate on in-domain data, as e.g. in the work of Luong and Manning (2015). Since we were aiming at covering all possible film genres, we did not perform this additional fine-tuning in our experiments. We also did not use any back-translated target language monolingual data.

4.2 Handling language variety

Most MT systems do not differentiate between European and Latin American (LA) Spanish as the target language, providing a single system for translation into Spanish. However, significant differences between the two language varieties require the creation of separate subtitles for audiences in Latin America and Spain.

Almost no parallel corpora are available for training NMT systems, in which the target language is explicitly marked as Latin American Spanish, and the majority of the public corpora represent European Spanish (such as proceedings of the European Parliament). However, large portions of the in-domain OpenSubtitles corpus contain Latin American Spanish subtitles. We follow a rule-based approach to label those documents/movies from the OpenSubtitles corpus as

translations into LA Spanish. If the plural form of the word "you" is "ustedes" that is used in Latin American Spanish, then we mark the whole document as belonging to this language variety. Since this word is used frequently in movie dialogues, we can label a significant number of documents as belonging to LA Spanish (a total of 192M running words when counted on the Spanish side of the parallel data).

We then train a multilingual system similarly to Firat et al. (2016). We do not change the neural architecture, but add a special token at the beginning of the source sentence to signal LA Spanish output for all training sentence pairs which we labeled as translations into LA Spanish with the rule-based method described above. This is also similar to using tokens for domain control as in the work of Kobus et al. (2016). We used a development set labeled as having translations into LA Spanish to track convergence and for selection of the final training epoch.

An alternative approach that was applied to low-resource language pairs by Neubig and Hu (2018) would have been to pre-train the model on all English-Spanish data, and then continue training on sentence pairs with LA Spanish targets. However, we did not follow this approach to avoid overfitting to the style of the OpenSubtitles corpus instead of adapting to the LA Spanish language variety.

4.3 Towards document-level translation

Subtitles often contain short sentences which, when translated by NMT individually, provide very little context for correct translation of certain words and phrases, such as pronouns. Yet this context is available in preceding sentences. As a step towards document-level translation, we created a training corpus of OpenSubtitles in which we spliced two or more consecutive subtitles from the same film, as well as their translations, until a maximum length of K tokens was reached on the source side. We inserted a special separator symbol between each pair of spliced sentences both on the source and the target side. The idea was that the NMT system can learn to produce these separator symbols and learn not to re-order words across them, so that the original sentence segmentation can be restored. At the same time, because of the nature of the recurrent model, the context of the previous sentences would also be memorized by the system and would affect the translation quality of the current sentence[3].

We created two copies of OpenSubtitles corpus of only spliced sentence pairs with $K = 20$ and $K = 30$, respectively, and used this corpus in training together with all the other data described in Section 4.1. During inference, we also spliced consecutive short sentences from the same film until a threshold of $K = 20$ tokens was reached and then translated the resulting test set. Thus, each sentence was translated only once, either as part of a spliced sentence sequence or as an individual (long) sentence. A possibly better, but more redundant approach would have been to cut out the translation of only the last sentence in a spliced sequence, and then re-send the corresponding source sentence as context for translating the next sentence. However, for time reasons we did not test this approach. In the future, we also plan to expand on the existing research on document-level translation (Miculicich et al., 2018; Wang et al., 2017) and encode the previous inter-sentence context in a separate neural component. Even the first step towards expanding context beyond a single sentence described above led to some improvements in translation, and in particular pronoun disambiguation, as will be seen in Section 6.

5 Subtitle Segmentation

The output of the NMT system has to be formatted in an appropriate way when displayed on the screen. Typically, there exists a fixed character limit per subtitle line, the number of lines should not exceed two, and the text in a subtitle has to be as long as needed to match the user's reading speed, so that it is possible for viewers to read the subtitle and also watch the film at the same time. Beyond that, we want line and subtitle boundaries to occur in places where the flow of reading is harmed as little as possible. While the first two requirements can be implemented as hard rules, optimizing boundaries for readability is more subtle and a lack thereof can easily expose the subtitle as being machine generated, especially when compared to a professionally created one. Punctuation and part-of-speech information can indicate possible segmentation points. However, in general finding good boundaries is not straight-forward and

depends on syntax and semantics.

We therefore employ a neural model to predict segment boundaries. It consists of a 128-dimensional word embedding layer and two 256-dimensional bi-directional LSTM layers, followed by a softmax. The output is a binary decision, i.e. we generate two probabilities per input word w_i: the probability $p_{B,i}$ of inserting a segment boundary after position i, and the probability $1 - p_{B,i}$ of the complementary event.

We train the model on the Spanish OpenSubtitles 2018 corpora of the OPUS Project (Lison and Tiedemann, 2016), which we tokenize and convert to lower-case. The data comes in XML format, including annotated sentence boundaries and timestamps for the subtitle units. We use all subtitle boundaries occurring in between words of a sentence as ground truth labels. Training is performed on all sentences containing at least one subtitle boundary, leading to a corpus size of 16.7M sentences.

To enforce the additional requirements mentioned above, we integrate the neural segmentation model into a beam search decoder. The search happens synchronous to the word positions of the input. At each step there are three possible expansions of a partial hypothesis: no boundary, line boundary, or subtitle boundary after the current word. The natural logarithm of the segmentation model probability is used as score (making no distinction between line and subtitle boundaries). Penalties for the following auxiliary features are subtracted:

1. *character limit*: penalty $q_1 = \infty$ if a line is longer than allowed;

2. *number of lines*: penalty q_2 for every line exceeding two in a given subtitle;

3. *similar line lengths*: penalty q_3 per difference in length of subsequent lines within a subtitle, measured in characters;

4. *expected subtitle lengths*: penalty q_4 per deviation from expected subtitle lengths, measured in characters; we expect subtitle lengths to be as in the source language, only scaled according to the difference in sentence length between the source sentence and its translation.

The third feature is supposed to lead to geometrically pleasing line lengths. In particular, it avoids

---

[3]We came up with this approach on our own, but later found it to be similar to the work of Tiedemann and Scherrer (2017), who include a single previous translation unit with a separator symbol as additional context.

orphans, i.e. lines with very few words in them. The forth feature attempts to keep the translation in sync with the video by keeping the number of characters in a subtitle similar to the source language. This also means that the subtitle duration will be suited for a similar reading speed as the one set in the source file. As a side effect, this feature ensures that we predict the right number of subtitle boundaries for a given sentence.

We use a beam size of 100. The penalties are set to $q_2 = 10$, $q_3 = 0.1$ and $q_4 = 1$. Furthermore, we use a margin of 20% and 30% of the line and subtitle lengths for features 3 and 4, respectively, in which no penalty is applied.

For the baseline approach, we do the segmentation using the four heuristics only, i.e. without the neural segmentation model. This is similar to algorithms used in existing subtitling tools and makes a direct analysis of the effect of the segmentation model possible.

6 Experimental Results

6.1 User experience

To confirm the improvement in quality described in Sections 3 and 4 and the usability of the ensuing output we sought the feedback of professional translators. We selected the language pair US English into LA Spanish for our case study and used video materials of two different genres:

- *Home*[4], a documentary about Earth, composed of aerial shots of our planet and narrated by a single voice over narrator, in a paced manner with well-structured sentences;

- *Lucy: The Bean Queen*[5], an all-time classic sitcom, full of puns and idiomatic language.

We asked an experienced English subtitler to create subtitle files to be used as input for machine translation purposes, with 6.6K running words for *Home* and 2.7K running words for *Lucy*, following well-established subtitling conventions in the source audio language (English). These subtitle files were subsequently machine translated into LA Spanish using both the baseline and the adapted MT systems described in previous sections, the latter including the inter-sentence context for short sentences and the proposed novel subtitle segmentation algorithm.

We asked two translators to perform a post-editing evaluation of the two MT outputs. Both have between 11-20 years of experience each in all types of subtitling work. PE1 comes from Colombia and PE2 from Argentina. Both have experience with MT of general texts and PE1 had limited prior experience with the use of MT in subtitling. We split the two source files in three roughly equal sections and asked the translators to perform the following tasks:

- Translate Part 1 straight from the template file, without deviating from the set timings, subtitle number and segmentation;

- Post-edit Part 2 using output from the baseline MT system;

- Post-edit Part 3 using output from the adapted MT system.

The translators did not know the output of which system they were post-editing. We asked the translators to work consecutively, as they normally would, taking as few breaks as possible and recording their actual work time to the nearest minute. We asked them to include the time for research they would normally perform as part of their translation task in this measurement and review their work one final time before submitting it, as they would under live working conditions in order to submit a file of publishable quality level. We then asked the translators to answer a survey, which included answers to the demographic information mentioned above, plus a qualitative survey of the machine translation output and the post-editing experience, using a combination of ranking scale scores and free-text questions.

6.2 Translation speed benchmarking

Both translators were asked to translate "from scratch" Part 1 of each of the two template files, totaling 24 minutes/220 subtitles for *Home* and 8 minutes/118 subtitles for *Lucy*, in order to obtain their benchmark speed for each type of material. PE1 with 2.08/2.0 subtitles per minute for Home and Lucy, respectively, turned out to be significantly faster than PE2 (1.18/1.44 subtitles per minute) and maintained similar speed irrespective of the film genre. Their translated files for Part 1 of the templates were used as gold reference for performing automatic MT evaluation, with its results shown in the next section.

---

[4]https://archive.org/details/HOME_English
[5]https://archive.org/details/TLS_Lucy_The_Bean_Queen

Mode	System	BLEU [%]	TER [%]	charTER [%]
W	baseline	52.3	50.3	42.8
	adapted	53.6	49.2	41.2
S	baseline	49.9	58.5	51.8
	adapted	54.7	49.3	41.9
	base segm.	50.8	57.8	52.4
L	baseline	37.2	60.1	53.4
	adapted	44.0	49.3	42.1
	base segm.	38.2	59.4	53.4

Table 1: Case-sensitive MT error measures on part 1 of the *Home* documentary computed in 3 different modes: using full sentences with real words only (W), on the level of subtitles (S), or on the level of subtitles with line breaks within a subtitle marked with a special token BR both in MT output and reference translation. The BLEU scores are computed against two human reference translations created "from scratch", other measures against the translation of PE1.

Mode	System	BLEU [%]	TER [%]	charTER [%]
W	baseline	26.3	68.4	61.3
	adapted	30.3	61.5	56.8
	sent-level	30.2	62.8	54.8
S	baseline	26.6	85.6	60.4
	adapted	31.1	76.1	56.4
	sent-level	30.5	77.3	54.9
	base segm.	31.0	78.2	58.8
L	baseline	21.8	85.7	61.6
	adapted	30.4	75.6	56.6
	base segm.	25.7	79.4	59.4

Table 2: Case-sensitive MT error measures on part 1 of the *Lucy: The Bean Queen* documentary computed as in Table 1.

6.3 Automatic evaluation

We computed automatic MT metrics BLEU (Papineni et al., 2002), TER (Snover et al., 2006), and CharacTER (Wang et al., 2016) on the first part of each template for which we now had two independent human reference translations. We computed the scores three times using different evaluation modes. In the mode (W), we computed the scores and error rates on the full sentences; thus, pure MT quality is evaluated, and any segmentation decisions are ignored. In the (S) mode, we compared the subtitles with each other. Thus, any words and phrases wrongly placed in a different (e.g. previous or next) subtitle would count as errors. Finally, in the (L) mode we additionally add a special symbol to represent a line break (in rare cases, two breaks) within a subtitle. Thus, an incorrect line break is an extra token error that directly affects all error metrics. To summarize, the (S) and (L) evaluation modes jointly judge the MT and segmentation quality, whereas the (W) mode only judges the MT quality.

Table 1 shows these results for the *Home* video. We observe an improvement in BLEU from 52.3 to 53.6%, as computed with two reference translations, when comparing the baseline system with the adapted one that uses previous sentence context. This improvement becomes much larger in the (S) and (L) evaluation modes, which confirms the quality of the segmentation algorithm as compared with the baseline heuristics-only segmentation. The other error measures improve similarly with the adapted MT output and the proposed segmentation algorithm. We also show the result of the adapted system, but with the baseline segmentation. The result for this system is slightly better than for the baseline due to the generally better MT quality, but because of the incorrect segmentation it is very far from human references when the evaluation is performed on the level of subtitles.

On part 1 of the *Lucy* sitcom (Table 2), the improvements with the adapted system are more significant when the MT quality alone is evaluated. This is expected, since the style of the input is further away from the general-domain (news) data that was used to train the baseline system. On the other hand, the improvements with the new segmentation algorithm w.r.t baseline segmentation seem to be significant, but less pronounced, since here we are dealing with generally shorter subtitles, many of them one-liners. Nevertheless, the improvement in the (L) evaluation mode, where incorrect line breaks within a subtitle are considered as errors, is as large as 8 BLEU percentage points absolute, from 21.8 to 30.4%. Table 2 also shows the results for the adapted system, but when translating individual sentences without inter-sentence context (lines *sent-level*). We observed only insignificant reduction of the pure MT quality in BLEU and TER; the CharacTER even improved. The test sample was too small to make any conclusions here. Nevertheless, we observed cases where the translation of some words (e.g., pronouns) was better when consecutive short sentences were translated as a single unit as described

Test set/system	HTER [%]		SER [%]	
	PE1	PE2	PE1	PE2
p. 2 baseline	36.7	51.4	88.0	99.0
p. 3 adapted	27.8	44.2	67.2	79.6
p. 2 adapted*	36.2	46.5	83.6	88.7

Table 3: Case-sensitive Human Translation Edit Rate (HTER) and Subtitle Edit Rate (SER) on the post-edited parts 2 and 3 of the *Home* documentary. *The comparison of the adapted NMT on section 2 is against the human post-editing of the baseline NMT output.

Test set/system	HTER [%]		SER [%]	
	PE1	PE2	PE1	PE2
p. 2 baseline	73.8	82.7	89.4	91.7
p. 3 adapted	44.0	59.5	71.9	80.5
p. 2 adapted*	60.6	72.0	87.9	90.9

Table 4: Case-sensitive Human Translation Edit Rate (HTER) and Subtitle Edit Rate (SER) on the post-edited parts 2 and 3 of the *Lucy: The Bean Queen* documentary. *The comparison of the adapted NMT on part 2 is against the human post-editing of the baseline NMT output.

in Section 4.3, and the improvement could only be explained by the additional context.

6.4 Evaluation of human post-editing effort

We computed the HTER scores (TER against the post-edited MT output) for the parts 2 and 3 of both files. We also computed the *subtitle error rate* (SER), that we defined as the percentage of subtitles which were changed by the post-editor (not counting possible corrections of the line breaks within a subtitle). Table 3 shows the HTER and SER results for the *Home* documentary. We see that the HTER is consistently better for both post-editors when the adapted MT output is used. PE1 especially finds the adapted MT output acceptable and keeps approximately $1/3$ of the subtitles completely unchanged. The second post-editor makes more corrections in general, but also for him the number of corrections made on the adapted MT output is significantly lower. The numbers above have to be taken with a grain of salt, since there was no other way but to compare the post-editing effort on different parts of the file. However, even when we compare the adapted MT output on part 2 against the post-edited baseline MT output, we obtain lower HTER and SER scores than for the baseline MT output itself. This again underlines the high quality of the adapted MT output with proper subtitle segmentation.

Similar conclusions can be made from the HTER and SER results in Table 4 for the *Lucy* sitcom. Here, the number of corrections is generally higher, but the reduction of the post-editing effort when post-editing the adapted vs. baseline MT is very significant, e.g. from 73.8 to 44.0% HTER for PE1 (as measured on different parts of the file with similar translation difficulty).

File	Post-editor	PE speed subs/min	Gain (%)	
			Product.	Time
Home	PE1	1.36	15.98	13.78
baseline	PE2	2.00	-3.64	-3.77
Lucy	PE1	1.43	-0.29	-0.30
baseline	PE2	2.28	13.79	12.12
Home	PE1	1.87	58.70	36.99
adapted	PE2	2.15	3.75	3.62
Lucy	PE1	1.86	28.91	22.43
adapted	PE2	3.12	56.10	35.94

Table 5: Productivity and time gain by using baseline/adapted MT output as compared to translating "from scratch".

6.5 Post-editing efficiency

We also performed an analysis of productivity gain and time efficiency by comparing translator speeds when post-editing the baseline and adapted MT outputs against their benchmark speed (Section 6.2). The results are presented in Table 5.

Productivity gain is the estimated percentage of additional work a translator would be able to complete when performing an MTPE task versus translating the same text from scratch. Time efficiency is the estimated percentage of time a translator would save when performing an MTPE task versus translating the same material from scratch.

As we can see, both productivity gain and time efficiency were achieved for both post-editors overall. The average productivity gain was 6.46% on the baseline MT output and 36.87% on the adapted MT output, the time efficiency increased by 5.46% and 24.74%, respectively. There were borderline productivity losses in one file per translator when working on the baseline output, but more than significant productivity increases on the adapted output. The same trend is observed with time efficiency as well, verifying our initial hypothesis regarding the usability of the adapted MT output.

Though no conclusion may be drawn from the results of two post-editors only, but given that their overall profiles are quite similar with a marked difference in their translation speed, it is interesting to note that the slower of the two benefits more overall in an MTPE workflow. It should be pointed out, however, that PE1 did have some experience with MT in subtitles, whereas PE2 did not, which might indicate that PE2 had to go through a learning curve and, hence, explain his slow speed on *Home* and the large increase in his post-editing speed on *Lucy*.

The % of subtitles changed (SER) is analyzed in Section 6.4. 100-SER is the percentage of subtitles that were left unchanged after post-editing, including both punctuation and capitalization aspects. This metric does not take into account the pertinence or complexity of the changes made by a post-editor to the rest of the subtitle file. As a result, from a time efficiency perspective, it does not necessarily indicate the effort a post-editor needs to invest when post-editing the entire file. It is still expected though that with lower SER, a translator's time efficiency is likely to increase. The results above corroborate this assumption, and we note that where translators saved more time when performing an MTPE task, they were also using more of the MT output without making any changes to it. A marked increase in the usage of MT output with zero edits was noted in the adapted MT output with the average overall subtitles unchanged at 25% across all files and both post-editors versus 8% for the baseline MT output.

6.6 User survey

A qualitative evaluation with the two translators that were involved in the MTPE task was also performed, in the form of a survey. The MQM[6] framework was used to define the dimensions of MT output quality the translators were asked about, and the following definitions were provided to them:

- Accuracy: Meaning, e.g. mistranslations, omissions, additions, untranslated words

- Fluency: Well-formedness of text, e.g. spelling, grammar, word order, consistency, typography, style

- Design: Physical presentation of text, e.g. line length, readability, line and subtitle breaks

The translators were asked to rank the MT outputs they worked on with respect to each of the three quality dimensions above, as well as on the basis of the overall MT quality and regarding the post-editing experience itself. A ranking scale of 1-5 was used in this survey (5 being best). All results were consistent, with translators ranking both quality and post-editing experience for the baseline MT output as a 2 on average, i.e. poor, and for the adapted MT output as 3, i.e. fair.

The translators confirmed the improvement in quality in the adapted MT output, which corroborates previous findings and our initial hypothesis for this case study. When asked additional questions regarding the perceived MT impact on their productivity and on the quality of the final product, PE2 confirmed he "felt" the increase in productivity he witnessed on *Lucy* and explained that his experience with *Home* would have been similar had it not been for a particularly difficult section in the source text in the last part of *Home* that slowed him down substantially. Yet PE2 felt it was only the easier parts of *Lucy*, the simpler sentences, on which the MT was perfect, while it still translated most of the slang and puns (i.e. the creative part) wrongly.

PE1 noted the difficulty in finding his own writing style when post-editing, but also explained that he became much faster once he understood what to expect from the MT and found a rhythm. He was impressed by the correct terminology in the MT output of *Home*, one of the main reasons why both translators reported they would consider using output such as that of the adapted MT on documentary genres like *Home* in their daily work.

Both subtitlers raised concerns about the influence the MT has on their productivity (PE1) and on the quality of the final product (PE2) as uncommon but correct translations in the target language would not be corrected in a post-editing workflow, potentially affecting the overall result[7]. Finally, both translators said that there were only few cases in the baseline MT output where expressions from European Spanish were used and had to be corrected; they reported only one such case in the adapted MT output (see Section 4.2 on why).

___

[6]http://www.qt21.eu/mqm-definition/definition-2014-06-06.html

[7]Cf. also the findings of Farrell (2018) on this matter.

6.7 Discussion

Both the automatic measures as well as the productivity/time gain evaluation with independent subtitlers indicate that the adapted MT output significantly outperformed the baseline MT in terms of quality. All of the metrics, whether on Part 1 against a gold reference file, or on Parts 2 and 3, against the post-edited files correlate and verify the conclusion above. A ranking scale qualitative evaluation by the translators also confirmed the above findings, and translators provided further insights as to the post-editing process itself.

7 Conclusions

In this paper, we described how a state-of-the-art NMT system can be effectively customized for subtitling. We proposed a simple way to integrate inter-sentence context for translation of short utterances and dialog turns, adapted the NMT system to language variation (Latin American Spanish) and subtitling style and domain. We introduced a novel algorithm for subtitle segmentation that combines a recurrent neural network model with hard and soft subtitle length and duration constraints in a beam search. We performed an extensive automatic and human evaluation, which showed notable improvements in quality of the adapted MT output segmented into subtitles with our proposed algorithm as compared to the baseline MT system output with heuristics-based line breaks. This quality improvement led to significant productivity and time gains when the adapted MT output was post-edited by independent professional translators, compared both to translation from scratch and post-editing the translations of the baseline MT system. Finally, we received positive qualitative feedback on the adapted MT output from the post-editors involved in our study.

In the future, we plan to use more sophisticated document-level features for better consistency of the translations. We also started to expand the language coverage and trained similar adapted systems with learned segmentation for the language pairs Spanish-to-English and English-to-Russian. Examples of automatic subtitles created by these systems when using or ignoring inter-sentence context are shown in Figure 1 and examples of heuristics-based vs. model-based segmentation for En→Es, Es→En, and En→Ru NMT output are shown in Figure 2 in the Appendix.

References

Martín Abadi, Ashish Agarwal, Paul Barham, Eugene Brevdo, Zhifeng Chen, Craig Citro, Greg S. Corrado, Andy Davis, Jeffrey Dean, Matthieu Devin, Sanjay Ghemawat, Ian Goodfellow, Andrew Harp, Geoffrey Irving, Michael Isard, Yangqing Jia, Rafal Jozefowicz, Lukasz Kaiser, Manjunath Kudlur, Josh Levenberg, Dandelion Mané, Rajat Monga, Sherry Moore, Derek Murray, Chris Olah, Mike Schuster, Jonathon Shlens, Benoit Steiner, Ilya Sutskever, Kunal Talwar, Paul Tucker, Vincent Vanhoucke, Vijay Vasudevan, Fernanda Viégas, Oriol Vinyals, Pete Warden, Martin Wattenberg, Martin Wicke, Yuan Yu, and Xiaoqiang Zheng. 2015. TensorFlow: Large-scale machine learning on heterogeneous systems. Software available from tensorflow.org.

Aitor Álvarez, Carlos-D Martínez-Hinarejos, Haritz Arzelus, Marina Balenciaga, and Arantza del Pozo. 2017. Improving the automatic segmentation of subtitles through conditional random field. *Speech Communication*, 88:83–95.

Aitor Álvarez Muniain, Marina Balenciaga, Arantza del Pozo Echezarreta, Haritz Arzelus Irazusta, Anna Matamala, and Carlos D Martínez Hinarejos. 2016. Impact of automatic segmentation on the quality, productivity and self-reported post-editing effort of intralingual subtitles. In *Proceedings of the Tenth International Conference on Language Resources and Evaluation (LREC 2016)*, pages 3049–3053.

Parnia Bahar, Jan Rosendahl, Nick Rossenbach, and Hermann Ney. 2017. The RWTH Aachen machine translation systems for IWSLT 2017. In *Proceedings of the 14th International Workshop on Spoken Language Translation*, pages 29–34.

Dzmitry Bahdanau, Kyunghyun Cho, and Yoshua Bengio. 2015. Neural machine translation by jointly learning to align and translate. In *Proceedings of the International Conference on Learning Representations (ICLR)*.

Thierry Etchegoyhen, Lindsay Bywood, Mark Fishel, Panayota Georgakopoulou, Jie Jiang, Gerard Van Loenhout, Arantza Del Pozo, Mirjam Sepesy Maucec, Anja Turner, and Martin Volk. 2014. Machine translation for subtitling: A large-scale evaluation. In *LREC*, pages 46–53.

Michael Farrell. 2018. Machine translation markers in post-edited machine translation output. In *The 40th Conference Translating and the Computer, London, United Kingdom*, pages 15–16.

Orhan Firat, Kyunghyun Cho, and Yoshua Bengio. 2016. Multi-way, multilingual neural machine translation with a shared attention mechanism. *arXiv preprint arXiv:1601.01073*.

Armand Joulin, Edouard Grave, Piotr Bojanowski, and Tomas Mikolov. 2016. Bag of tricks for efficient text classification. *arXiv preprint arXiv:1607.01759*.

Diederik P. Kingma and Jimmy Ba. 2015. Adam: A method for stochastic optimization. In *Proceedings of the International Conference on Learning Representations (ICLR)*, San Diego, CA, USA.

Catherine Kobus, Josep Crego, and Jean Senellart. 2016. Domain control for neural machine translation. *arXiv preprint arXiv:1612.06140*.

Taku Kudo and John Richardson. 2018. Sentencepiece: A simple and language independent subword tokenizer and detokenizer for neural text processing. In *Proceedings of the 2018 Conference on Empirical Methods in Natural Language Processing: System Demonstrations*, pages 66–71.

Pierre Lison and Raveesh Meena. 2016. Automatic turn segmentation for movie & TV subtitles. In *2016 IEEE Spoken Language Technology Workshop (SLT)*, pages 245–252. IEEE.

Pierre Lison and Jörg Tiedemann. 2016. OpenSubtitles2016: Extracting large parallel corpora from movie and TV subtitles. In *Proceedings of the 10th International Conference on Language Resources and Evaluation (LREC 2016)*. European Language Resources Association.

Minh-Thang Luong and Christopher D Manning. 2015. Stanford neural machine translation systems for spoken language domains. In *Proceedings of the International Workshop on Spoken Language Translation*, pages 76–79.

Lesly Miculicich, Dhananjay Ram, Nikolaos Pappas, and James Henderson. 2018. Document-level neural machine translation with hierarchical attention networks. In *Proceedings of the 2018 Conference on Empirical Methods in Natural Language Processing*, pages 2947–2954, Brussels, Belgium. Association for Computational Linguistics.

Mathias Müller and Martin Volk. 2013. Statistical machine translation of subtitles: From OpenSubtitles to TED. In *Language processing and knowledge in the Web*, pages 132–138. Springer.

Graham Neubig and Junjie Hu. 2018. Rapid adaptation of neural machine translation to new languages. *arXiv preprint arXiv:1808.04189*.

Kishore Papineni, Salim Roukos, Todd Ward, and Wei-Jing Zhu. 2002. BLEU: a Method for Automatic Evaluation of Machine Translation. In *Proceedings of the 41st Annual Meeting of the Association for Computational Linguistics*, pages 311–318, Philadelphia, Pennsylvania, USA.

Gabriel Pereyra, George Tucker, Jan Chorowski, Lukasz Kaiser, and Geoffrey E. Hinton. 2017. Regularizing neural networks by penalizing confident output distributions. *CoRR*, abs/1701.06548.

Matthew Snover, Bonnie Dorr, Richard Schwartz, Linnea Micciulla, and John Makhoul. 2006. A Study of Translation Edit Rate with Targeted Human Annotation. In *Proceedings of the 7th Conference of the Association for Machine Translation in the Americas*, pages 223–231, Cambridge, Massachusetts, USA.

Hye-Jeong Song, Hong-Ki Kim, Jong-Dae Kim, Chan-Young Park, and Yu-Seop Kim. 2019. Inter-sentence segmentation of YouTube subtitles using long-short term memory (LSTM). *Applied Sciences*, 9(7):1504.

Jörg Tiedemann and Yves Scherrer. 2017. Neural machine translation with extended context. *arXiv preprint arXiv:1708.05943*.

Ottokar Tilk and Tanel Alumäe. 2015. LSTM for punctuation restoration in speech transcripts. In *Sixteenth annual conference of the international speech communication association*.

Zhaopeng Tu, Zhengdong Lu, Yang Liu, Xiaohua Liu, and Hang Li. 2016. Coverage-based neural machine translation. *CoRR*, abs/1601.04811.

Martin Volk, Rico Sennrich, Christian Hardmeier, and Frida Tidström. 2010. Machine translation of TV subtitles for large scale production. In *JEC 2010; November 4th, 2010; Denver, CO, USA*, pages 53–62. Association for Machine Translation in the Americas.

Longyue Wang, Zhaopeng Tu, Andy Way, and Qun Liu. 2017. Exploiting cross-sentence context for neural machine translation. *arXiv preprint arXiv:1704.04347*.

Weiyue Wang, Jan-Thorsten Peter, Hendrik Rosendahl, and Hermann Ney. 2016. CharacTER: Translation edit rate on character level. In *Proceedings of the First Conference on Machine Translation: Volume 2, Shared Task Papers*, volume 2, pages 505–510.

Albert Zeyer, Tamer Alkhouli, and Hermann Ney. 2018. RETURNN as a generic flexible neural toolkit with application to translation and speech recognition. In *Proceedings of ACL 2018, Melbourne, Australia, July 15-20, 2018, System Demonstrations*, pages 128–133.

A Supplementary Material

Source text:	MT without context:	Document-level MT:
18 00:05:43,751 --> 00:05:45,083 ¿Y por qué lo aceptaste?	18 00:05:43,751 --> 00:05:45,083 And why did you accept it?	18 00:05:43,751 --> 00:05:45,083 Then why did you accept it?
19 00:05:45,125 --> 00:05:47,792 Porque hablé con él. Creo que es inocente.	19 00:05:45,125 --> 00:05:47,792 Because I talked to him. I think he's innocent.	19 00:05:45,125 --> 00:05:47,792 Because I talked to him. I think he's innocent.
20 00:05:47,876 --> 00:05:49,250 No, yo no estoy tan segura.	20 00:05:47,876 --> 00:05:49,250 No, I'm not so sure.	20 00:05:47,876 --> 00:05:49,250 No, I'm not so sure.
21 00:05:49,292 --> 00:05:50,959 Todas las pruebas están en su contra.	21 00:05:49,292 --> 00:05:50,959 All the evidence is against you.	21 00:05:49,292 --> 00:05:50,959 All the evidence is against him.
22 00:05:51,083 --> 00:05:53,417 Pasó la noche con ella. Fue el último que la vio con vida.	22 00:05:51,083 --> 00:05:53,417 She spent the night with her. He was the last one to see her alive.	22 00:05:51,083 --> 00:05:53,417 He spent the night with her. He was the last one to see her alive.
23 00:05:53,542 --> 00:05:54,501 De acuerdo.	23 00:05:53,542 --> 00:05:54,501 Okay.	23 00:05:53,542 --> 00:05:54,501 Agreed.
27 00:06:02,501 --> 00:06:07,626 Sin embargo, Carlos conoció a esa mujer esa misma noche.	27 00:06:02,501 --> 00:06:07,626 However, Carlos met that woman that same night.	27 00:06:02,501 --> 00:06:07,626 However, Carlos met that woman that same night.
28 00:06:08,584 --> 00:06:10,626 Al día siguiente, se iba a casar con Alejandra.	28 00:06:08,584 --> 00:06:10,626 The next day, he was going to marry Alejandra.	28 00:06:08,584 --> 00:06:10,626 The next day, she was marrying Alejandra.
29 00:06:10,667 --> 00:06:12,542 ¿Qué motivos tendría para matarla?	29 00:06:10,667 --> 00:06:12,542 What's the point of killing her?	29 00:06:10,667 --> 00:06:12,542 What motive would she have to kill her?
30 00:06:12,667 --> 00:06:14,417 -Yo no lo sé. -Ninguno.	30 00:06:12,667 --> 00:06:14,417 - I don't know. - None.	30 00:06:12,667 --> 00:06:14,417 -I don't know. -None.

Figure 1: Examples of Spanish-to-English subtitle translation with and without inter-sentence context available to the NMT system.

Source text:	MT without segmentation algorithm:	MT with segmentation algorithm:
17 00:01:39,160 --> 00:01:42,400 You can skip the eulogy, I'm not gone yet.	17 00:01:39,160 --> 00:01:42,400 Можешь пропустить надгробную речь, я еще не ушел.	17 00:01:39,160 --> 00:01:42,400 Можешь пропустить надгробную речь, я еще не ушел.
35 00:02:48,400 --> 00:02:51,480 That proves that you have confidence in my work.	35 00:02:48,400 --> 00:02:51,480 Это доказывает, что ты уверен в моей работе.	35 00:02:48,400 --> 00:02:51,480 Это доказывает, что ты уверен в моей работе.
42 00:03:11,440 --> 00:03:16,480 A contract with the Royal Furniture Company for $1,500?	42 00:03:11,440 --> 00:03:16,480 Контракт с Королевской мебельной компанией за $1500?	42 00:03:11,440 --> 00:03:16,480 Контракт с Королевской мебельной компанией за $1500?
45 00:07:29,040 --> 00:07:32,800 Thanks to them, the carbon drained from the atmosphere 46 00:07:32,920 --> 00:07:35,400 and other life forms could develop.	45 00:07:29,040 --> 00:07:32,800 Gracias a ellos, el carbono drenado de la atmósfera y otras formas de vida 46 00:07:32,920 --> 00:07:35,400 podrían desarrollarse.	45 00:07:29,040 --> 00:07:32,800 Gracias a ellos, el carbono drenado de la atmósfera 46 00:07:32,920 --> 00:07:35,400 y otras formas de vida podrían desarrollarse.
49 00:07:47,240 --> 00:07:50,200 which enabled it to break apart the water molecule 50 00:07:50,320 --> 00:07:52,240 and take the oxygen.	49 00:07:47,240 --> 00:07:50,200 lo que le permitió romper 50 00:07:50,320 --> 00:07:52,240 la molécula de agua y tomar el oxígeno.	49 00:07:47,240 --> 00:07:50,200 lo que le permitió romper la molécula de agua 50 00:07:50,320 --> 00:07:52,240 y tomar el oxígeno.
10 00:05:24,000 --> 00:05:27,125 No, bueno, es que todos fueron a comer 11 00:05:27,375 --> 00:05:29,918 y te quería decir que, si quieres, podemos salir a comer juntos.	10 00:05:24,000 --> 00:05:27,125 No, well, they all went to eat and I wanted to tell you, if you want, 11 00:05:27,375 --> 00:05:29,918 we can go out and eat together.	10 00:05:24,000 --> 00:05:27,125 No, well, they all went to eat 11 00:05:27,375 --> 00:05:29,918 and I wanted to tell you, if you want, we can go out and eat together.
13 00:05:32,000 --> 00:05:34,083 Tengo mucho trabajo. Y con esto del caso de Ibarra, 14 00:05:34,209 --> 00:05:35,876 estoy saturado, Olivia.	13 00:05:32,000 --> 00:05:34,083 I have a lot of work. 14 00:05:32,000 --> 00:05:34,083 And with this Ibarra case, 15 00:05:34,209 --> 00:05:35,876 I'm saturated, Olivia.	13 00:05:32,000 --> 00:05:34,083 I have a lot of work. And with this Ibarra case, 14 00:05:34,209 --> 00:05:35,876 I'm saturated, Olivia.

Figure 2: Examples of subtitle segmentation using model-based approach vs. heuristics-based approach (English-to-Russian, English-to-Spanish, and Spanish-to-English translation).

Integration of Dubbing Constraints into Machine Translation

Ashutosh Saboo
BITS Pilani, K.K. Birla Goa Campus[*]
Goa, India
ashutosh.saboo96@gmail.com

Timo Baumann
Department of Informatics,
Universität Hamburg, Germany
baumann@informatik.uni-hamburg.de

Abstract

Translation systems aim to perform a meaning-preserving conversion of linguistic material (typically text but also speech) from a source to a target language (and, to a lesser degree, the corresponding socio-cultural contexts). Dubbing, i.e., the lip-synchronous translation and revoicing of speech adds to this constraints about the close matching of phonetic and resulting visemic synchrony characteristics of source and target material. There is an inherent conflict between a translation's meaning preservation and its 'dubbability' and the resulting trade-off can be controlled by weighing the synchrony constraints. We introduce our work, which to the best of our knowledge is the first of its kind, on integrating synchrony constraints into the machine translation paradigm. We present first results for the integration of synchrony constraints into encoder decoder-based neural machine translation and show that considerably more 'dubbable' translations can be achieved with only a small impact on BLEU score, and dubbability improves more steeply than BLEU degrades.

1 Introduction

Dubbing, the lip-synchronous translation and re-voicing of audio-visual media, is essential for the full-fledged reception of foreign movies, TV shows, instructional videos, advertisements, or short social media clips. Dubbing does not contend for the viewers' visual attention like subtitles (Díaz-Cintas and Remael, 2014) do, and unlike voice-over or asynchronous speech there is no (or only little) mismatch of visual and auditory impression where the resulting cognitive dissonance would otherwise increase the viewers' cognitive load, or even lead to understanding errors (McGurk and Macdonald,

1976). Dubbing is still primarily studied in audio-visual translation (Orero, 2004; Chaume, 2012) and performed manually, unlike textual translation, which is largely being automated or supported by computer-aided translation (Koehn, 2009).

Recent break-throughs in speech-to-speech translation (Jia et al., 2019), do not yield translations that systematically observe dubbing constraints, i.e. do not match phonetically (or rather: visemically) the original source (we call this 'dubbability'). It is our goal to create MT systems where the dubbability of the translation can be controlled so as to optimize the trade-off between translation quality and lip-synchrony of the dubbed speech. We hope that more widely available dubbing across languages will help to stimulate access to foreign media and foster inter-cultural exchange.

We argue that dubbable MT will not simply emerge from training on dubbed audio-visual corpora, i.e. implicitly. By comparison, audio-visual corpora will always remain smaller than pure text-to-text translation corpora. As a result, merely relying on training a conventional MT system on large amounts of dubbing texts is bound to severely limit performance. What's more, the task of dubbing combines the constraints of several areas (meaning-preserving as well as prosodically similar translation) which have different properties. For example, for speech from the off or without the speaker's face visible, there are no limitations on prosodic similarity while it may be critical in close-up scenes; the *translation* system would thus need to consider video as well (but only very selectively so). Thus, we are looking for a flexible weighing of these two aspects which we achieve by introducing *phonetic synchrony constraints* that describe the 'dubbability' of a proposed translation, i.e., how well it is expected to allow for lip-synchronous revoicing in

---

[*]This work was performed during an internship at Universität Hamburg, Germany.

Proceedings of the Fourth Conference on Machine Translation (WMT), Volume 1: Research Papers, pages 94–101
Florence, Italy, August 1-2, 2019. ©2019 Association for Computational Linguistics

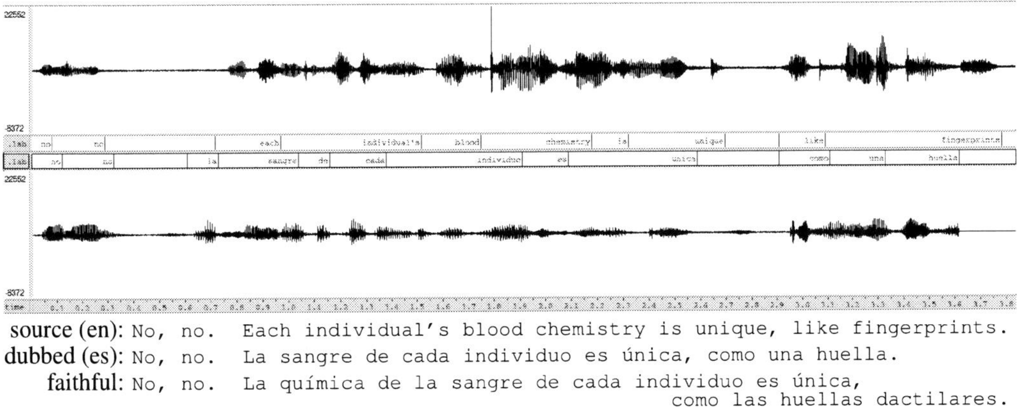

```
source (en): No, no.   Each individual's blood chemistry is unique, like fingerprints.
dubbed (es): No, no.   La sangre de cada individuo es única, como una huella.
   faithful: No, no.   La química de la sangre de cada individuo es única,
                                          como las huellas dactilares.
```

Figure 1: Example dubbing in the show "Heroes" (season 3, episode 1, starting at 29'15", from Öktem et al. (2018)); 'faithful' meaning-preserving translation based on Google Translate.

the target language.[1]

An example of the weighing of lip synchrony and faithful translation in dubbing is shown in Figure 1 which shows an example utterance in the HEROes corpus[2] (Öktem et al., 2018) in its English original and Spanish dubbed revoicing, as well as a meaning-preserving translation. The latter results in about 70 % too many syllables (32 vs. 19 in the source), and would be next to impossible to revoice in a lip-synchronous manner. The human translator (and dubbing expert) resolved the issue by sacrificing some detail in the translation: two terms, "blood chemistry" and "fingerprints" can easily be translated slightly differently (leaving out the "chemistry" and "finger" aspects, as well as singularizing "prints") which reduces the syllable difference down to 20 % without sacrificing the overall meaning conveyed by the utterance.

We describe how synchrony constraints can be included in the MT process, in particular in the search/decoding process of neural MT, in the following section and then describe our implemented system in Section 3 and present results of our experimentation in Section 5. We conclude in Section 6 where we also present our plans for future work.

2   Integration of Dubbing Constraints

Given a source language sentence S, both statistical MT and neural MT perform a search among many different possible candidate utterances C in the target language, wrt. constraints that represent the faithfulness of the translation, $score_t(C, S)$, with the best scoring candidate picked as the result.

Given the source sentence and a candidate translation, we can compute a phonetic (or visemic) synchrony $score_p(C, S)$. Then, for dubbing-optimized machine translation, we simply compute a dubbing-optimal $score_d$ that combines both sub-scores using a weight α that indicates the relative importance of phonetic synchrony vs. translation faithfulness:

$$score_d^\alpha(C, S) =$$
$$(1 - \alpha) * score_t(C, S) + \alpha * score_p(C, S).$$

In application, α can be varied, e. g. according to whether the speaker's face is visible on screen.

MT systems gradually construct and prune the search space as their scoring functions work well locally, i.e., already do well for partial translations.[3] In contrast, synchrony scoring requires a global perspective, in particular for a constraint such as the relative deviation in syllable number between a candidate and the source, i.e. for

$$score_p(C, S) = abs(syll(C) - syll(S))/syll(S).$$

It is not easy to compute this for only a prefix of C as it is typically unclear which words in the source have already been accounted for and as syllables can be shifted between words (only the total matters).

To integrate phonetic constraints into the search

---

[1]In this paper, we use the relative difference of syllable count estimates between source and target material as the similarity constraint. We expect that more elaborate constraints, e. g. based on accentuation, stress marks, expected speech durations, articulatory and prosodic features, visemes, etc. will be needed to match human dubbing performance.

[2]http://hdl.handle.net/10230/35572

[3]However, He et al. (2017) use a similar technique as outlined below for BLEU-optimal decoding for NMT.

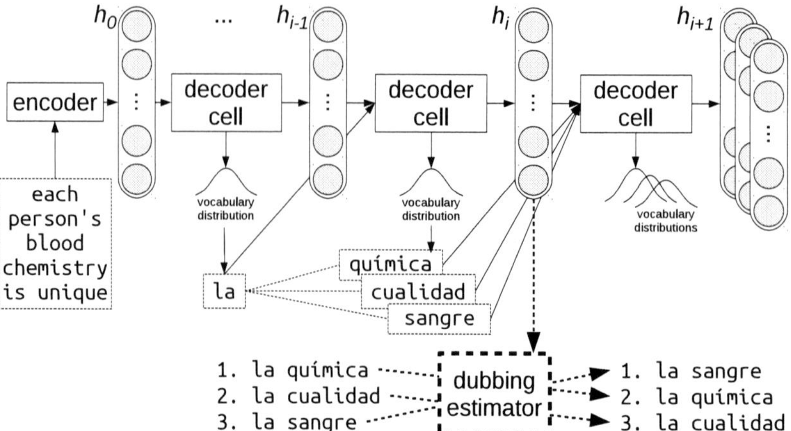

Figure 2: Integration of dubbing constraints into the MT decoder: the beam is re-scored by a combined score of the phonetic similarity of the decoded prefix as well as a heuristic estimate for what remains in the search state.

process, we propose a heuristic dubbing estimator that breaks down the task of phonetic similarity scoring into (a) the known phonetic score for the prefix that has already been generated, and (b) a heuristic $\widehat{score}_p$ based on the internal state of the decoder for how well the yet untranslated part of the utterance will score. Different prefixes correspond to different decoder states and states are known to capture the remaining length of the translation (Shi et al., 2016). Our method extends over that of Chatterjee et al. (2017), which scores constraints only once all necessary information is available in the decoded prefix. The resulting beam search then performs similarly to A* (Hart et al., 1968).

Figure 2 depicts our method, without loss of generality, for NMT. In the example, the decoding of an utterance at decoding stage i is shown. At i, the decoder may consider to add a word to faithfully translate the phrase "blood chemistry", and as an alternate hypothesis consider translating just "blood" as a shorter form of conveying the same message. All alternatives are placed in the MT system's beam which is then re-scored by the *dubbing estimator* which takes each word sequence in the beam to compute the phonetic score of the prefix, as well as the decoder's hidden state h_i to estimate the score for what will still have to be translated. In this case, we can imagine that "sangre" will re-score to a higher position as its brevity is preferred (whereas the alternatives would still need to add "sangre" in a later decoding stage, thus their states will be estimated as containing more material to come yielding an overall higher estimate and a lower score).

The integration of synchrony constraints into the decoder enables a dubbing-optimal search with very little decoding overhead, however with some implementation effort. In addition, the heuristics $\widehat{score}_p$ could turn out to be be problematic given little training material or domain mismatches (see below). A similar result at low code complexity but potentially longer run time can be achieved by post-hoc rescoring based on a relatively large beam size from a standard NMT decoder. This approach is implemented in our first prototype which will be described in the next section.

3 Implemented System

We first describe our NMT model and training setup in detail, which yields an MT system that is competitive with the state of the art. Overall, our goal is not to create a heavily optimized system that gives us the highest possible performance in our domain but merely to yield a plausible baseline. We then describe our amendments for dubbing-optimal decoding.

We implement a convolutional encoder-decoder NMT model (Gehring et al., 2017). Given the relatively lesser training data (see below), we use a smaller model than Gehring et al. (2017), inspired by Edunov et al. (2018) and hence adapt certain hyperparameter values as described in Table 1.

We pre-process textual data as follows: we perform tokenization using the scripts from the open-source package Moses[4] (Koehn et al., 2007)

---

[4] `https://github.com/moses-smt/mosesdecoder`

followed by a byte-pair encoding compression algorithm to reduce the vocabulary size (Sennrich et al., 2016) using the open-source package `subword-nmt`[5]. We denote words not included in the vocabulary as `<UNK>`. We do not apply any lowercasing or stemming.

We train our model with `fairseq`[6] (Ott et al., 2019) for the default 34 epochs with training objectives and search settings as found to be optimal by Edunov et al. (2018) for a similar MT task.

Our standard decoder uses a beam-size of 50 (which is larger than typically used, but see next section for results).

For **dubbing-optimal decoding**, we rescore the N-best list from standard decoding $\mathbf{B}_t$ by the method outlined in Section 2: We estimate the number of syllables in each candidate and the source sentence and take the difference ($\mathrm{sylldiff}(C, S) = abs(syll(C) - syll(S))$) and convert this to a $\mathrm{score}_p(C, S) = 1/(1+\mathrm{sylldiff}(C, S))$ that is highest for identical syllable counts. We then reweigh the sub-scores for translation and synchrony with a weight α, yielding a rescored beam $\mathbf{B}_d$ of which we take the best-ranked translation as being the dubbing-optimal translation. The full algorithm for rescoring is described in Algorithm 1. We use `Pyphen`[7] for estimating the syllable count for both English (source language) and Spanish (target language).

---

[5] `https://github.com/rsennrich/subword-nmt`
[6] `https://github.com/pytorch/fairseq`
[7] `https://pyphen.org/`

Table 1: Custom hyperparameters of our convolutional encoder-decoder model; all other hyperparameters are set as by Gehring et al. (2017).

Hyperparameter	Value
Encoder embedding dimension	256
Encoder hidden units in each layer	256
Kernel size for each encoder layer	3
Encoder layers	4
Dropout rate	0.2
Decoder embedding dimension	256
Decoder hidden units in each layer	256
Kernel size for each decoder layer	3
Decoder layers	3

Algorithm 1 N-Best Rescoring with Dubbing Constraints

1: **Input:** Translation model $P(y|x)$, Test Batch Input T, Rescoring Factor α
2: $\mathbf{B}_t \leftarrow \forall_{e \in T} StandardBeamSearch(e)$
3: **for all** candidate C in $\mathbf{B}_t$ **do**
4:     $\mathrm{score}_t(C) \leftarrow C.score$
5:     $\mathrm{score}_p(C) \leftarrow 1/(1+ \mathrm{sylldiff}(C, S))$
6:     $\mathrm{score}_d(C) \leftarrow (1 - \alpha) * \mathrm{score}_t(C) + \alpha * \mathrm{score}_p(C)$
7: **Output:** Rescored Beam Output $\mathbf{B}_d$
8: **Select:** Best-ranked candidate from $\mathbf{B}_d$

---

4 Setup and Evaluation Method

Ideally, a dubbing-optimal translation system should be evaluated on dubbed material. We use the HEROes dubbing corpus (Öktem et al., 2018) a corpus of the TV show with the same name with the source (English) and dubbing into Spanish. The corpus contains a total of 7000 manually aligned utterance pairs in 9.5 hours of speech and based on forced alignment of video subtitles to the audio tracks. The audio material (in both English and Spanish) is not yet used in the experiments reported below.

We find that the HEROes corpus contains 85,767 (resp. 83,561) syllables for English (resp. dubbed Spanish), as computed with `Pyphen`. The average number of syllables per utterance is 12.25 for English and 11.94 for Spanish. We conclude that, on average, both languages use almost the same number of syllables and hence our phonetic similarity measure based on syllables should be useful. (It would be possible, for other language pairs where the notion of syllable differs, e. g. when considering the mora-driven Japanese, to compute some sort of correction factor between the languages. In our case, we simply ignore the relative difference in syllables of $< 3\%$ between the languages.)

Although large for a dubbing corpus, the 7,000 utterances are far too little to train an NMT model on. We hence use the English $\rightarrow$ Spanish parallel data in the Europarl corpus (Koehn, 2005) for training and will evaluate on both the dubbing corpus and a test set based on the Europarl corpus. The genre of science fiction TV shows may differ radically from parliament proceedings. However, this merely results in lower BLEU performance on the out-of-domain data. We believe that model adaptation (e.g. Chu and Wang, 2018) or relatively more in-domain training material (e.g. Lison and Tiedemann, 2016) would work orthogonal to the dubbing-specific improvements in our paper. Text pre-processing is identical for both corpora.

We measure the translation performance in terms of BLEU (Papineni et al., 2002) as computed with the SacreBLEU software[8] (Post, 2018). Dubbing-optimality of translations in the test-set T is determined by micro-averaging the dubbing-scores as follows: by *synchrony-score* for test-set T defined as:

$$synchrony\text{-}score(T) =$$
$$\frac{\sum_{e \in T} abs(syll(\text{NMT}(e)) - syll(e))}{\sum_{e \in T} syll(e)}$$

where $\text{NMT}(e)$ is the target translation given by the NMT model $P(y|x)$ (with or without dubbing constraints applied) for English source text e.

As is evident, the lower the synchrony score the better is the dubbing optimality. We run our experiment to analyze the variation of BLEU vs. synchrony score for different rescoring factors α.

We use the trained NMT model as described in the above section. Our decoding algorithm is as described in Algorithm 1, which we use to compute the relation between translation performance and dubbing-optimality of translations.

5 Experiment and Results

It has previously been pointed out that NMT performance suffers from a beam search size beyond 5 or 10 (Koehn and Knowles, 2017; Tu et al., 2017) and numerous methods have been proposed to circumvent this (Huang et al., 2017; Ott et al., 2018; Yang et al., 2018). However, for our present way of dubbing-optimization based on N-best rescoring, high beam sizes are essential for the dubbing-rescoring described in Algorithm 1 to have some material to work with. With only few candidates to be rescored, it might not necessarily give us the most 'dubbable' result.

We experimented with various beam sizes and found no BLEU degradation for a beam size of 50. Larger beams may eventually lead to a degradation and run time would become overly long as it linearly increases with the beam size. Owing to the best of both worlds, we resort to a beam size of 50 for the experiments reported below.

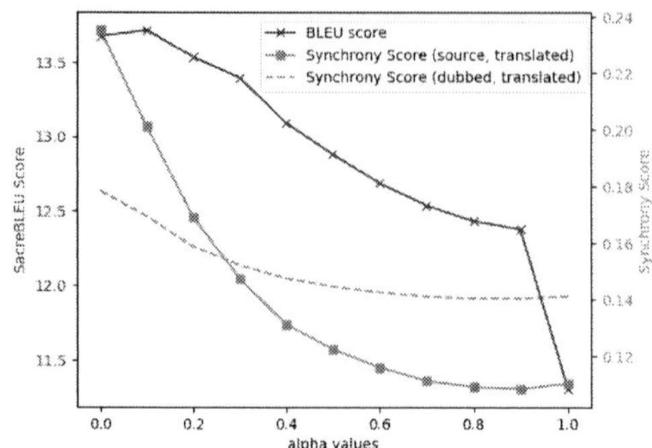

Figure 3: Evaluation results for the HEROes corpus.

5.1 Evaluation on Dubbing Material

Figure 3 shows BLEU scores (left scale, higher is better) and synchrony score (right scale, lower is better) of our proposed system for a range of α between 0 and 1. Notice that $\alpha = 0$ corresponds to no rescoring, i. e. the baseline system.

The relatively low BLEU score of 13.67 for the baseline system reflects the domain-mismatch between HEROes and Europarl.[9] We find that BLEU score is impacted only moderately for relatively low values of α, with a relative decrease of 2 % for $\alpha = .3$. At the same time, we find the synchrony score to improve drastically already with small values of α: while the difference in syllables between source and target is almost one quarter in the baseline system, this is almost halved, down to 14 % for $\alpha = .3$.

Figure 3 also contains the synchrony score of the proposed translations vs. the actual gold-standard dubbed texts (dotted line in the figure). As can be seen, the similarity increases up to about $\alpha = .3$ and then flattens out. This is in line with our observation that, while source and target number of syllables correlate highly, there is no perfect match, indicating that our synchrony constraint has only limited value. However, it also points to the fact that a human dubbing expert needs to find the middle ground between faithful translation and perfect synchrony. Given that two differing linguistic systems are involved, a perfect synchrony is simply impossible if the meaning is to remain approximately correct.

---

[8] https://github.com/mjpost/sacreBLEU

[9] To the great relief of the authors, the European parliament does *not* speak like supernatural figures in a mystery TV show that was scrapped after only 4 seasons due to the harsh criticism on its ludicrous nature.

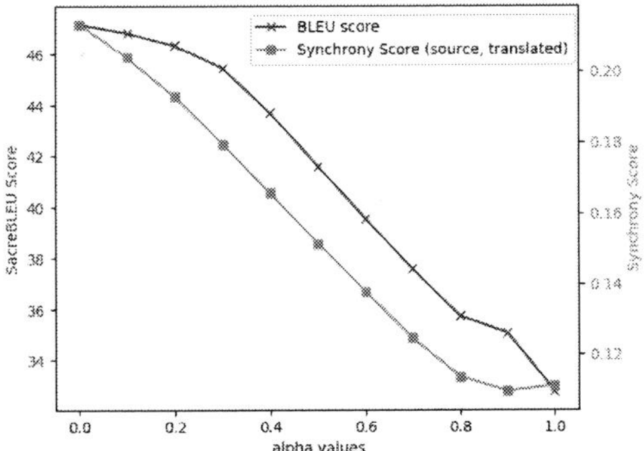

Figure 4: In-domain evaluation results for Europarl.

5.2 In-Domain Evaluation

We also evaluate our method *in-domain*, on test data sampled from Europarl (excluded from training). In particular, we use those source sentences for which multiple reference translations are contained in the corpus (about 18k instances). Europarl translations, of course, are not transcripts of lip-synchronously dubbed speech. Thus, our expectations for synchrony constraints are somewhat lower. However, testing in-domain still helps greatly to validate our out-of-domain results above.

As can be seen in Figure 4, we see a similar decrease in BLEU scores (and only very gradually for small α values) and more strongly improving synchrony scores. This again points towards a useful trade-off when combining synchrony constraints with the requirement of meaning-preserving translations. There is a range of possible reasons why our method does not work as well for Europarl as for the HEROes corpus. In particular, Europarl is not transcribed speech and hence may be less 'dubbable' by nature; many phrases in Europarl may translate to phrases with a different number of syllables in the target language, yet the model is reluctant to give up this translation in the in-domain condition; the proxy-target of syllables may work less well for longer, more specific words as found in legal texts, where a focus on only accentuated syllables may be more useful.

6 Conclusion and Future Work

We have explored the task of *dubbing-optimal* machine translation, i. e. machine translation that unifies the constraints of faithfulness in translation with the constraint of lip-synchrony for revoicing of audio-visual media. We have, so far, limited our synchrony constraint to counting syllables (which acts as a proxy to jaw openings that would be a major factor in visemic characteristics of speech).

We have outlined how one can integrate *synchrony constraints* into to the search during decoding by estimating the amount of syllables that are still remaining in the hidden state of the encoder-decoder model. We have implemented a simpler prototype system that instead rescores a conventional system's final N-best list.

Using the (as far as we know) largest corpus of dubbed speech available, the HEROes corpus (Öktem et al., 2018), we have shown our method to yield much more 'dubbable' translations than those that result from a standard MT system. In fact, while the manual dubbing for the sentence in Figure 1 abbreviates the phrase "blood chemistry" to plain "sangre", our model instead chooses "la *química* de cada persona es única" which is still a reasonable translation of "blood chemistry" and comes very close in terms of syllable count.

In the future, we intend to implement the fully integrated search as described in Section 2, as well as implement more powerful synchrony metrics that could also ground in the source audio (e. g. to find out what syllables were stressed) or the source video (e. g. to find out how well the face is visible), and could also consider detailed aspects of the target speech (e. g. via speech synthesis cost estimates for forcing the target text on the observed visemes).

One interesting and relevant aspect of teaching humans interpreting is the task of rewording material in the target language (Gile, 2005). A model that can be trained towards an ability of coming up with alternate wordings for the same concept (but with different synchrony-related properties) would potentially yield much better candidates for 'dubbability' assessment.

Acknowledgments

This work is partially supported by Volkswagen Foundation under the funding codes 91926 and 93255. We thank the 3 anonymous reviewers for their insightful remarks.

References

Rajen Chatterjee, Matteo Negri, Marco Turchi, Marcello Federico, Lucia Specia, and Frédéric Blain. 2017. Guiding neural machine translation decoding with external knowledge. In *Proceedings of the Second Conference on Machine Translation*, pages 157–

168, Copenhagen, Denmark. Association for Computational Linguistics.

Frederic Chaume. 2012. *Audiovisual translation: Dubbing*. St. Jerome Publishing, Manchester.

Chenhui Chu and Rui Wang. 2018. A survey of domain adaptation for neural machine translation. In *Proceedings of the 27th International Conference on Computational Linguistics*, pages 1304–1319, Santa Fe, USA. Association for Computational Linguistics.

Jorge Díaz-Cintas and Aline Remael. 2014. *Audiovisual Translation, Subtitling*. Routledge, London.

Sergey Edunov, Myle Ott, Michael Auli, David Grangier, and Marc'Aurelio Ranzato. 2018. Classical structured prediction losses for sequence to sequence learning. In *Proceedings of the 2018 Conference of the North American Chapter of the Association for Computational Linguistics: Human Language Technologies, Volume 1 (Long Papers)*, pages 355–364, New Orleans, USA. Association for Computational Linguistics.

Jonas Gehring, Michael Auli, David Grangier, Denis Yarats, and Yann N. Dauphin. 2017. Convolutional sequence to sequence learning. In *Proceedings of the 34th International Conference on Machine Learning - Volume 70*, pages 1243–1252.

Daniel Gile. 2005. Teaching conference interpreting. In *Training for the New Millennium*, pages 127–151. John Benjamins Publishing Company, Amsterdam.

P. E. Hart, N. J. Nilsson, and B. Raphael. 1968. A formal basis for the heuristic determination of minimum cost paths. *IEEE Transactions on Systems Science and Cybernetics*, 4(2):100–107.

Di He, Hanqing Lu, Yingce Xia, Tao Qin, Liwei Wang, and Tie-Yan Liu. 2017. Decoding with value networks for neural machine translation. In I. Guyon, U. V. Luxburg, S. Bengio, H. Wallach, R. Fergus, S. Vishwanathan, and R. Garnett, editors, *Advances in Neural Information Processing Systems 30*, pages 178–187.

Liang Huang, Kai Zhao, and Mingbo Ma. 2017. When to finish? optimal beam search for neural text generation (modulo beam size). In *Proceedings of the 2017 Conference on Empirical Methods in Natural Language Processing*, pages 2134–2139, Copenhagen, Denmark. Association for Computational Linguistics.

Ye Jia, Ron J. Weiss, Fadi Biadsy, Wolfgang Macherey, Melvin Johnson, Zhifeng Chen, and Yonghui Wu. 2019. Direct speech-to-speech translation with a sequence-to-sequence model. *CoRR*, abs/1904.06037.

Philipp Koehn. 2005. Europarl: A Parallel Corpus for Statistical Machine Translation. In *Conference Proceedings: the tenth Machine Translation Summit*, pages 79–86, Phuket, Thailand. AAMT, AAMT.

Philipp Koehn. 2009. A process study of computer-aided translation. *Machine Translation*, 23(4):241–263.

Philipp Koehn, Hieu Hoang, Alexandra Birch, Chris Callison-Burch, Marcello Federico, Nicola Bertoldi, Brooke Cowan, Wade Shen, Christine Moran, Richard Zens, Chris Dyer, Ondřej Bojar, Alexandra Constantin, and Evan Herbst. 2007. Moses: Open source toolkit for statistical machine translation. In *Proceedings of the 45th Annual Meeting of the Association for Computational Linguistics Companion Volume Proceedings of the Demo and Poster Sessions*, pages 177–180, Prague, Czech Republic. Association for Computational Linguistics.

Philipp Koehn and Rebecca Knowles. 2017. Six challenges for neural machine translation. In *Proceedings of the First Workshop on Neural Machine Translation*, pages 28–39, Vancouver, Canada. Association for Computational Linguistics.

Pierre Lison and Jörg Tiedemann. 2016. Opensubtitles2016: Extracting large parallel corpora from movie and tv subtitles. In *Proceedings of the Tenth International Conference on Language Resources and Evaluation (LREC 2016)*, Portorož, Slovenia. European Language Resources Association (ELRA).

Harry McGurk and John Macdonald. 1976. Hearing lips and seeing voices. *Nature*, 264(5588):746–748.

Alp Öktem, Mireia Farrús, and Antonio Bonafonte. 2018. Bilingual Prosodic Dataset Compilation for Spoken Language Translation. In *Proc. Iber-SPEECH 2018*, pages 20–24.

Pilar Orero, editor. 2004. *Topics in Audiovisual Translation*. John Benjamins Publishing Company.

Myle Ott, Michael Auli, David Grangier, and Marc'Aurelio Ranzato. 2018. Analyzing uncertainty in neural machine translation. In *Proceedings of the 35th International Conference on Machine Learning*, volume 80 of *Proceedings of Machine Learning Research*, pages 3956–3965, Stockholmsmässan, Stockholm Sweden. PMLR.

Myle Ott, Sergey Edunov, Alexei Baevski, Angela Fan, Sam Gross, Nathan Ng, David Grangier, and Michael Auli. 2019. fairseq: A fast, extensible toolkit for sequence modeling. In *Proceedings of the 2019 Conference of the North American Chapter of the Association for Computational Linguistics (Demonstrations)*, pages 48–53, Minneapolis, USA. Association for Computational Linguistics.

Kishore Papineni, Salim Roukos, Todd Ward, and Wei-Jing Zhu. 2002. Bleu: A method for automatic evaluation of machine translation. In *Proceedings of the 40th Annual Meeting on Association for Computational Linguistics*, ACL '02, pages 311–318, Philadelphia, Pennsylvania. Association for Computational Linguistics.

Matt Post. 2018. A call for clarity in reporting BLEU scores. In *Proceedings of the Third Conference on Machine Translation: Research Papers*, pages 186–191, Belgium, Brussels. Association for Computational Linguistics.

Rico Sennrich, Barry Haddow, and Alexandra Birch. 2016. Neural machine translation of rare words with subword units. In *Proceedings of the 54th Annual Meeting of the Association for Computational Linguistics (Volume 1: Long Papers)*, pages 1715–1725, Berlin, Germany. Association for Computational Linguistics.

Xing Shi, Kevin Knight, and Deniz Yuret. 2016. Why neural translations are the right length. In *Proceedings of the 2016 Conference on Empirical Methods in Natural Language Processing*, pages 2278–2282, Austin, USA. Association for Computational Linguistics.

Zhaopeng Tu, Yang Liu, Lifeng Shang, Xiaohua Liu, and Hang Li. 2017. Neural machine translation with reconstruction.

Yilin Yang, Liang Huang, and Mingbo Ma. 2018. Breaking the beam search curse: A study of (re-)scoring methods and stopping criteria for neural machine translation. In *Proceedings of the 2018 Conference on Empirical Methods in Natural Language Processing*, pages 3054–3059, Brussels, Belgium. Association for Computational Linguistics.

Widening the Representation Bottleneck in Neural Machine Translation with Lexical Shortcuts

Denis Emelin[1], Ivan Titov[1, 2], and Rico Sennrich[1, 3]

[1]University of Edinburgh, Scotland
[2]University of Amsterdam, Netherlands
[3]University of Zurich, Switzerland
D.Emelin@sms.ed.ac.uk
ititov@inf.ed.ac.uk rico.sennrich@ed.ac.uk

Abstract

The transformer is a state-of-the-art neural translation model that uses attention to iteratively refine lexical representations with information drawn from the surrounding context. Lexical features are fed into the first layer and propagated through a deep network of hidden layers. We argue that the need to represent and propagate lexical features in each layer limits the model's capacity for learning and representing other information relevant to the task. To alleviate this bottleneck, we introduce gated shortcut connections between the embedding layer and each subsequent layer within the encoder and decoder. This enables the model to access relevant lexical content dynamically, without expending limited resources on storing it within intermediate states. We show that the proposed modification yields consistent improvements over a baseline transformer on standard WMT translation tasks in 5 translation directions (0.9 BLEU on average) and reduces the amount of lexical information passed along the hidden layers. We furthermore evaluate different ways to integrate lexical connections into the transformer architecture and present ablation experiments exploring the effect of proposed shortcuts on model behavior.[1]

1 Introduction

Since it was first proposed, the transformer model (Vaswani et al., 2017) has quickly established itself as a popular choice for neural machine translation, where it has been found to deliver state-of-the-art results on various translation tasks (Bojar et al., 2018). Its success can be attributed to the model's high parallelizability allowing for significantly faster training compared to recurrent neural networks (Chen et al., 2018), superior ability to perform lexical disambiguation, and capacity for capturing long-distance dependencies on par with existing alternatives (Tang et al., 2018).

Recently, several studies have investigated the nature of features encoded within individual layers of neural translation models (Belinkov et al., 2017, 2018). One central finding reported in this body of work is that, in recurrent architectures, different layers prioritize different information types. As such, lower layers appear to predominantly perform morphological and syntactic processing, whereas semantic features reach their highest concentration towards the top of the layer stack. One necessary consequence of this distributed learning is that different types of information encoded within input representations received by the translation model have to be transported to the layers specialized in exploiting them.

Within the transformer encoder and decoder alike, information exchange proceeds in a strictly sequential manner, whereby each layer attends over the output of the immediately preceding layer, complemented by a shallow residual connection. For input features to be successfully propagated to the uppermost layers, the translation model must therefore store them in its intermediate representations until they can be processed. By retaining lexical content, the model is unable to leverage its full representational capacity for learning new information from other sources, such as the surrounding sentence context. We refer to this limitation as the representation bottleneck.

To alleviate this bottleneck, we propose extending the standard transformer architecture with lexical shortcuts which connect the embedding layer with each subsequent self-attention sub-layer in both encoder and decoder. The shortcuts are defined as gated skip connections, allowing the model to access relevant lexical information at any

---

[1]Our code is publicly available to aid the reproduction of the reported results: https://github.com/demelin/transformer_lexical_shortcuts

Proceedings of the Fourth Conference on Machine Translation (WMT), Volume 1: Research Papers, pages 102–115
Florence, Italy, August 1-2, 2019. ©2019 Association for Computational Linguistics

point, instead of propagating it upwards from the embedding layer along the hidden states.

We evaluate the resulting model's performance on multiple language pairs and varying corpus sizes, showing a consistent improvement in translation quality over the unmodified transformer baseline. Moreover, we examine the distribution of lexical information across the hidden layers of the transformer model in its standard configuration and with added shortcut connections. The presented experiments provide quantitative evidence for the presence of a representation bottleneck in the standard transformer and its reduction following the integration of lexical shortcuts.

While our experimental efforts are centered around the transformer, the proposed components are compatible with other multi-layer NMT architectures.

The contributions of our work are as follows:

1. We propose the use of lexical shortcuts as a simple strategy for alleviating the representation bottleneck in NMT models.

2. We demonstrate significant improvements in translation quality across multiple language pairs as a result of equipping the transformer with lexical shortcut connections.

3. We conduct a series of ablation studies, showing that shortcuts are best applied to the self-attention mechanism in both encoder and decoder.

4. We report a positive impact of our modification on the model's ability to perform word sense disambiguation.

2 Proposed Method

2.1 Background: The transformer

As defined in (Vaswani et al., 2017), the transformer is comprised of two sub-networks, the encoder and the decoder. The encoder converts the received source language sentence into a sequence of continuous representations containing translation-relevant features. The decoder, on the other hand, generates the target language sequence, whereby each translation step is conditioned on the encoder's output as well as the translation prefix produced up to that point.

Both encoder and decoder are composed of a series of identical layers. Each encoder layer contains two sub-layers: A self-attention mechanism

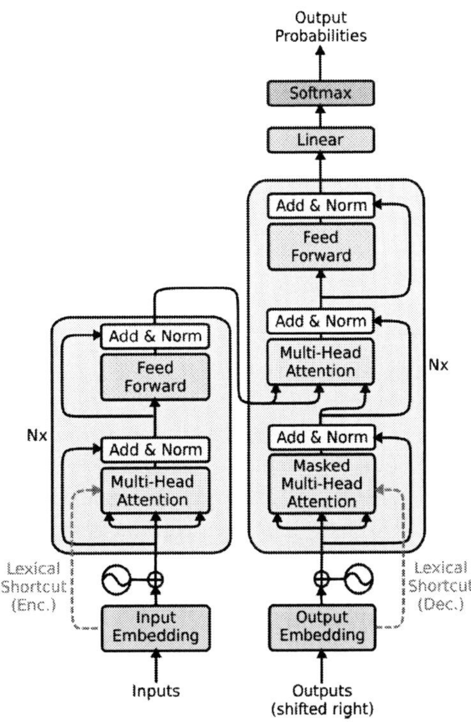

Figure 1: Integration of lexical shortcut connections into the overall transformer architecture.

and a position-wise fully connected feed-forward network. Within the decoder, each layer is extended with a third sub-layer responsible for attending over the encoder's output. In each case, the attention mechanism is implemented as multi-head, scaled dot-product attention, which allows the model to simultaneously consider different context sub-spaces. Additionally, residual connections between layer inputs and outputs are employed to aid with signal propagation.

In order for the dot-product attention mechanism to be effective, its inputs first have to be projected into a common representation sub-space. This is accomplished by multiplying the input arrays H^S and H^T by one of the three weight matrices K, V, and Q, as shown in Eqn. 1-3, producing attention keys, values, and queries, respectively. In case of multi-head attention, each head is assigned its own set of keys, values, and queries with the associated learned projection weights.

$$Q = W^Q H^S \qquad (1)$$
$$K = W^K H^T \qquad (2)$$
$$V = W^V H^T \qquad (3)$$

In case of encoder-to-decoder attention, H^T

corresponds to the final encoder states, whereas H^S is the context vector generated by the preceding self-attention sub-layer. For self-attention, on the other hand, all three operations are given the output of the preceding layer as their input. Eqn. 4 defines attention as a function over the projected representations.

$$Attention(Q, K, V) = \text{softmax}(\frac{QK^T}{\sqrt{d_k}})V \quad (4)$$

To prevent the magnitude of the pre-softmax dot-product from becoming too large, it is divided by the square root of the total key dimensionality d_k. Finally, the translated sequence is obtained by feeding the output of the decoder through a softmax activation function and sampling from the produced distribution over target language tokens.

2.2 Lexical shortcuts

Given that the attention mechanism represents the primary means of establishing parameterized connections between the different layers within the transformer, it is well suited for the re-introduction of lexical content. We achieve this by adding gated connections between the embedding layer and each subsequent self-attention sub-layer within the encoder and the decoder, as shown in Figure 1.

To ensure that lexical features are compatible with the learned hidden representations, the retrieved embeddings are projected into the appropriate latent space, by multiplying them with the layer-specific weight matrices $W_l^{K^{SC}}$ and $W_l^{V^{SC}}$. We account for the potentially variable importance of lexical features by equipping each added connection with a binary gate inspired by the Gated Recurrent Unit (Cho et al., 2014). Functionally, our lexical shortcuts are equivalent to highway connections of (Srivastava et al., 2015) that span an arbitrary number of intermediate layers.

$$K_l^{SC} = W_l^{K^{SC}} E \quad (5)$$
$$V_l^{SC} = W_l^{V^{SC}} E \quad (6)$$
$$K_l = W_l^K H_{l-1} \quad (7)$$
$$V_l = W_l^V H_{l-1} \quad (8)$$

$$r_l^K = \text{sigmoid}(K_l^{SC} + K_l + b_l^K) \quad (9)$$
$$r_l^V = \text{sigmoid}(V_l^{SC} + V_l + b_l^V) \quad (10)$$

$$K_l' = r_l^K \odot K_l^{SC} + (1 - r_l^K) \odot K_l \quad (11)$$
$$V_l' = r_l^V \odot V_l^{SC} + (1 - r_l^V) \odot V_l \quad (12)$$

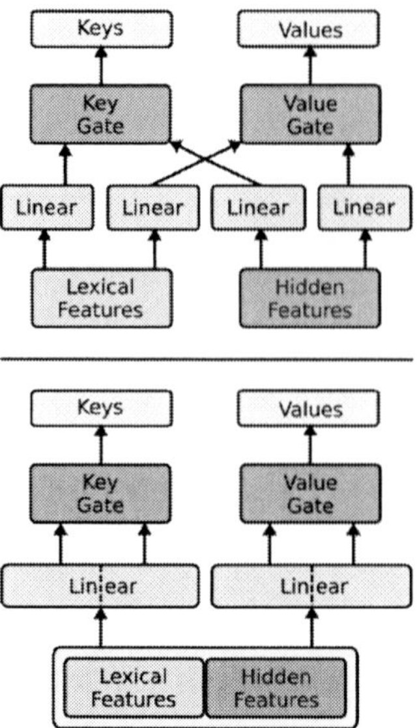

Figure 2: Modified attention inputs. Top: lexical shortcuts, bottom: lexical shortcuts + feature-fusion. Dashed lines denote splits along the feature dimension.

After situating the outputs of the immediately preceding layer H_{l-1} and the embeddings E within a shared representation space (Eqn. 5-8), the relevance of lexical information for the current attention step is estimated by comparing lexical and latent features, followed by the addition of a bias term b (Eqn. 9-10). The respective attention key arrays are denoted as K_l^{SC} and K_l, while V_l^{SC} and V_l represent the corresponding value arrays. The result is fed through a sigmoid function to obtain the lexical relevance weight r, used to calculate the weighted sum of the two sets of features (Eqn. 11-12), where $\odot$ denotes element-wise multiplication. Next, the key and value arrays K_l' and V_l' are passed to the multi-head attention function as defined in Eqn. 4, replacing the original K_l and V_l.

In an alternative formulation of the model, referred to as 'feature-fusion' from here on, we concatenate E and H_{l-1} before the initial linear projection, splitting the result in two halves along the feature dimension and leaving the rest of the shortcut definition unchanged[2]. This reduces Eqn. 5-8 to Eqn. 13-14, and enables the model to select relevant information by directly inter-relating lexical and hidden features. As such, both K_l^{SC} and K_l encode a mixture of embedding and hid-

---

[2]The feature-fusion mechanism is therefore based on the same principle as the Gated Linear Unit (Dauphin et al., 2017), while utilizing a more expressive gating function.

den features, as do the corresponding value arrays. While this arguably diminishes the contribution of the gating mechanism towards feature selection, preliminary experiments have shown that replacing gated shortcuts with gate-less residual connections (He et al., 2016) produces models that fail to converge, characterized by poor training and validation performance. For illustration purposes, figure 2 depicts the modified computation path of the lexically-enriched attention key and value vectors.

$$K_l^{SC}, K_l = W_l^K[E; H_{l-1}] \qquad (13)$$

$$V_l^{SC}, V_l = W_l^V[E; H_{l-1}] \qquad (14)$$

Other than the immediate accessibility of lexical information, one potential benefit afforded by the introduced shortcuts is the improved gradient flow during back-propagation. As noted in (Huang et al., 2017), the addition of skip connections between individual layers of a deep neural network results in an implicit 'deep supervision' effect (Lee et al., 2015), which aids the training process. In case of our modified transformer, this corresponds to the embedding layer receiving its learning signal from the model's overall optimization objective as well as from each layer it is connected to, making the model easier to train.

3 Experiments

3.1 Training

To evaluate the efficacy of the proposed approach, we re-implement the transformer model and extend it by applying lexical shortcuts to each self-attention layer in the encoder and decoder. A detailed account of our model configurations, data pre-processing steps, and training setup is given in the appendix (A.1-A.2).

3.2 Data

We investigate the potential benefits of lexical shortcuts on 5 WMT translation tasks: German → English (DE→EN), English → German (EN→DE), English → Russian (EN→RU), English → Czech (EN→CS), and English → Finnish (EN→FI). Our choice is motivated by the differences in size of the training corpora as well as by the typological diversity of the target languages.

To make our findings comparable to related work, we train EN↔DE models on the WMT14 news translation data which encompasses ∼4.5M sentence pairs. EN→RU models are trained on the WMT17 version of the news translation task, consisting of ∼24.8M sentence pairs. For EN→CS and EN→FI, we use the respective WMT18 parallel training corpora, with the former containing ∼50.4M and the latter ∼3.2M sentence pairs. We do not employ backtranslated data in any of our experiments to further facilitate comparisons to existing work.

Throughout training, model performance is validated on newstest2013 for EN↔DE, newstest2016 for EN→RU, and on newstest2017 for EN→CS and EN→FI. Final model performance is reported on multiple tests sets from the news domain for each direction.

3.3 Translation performance

The results of our translation experiments are summarized in Tables 1-2. To ensure their comparability, we evaluate translation quality using sacreBLEU (Post, 2018). As such, our baseline performance diverges from that reported in (Vaswani et al., 2017). We address this by evaluating our EN→DE models using the scoring script from the tensor2tensor toolkit[3] (Vaswani et al., 2018) on the tokenized model output, and list the corresponding BLEU scores in the first column of Table 1.

Our evaluation shows that the introduction of lexical shortcuts consistently improves translation quality of the transformer model across different test-sets and language pairs, outperforming transformer-BASE by 0.5 BLEU on average. With feature-fusion, we see even stronger improvements, yielding total performance gains over transformer-BASE of up to 1.4 BLEU for EN→DE (averaging to 1.0), and 0.8 BLEU on average for the other 4 translation directions. We furthermore observe that the relative improvements from the addition of lexical shortcuts are substantially smaller for transformer-BIG compared to transformer-BASE. One potential explanation for this drop in efficacy is the increased size of latent representations the wider model is able to learn, which we discuss in section 4.1.

Furthermore, it is worth noting that transformer-BASE equipped with lexical connections performs comparably to the standard transformer-BIG, despite containing fewer than half of its parameters and being only marginally slower to train than our unmodified transformer-BASE implementa-

---

[3]`https://github.com/tensorflow/tensor2tensor/blob/master/\tensor2tensor/utils/get_ende_bleu.sh`

Model	newstest2014 (tokenized BLEU)	sacreBLEU					
		newstest 2014	newstest 2015	newstest 2016	newstest 2017	newstest 2018	test mean
transformer-BASE	27.3	25.8	28.5	33.2	27.3	40.4	31.0
+ lexical shortcuts	27.6	26.1	29.5	33.3	27.5	41.1	31.5
+ feature-fusion	**28.3**	**26.8**	**29.9**	**34.0**	**27.7**	**41.6**	**32.0**
transformer-BIG	28.7	27.2	30.1	**34.0**	28.1	41.3	32.1
+ lexical shortcuts + feature-fusion	**29.4**	**27.8**	**30.3**	33.2	**28.4**	41.3	**32.2**

Table 1: BLEU scores for the EN→DE news translation task.

Model	DE→EN		EN→RU		EN→CS		EN→FI	
	newstest 2014	newstest 2017	newstest 2017	newstest 2018	newstest 2015	newstest 2018	newstest 2015	newstest 2018
transformer-BASE	31.1	32.3	27.9	24.2	23.4	21.1	18.7	14.0
+ lexical shortcuts	31.3	32.3	28.4	24.9	24.1	21.4	19.5	14.5
+ feature-fusion	**31.7**	**32.9**	**28.9**	**25.3**	**24.3**	**21.6**	**19.8**	**14.8**

Table 2: Effect of lexical shortcuts on translation quality for different language pairs, as measured by sacreBLEU.

tion. A detailed overview of model sizes and training speed is provided in the supplementary material (A.1).

Concerning the examined language pairs, the average increase in BLEU is highest for EN→RU (1.1 BLEU) and lowest for DE→EN (0.6 BLEU). A potential explanation for why this is the case could be the difference in language topology. Of all target languages we consider, English has the least complex morphological system where individual words carry little inflectional information, which stands in stark contrast to a highly inflectional language with a flexible word order such as Russian. It is plausible that lexical shortcuts are especially important for translation directions where the target language is morphologically rich and where the surrounding context is essential to accurately predicting a word's case and agreement. With the proposed shortcuts in place, the transformer has more capacity for modeling such context information.

To investigate the role of lexical connections within the transformer, we conduct a thorough examination of our models' internal representations and learning behaviour. The following analysis is based on models utilizing lexical shortcuts with feature-fusion, due to its superior performance.

4 Analysis

4.1 Representation bottleneck

The proposed approach is motivated by the hypothesis that the transformer retains lexical features within its individual layers, which limits its capacity for learning and representing other types of relevant information. Direct connections to the embedding layer alleviate this by providing the model with access to lexical features at each processing step, reducing the need for propagating them along hidden states. To investigate whether this is indeed the case, we perform a probing study, where we estimate the amount of lexical content present within each encoder and decoder state.

We examine the internal representations learned by our models by modifying the probing technique introduced in (Belinkov et al., 2017). Specifically, we train a separate lexical classifier for each layer of a frozen translation model. Each classifier receives hidden states extracted from the respective transformer layer[4] and is tasked with reconstructing the sub-word corresponding to the position of each hidden state. Encoder-specific classifiers learn to reconstruct sub-words in the source sen-

---

[4]We treat the output of the feed-forward sub-layer as that layer's hidden state.

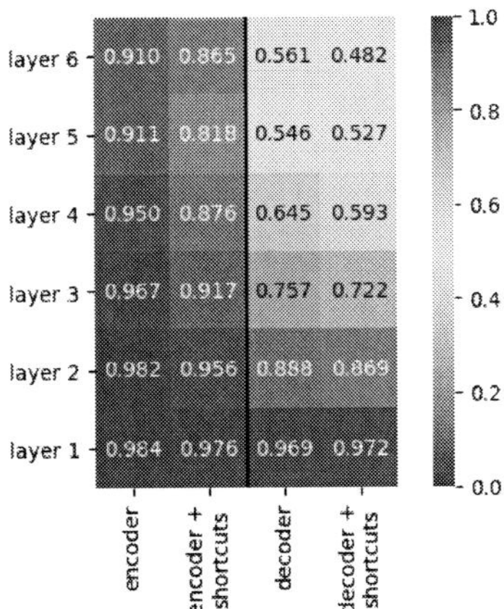

Figure 3: Layer-wise lexical probe accuracy measured on transformer-BASE for EN→DE (newstest2014).

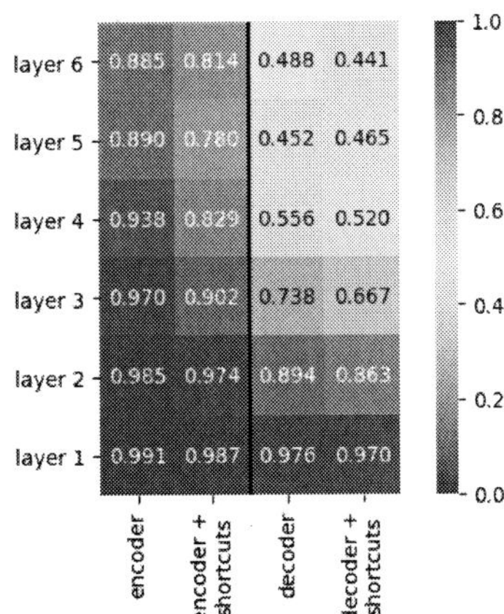

Figure 4: Layer-wise lexical probe accuracy measured on transformer-BASE for EN→RU (newstest2017).

tence, whereas classifiers trained on decoder states are trained to reconstruct target sub-words.

The accuracy of each layer-specific classifier on a withheld test set is assumed to be indicative of the lexical content encoded by the corresponding transformer layer. We expect classification accuracy to be high if the evaluated representations predominantly store information propagated upwards from the embeddings at the same position and to decrease proportionally to the amount of information drawn from the surrounding sentence context. Figures 3 and 4 offer a side-by-side comparison of the accuracy scores obtained for each layer of the base transformer and its variant equipped with lexical shortcut connections.

Based on the observed classification results, it appears that immediate access to lexical information does indeed alleviate the representation bottleneck by reducing the extent to which (sub-)word-level content is retained across encoder and decoder layers. By introducing shortcut connections, we effectively reduce the amount of lexical information the model retains within its intermediate states, thereby increasing its capacity for exploiting sentence context. The effect is consistent across multiple language pairs, supporting its generality. Additionally, to examine whether lexical retention depends on the specific properties of the input tokens, we track classification accuracy conditioned on part-of-speech tags and sub-word frequencies. While we do not discover a pronounced effect of either category on classification accuracy, we present a summary of our findings as part of the supplementary material for future reference (A.3).

Another observation arising from the probing

analysis is that the decoder retains fewer lexical features beyond its initial layers than the encoder. This may be due to the decoder having to represent information it receives from the encoder in addition to target-side content, necessitating a lower rate of lexical feature retention. Even so, by adding shortcut connections we can increase the dissimilarity between the embedding layer and the subsequent layers of the decoder, indicating a noticeable reduction in the retention and propagation of lexical features along the decoder's hidden states.

A similar trend can be observed when evaluating layer similarity directly, which we accomplish by calculating the cosine similarity between the embeddings and the hidden states of each transformer layer. Echoing our findings so far, the addition of lexical shortcuts reduces layer similarity relative to the baseline transformer for both encoder and decoder. The corresponding visualizations are also provided in the appendix (A.3).

Overall, the presented analysis supports the existence of a representation bottleneck in NMT models as one potential explanation for the efficacy of the proposed lexical shortcut connections.

Model	newstest 2017	newstest 2018	test mean
transformer-SMALL	25.2	37.0	28.6
+ lexical shortcuts	25.7	38.0	29.3
+ feature-fusion	**25.7**	**38.5**	**29.6**

Table 3: sacreBLEU scores for small EN→DE models; 'test mean' denotes the average of test-sets in table (1).

4.2 Model size

Next, we investigate the interaction between the number of model parameters and improvements in translation quality afforded by the proposed lexical connections. Following up on findings presented in section 3.1, we hypothesize that the benefit of lexical shortcuts diminishes once the model's capacity is sufficiently large. To establish whether this decline in effectiveness is gradual, we scale down the standard transformer, halving the size of its embeddings, hidden states, and feed-forward sub-layers. Table 3 shows that, on average, quality improvements are comparable for the small and standard transformer (1.0 BLEU for both), which is in contrast to our observations for transformer-BIG. One explanation is that given sufficient capacity, the model is capable of accommodating the upward propagation of lexical features without having to neglect other sources of information. However, as long as the model's representational capacity is within certain limits, the effect of lexical shortcuts remains comparable across a range of model sizes. With this in mind, the exact interaction between model scale and the types of information encoded in its hidden states remains to be fully explored. We leave a more fine-grained examination of this relationship to future research.

4.3 Shortcut variants

Until now, we focused on applying shortcuts to self-attention as a natural re-entry point for lexical content. However, previous studies suggest that providing the decoder with direct access to source sentences can improve translation adequacy, by conditioning decoding on relevant source tokens (Kuang et al., 2017; Nguyen and Chiang, 2017).

To investigate whether the proposed method can confer a similar benefit to the transformer, we apply lexical shortcuts to decoder-to-encoder attention, replacing or adding to shortcuts feeding into self-attention. Formally, this equates to fixing E to E^{enc} in Eqn. 5-6 and can be regarded as a variant of source-side bridging proposed by (Kuang et al., 2017). As Table 4 shows, while integrating shortcut connections into the decoder-to-encoder attention improves upon the base transformer, the improvement is smaller than when we modify self-attention. Interestingly, combining both methods yields worse translation quality than either one does in isolation, indicating that the decoder is un-

Model	newstest 2017	newstest 2018	test mean
transformer-BASE	27.3	40.4	31.0
+ self-attn. shortcuts	**27.7**	**41.6**	**32.0**
dec-to-enc shortcuts	27.6	40.7	31.5
+ self-attn. shortcuts	27.7	40.5	31.4
non-lexical shortcuts	27.1	40.6	31.3

Table 4: sacreBLEU for shortcut variants of EN→DE models; 'test mean' averages over test-sets in table (1).

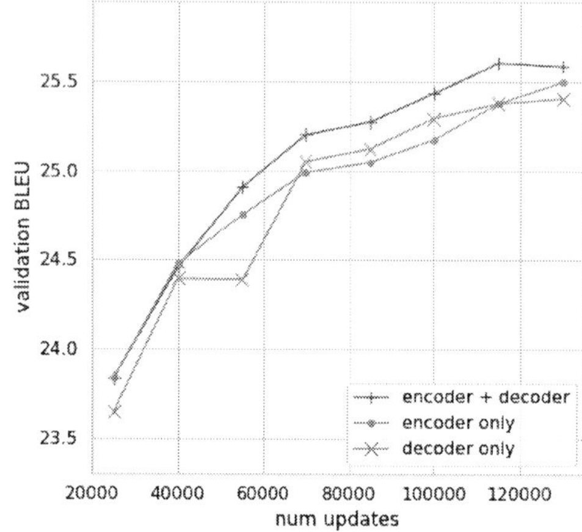

Figure 5: Effect of disabling shortcuts in either sub-network on validation BLEU.

able to effectively consolidate information from both source and target embeddings, which negatively impacts its learned latent representations. We therefore conclude that lexical shortcuts are most beneficial to self-attention.

A related question is whether the encoder and decoder benefit from the addition of lexical shortcuts to self-attention equally. We explore this by disabling shortcuts in either sub-network and comparing the so obtained translation models to one with intact connections. Figure 5 illustrates that best translation performance is obtained by enabling shortcuts in both encoder and decoder. This also improves training stability, as compared to the decoder-only ablated model. The latter may be explained by our use of tied embeddings which receive a stronger training signal from shortcut connections due to 'deep supervision', as this may bias learned embeddings against the sub-network lacking improved lexical connectivity.

While adding shortcuts improves translation

quality, it is not obvious whether this is predominantly due to improved accessibility of lexical content, rather than increased connectivity between network layers, as suggested in (Dou et al., 2018). To isolate the importance of lexical information, we equip the transformer with non-lexical shortcuts connecting each layer n to layer $n-2$, e.g. layer 6 to layer 4.[5] As a result, the number of added connections and parameters is kept identical to lexical shortcuts, whereas lexical accessibility is disabled, allowing for minimal comparison between the two configurations. Test-BLEU reported in Table 4 suggests that while non-lexical shortcuts improve over the baseline model, they perform noticeably worse than lexical connections. Therefore, the increase in translation quality associated with lexical shortcuts is not solely attributable to a better signal flow or the increased number of trainable parameters.

4.4 Word-sense disambiguation

Beyond the effects of lexical shortcuts on the transformer's learning dynamics, we are interested in how widening the representation bottleneck affects the properties of the produced translations. One challenging problem in translation which intuitively should benefit from the model's increased capacity for learning information drawn from sentence context is word-sense disambiguation.

We examine whether the addition of lexical shortcuts aids disambiguation by evaluating our trained DE→EN models on the *ContraWSD* corpus (Rios et al., 2017). The contrastive dataset is constructed by paring source sentences with multiple translations, varying the translated sense of selected source nouns between translation candidates. A competent model is expected to assign a higher probability to the translation hypothesis containing the appropriate word-sense.

While the standard transformer offers a strong baseline for the disambiguation task, we nonetheless observe improvements after adding direct connections to the embedding layers. Specifically, our baseline model reaches an accuracy of 88.8%, which improves to 89.5% with lexical shortcuts.

5 Related Work

Within recent literature, several strategies for altering the flow of information within the transformer

have been proposed, including adaptive model depth (Dehghani et al., 2018), layer-wise transparent attention (Bapna et al., 2018), and dense inter-layer connections (Dou et al., 2018). Our investigation bears strongest resemblance to the latter work, by introducing additional connectivity to the model. However, rather than establishing new connections between layers indiscriminately, we explicitly seek to facilitate the accessibility of lexical features across network layers. As a result, our proposed shortcuts remain sparse, while performing comparably to their best, more elaborate strategies that rely on multi-layer attention and hierarchical state aggregation.

Likewise, studies investigating the role of lexical features in NMT are highly relevant to our work. Among them, (Nguyen and Chiang, 2017) note that improving accessibility of source words in the decoder benefits translation quality for low-resource settings. In a similar vein, (Wu et al., 2018) attend both encoder hidden states and source embeddings as part of decoder-to-encoder attention, while (Kuang et al., 2017) provide the decoder-to-encoder attention mechanism with improved access to source word representations. We have found a variant of the latter method, which we adapted to the Transformer architecture, to be less effective than applying lexical shortcuts to self-attention, as discussed in section 4.3.

Another line of research from which we draw inspiration concerns itself with the analysis of the internal dynamics and learned representations within deep neural networks (Karpathy et al., 2015; Shi et al., 2016; Qian et al., 2016). Here, (Belinkov et al., 2017) and (Belinkov et al., 2018) serve as our primary points of reference by offering a thorough and principled investigation of the extent to which neural translation models are capable of learning linguistic properties from raw text.

Our view of the transformer as a model learning to refine input representations through the repeated application of attention is consistent with the iterative estimation paradigm introduced in (Greff et al., 2016). According to this interpretation, given a stack of connected layers sharing the same dimensionality and interlinked through highway or residual connections, the initial layer generates a rough version of the stack's final output, which is iteratively refined by successive layers, e.g. by enriching localized features with information drawn from the surrounding context. The re-

---

[5]The first layer is connected to the embedding layer, as there is no further antecedent.

sults of our probing studies support this analysis, further suggesting that different layers not only refine input features but also learn entirely new information given sufficient capacity, as evidenced by the decrease in similarity between embeddings and hidden states with increasing model depth.

6 Conclusion

In this paper, we have proposed a simple yet effective method for widening the representation bottleneck in the transformer by introducing lexical shortcuts. Our modified models achieve up to 1.4 BLEU (0.9 BLEU on average) improvement on 5 standard WMT datasets, at a small cost in computing time and model size. Our analysis suggests that lexical connections are useful to both encoder and decoder, and remain effective when included in smaller models. Moreover, the addition of shortcuts noticeably reduces the similarity of hidden states to the initial embeddings, indicating that dynamic lexical access aids the network in learning novel, diverse information. We also performed ablation studies comparing different shortcut variants and demonstrated that one effect of lexical shortcuts is an improved WSD capability.

The presented findings offer new insights into the nature of information encoded by the transformer layers, supporting the iterative refinement view of feature learning. In future work, we intend to explore other ways to better our understanding of the refinement process and to help translation models learn more diverse and meaningful internal representations.

7 Acknowledgments

Ivan Titov is supported by the European Union's Horizon 2020 research and innovation programme under grant agreement No 825299 (GoURMET). Computing resources were provided by the Alan Turing Institute under the EPSRCgrant EP/N510129/1.

References

Ankur Bapna, Mia Xu Chen, Orhan Firat, Yuan Cao, and Yonghui Wu. 2018. Training deeper neural machine translation models with transparent attention. *arXiv preprint arXiv:1808.07561*.

Yonatan Belinkov, Nadir Durrani, Fahim Dalvi, Hassan Sajjad, and James Glass. 2017. What do neural machine translation models learn about morphology? *arXiv preprint arXiv:1704.03471*.

Yonatan Belinkov, Lluís Màrquez, Hassan Sajjad, Nadir Durrani, Fahim Dalvi, and James Glass. 2018. Evaluating layers of representation in neural machine translation on part-of-speech and semantic tagging tasks. *arXiv preprint arXiv:1801.07772*.

Ondej Bojar, Christian Federmann, Mark Fishel, Yvette Graham, Barry Haddow, Matthias Huck, Philipp Koehn, and Christof Monz. 2018. Findings of the 2018 conference on machine translation (wmt18). In *Proceedings of the Third Conference on Machine Translation*, pages 272–307, Belgium, Brussels. Association for Computational Linguistics.

Mia Xu Chen, Orhan Firat, Ankur Bapna, Melvin Johnson, Wolfgang Macherey, George Foster, Llion Jones, Niki Parmar, Mike Schuster, Zhifeng Chen, et al. 2018. The best of both worlds: Combining recent advances in neural machine translation. *arXiv preprint arXiv:1804.09849*.

Kyunghyun Cho, Bart Van Merriënboer, Caglar Gulcehre, Dzmitry Bahdanau, Fethi Bougares, Holger Schwenk, and Yoshua Bengio. 2014. Learning phrase representations using rnn encoder-decoder for statistical machine translation. *arXiv preprint arXiv:1406.1078*.

Yann N Dauphin, Angela Fan, Michael Auli, and David Grangier. 2017. Language modeling with gated convolutional networks. In *Proceedings of the 34th International Conference on Machine Learning-Volume 70*, pages 933–941. JMLR. org.

Mostafa Dehghani, Stephan Gouws, Oriol Vinyals, Jakob Uszkoreit, and Łukasz Kaiser. 2018. Universal transformers. *arXiv preprint arXiv:1807.03819*.

Zi-Yi Dou, Zhaopeng Tu, Xing Wang, Shuming Shi, and Tong Zhang. 2018. Exploiting deep representations for neural machine translation. *arXiv preprint arXiv:1810.10181*.

Klaus Greff, Rupesh K Srivastava, and Jürgen Schmidhuber. 2016. Highway and residual networks learn unrolled iterative estimation. *arXiv preprint arXiv:1612.07771*.

Barry Haddow, Nikolay Bogoychev, Denis Emelin, Ulrich Germann, Roman Grundkiewicz, Kenneth Heafield, Antonio Valerio Miceli Barone, and Rico Sennrich. 2018. The university of edinburghs submissions to the wmt18 news translation task. In *Proceedings of the Third Conference on Machine Translation*, pages 403–413, Belgium, Brussels. Association for Computational Linguistics.

Kaiming He, Xiangyu Zhang, Shaoqing Ren, and Jian Sun. 2016. Deep residual learning for image recognition. In *Proceedings of the IEEE conference on computer vision and pattern recognition*, pages 770–778.

Gao Huang, Zhuang Liu, Laurens Van Der Maaten, and Kilian Q Weinberger. 2017. Densely connected convolutional networks. In *CVPR*, 2, page 3.

Andrej Karpathy, Justin Johnson, and Li Fei-Fei. 2015. Visualizing and understanding recurrent networks. *arXiv preprint arXiv:1506.02078*.

Diederik P Kingma and Jimmy Ba. 2014. Adam: A method for stochastic optimization. *arXiv preprint arXiv:1412.6980*.

Shaohui Kuang, Junhui Li, António Branco, Weihua Luo, and Deyi Xiong. 2017. Attention focusing for neural machine translation by bridging source and target embeddings. *arXiv preprint arXiv:1711.05380*.

Chen-Yu Lee, Saining Xie, Patrick Gallagher, Zhengyou Zhang, and Zhuowen Tu. 2015. Deeply-supervised nets. In *Artificial Intelligence and Statistics*, pages 562–570.

Toan Q Nguyen and David Chiang. 2017. Improving lexical choice in neural machine translation. *arXiv preprint arXiv:1710.01329*.

Matt Post. 2018. A call for clarity in reporting bleu scores. *arXiv preprint arXiv:1804.08771*.

Ofir Press and Lior Wolf. 2016. Using the output embedding to improve language models. *arXiv preprint arXiv:1608.05859*.

Peng Qian, Xipeng Qiu, and Xuanjing Huang. 2016. Analyzing linguistic knowledge in sequential model of sentence. In *Proceedings of the 2016 Conference on Empirical Methods in Natural Language Processing*, pages 826–835.

Annette Rios, Laura Mascarell, and Rico Sennrich. 2017. Improving word sense disambiguation in neural machine translation with sense embeddings. In *Proceedings of the 2nd Conference on Machine Translation, Copenhagen, Denmark*.

Danielle Saunders, Felix Stahlberg, Adria de Gispert, and Bill Byrne. 2018. Multi-representation ensembles and delayed sgd updates improve syntax-based nmt. *arXiv preprint arXiv:1805.00456*.

Helmut Schmid. 1999. Improvements in part-of-speech tagging with an application to german. In *Natural language processing using very large corpora*, pages 13–25. Springer.

Rico Sennrich, Barry Haddow, and Alexandra Birch. 2015. Neural machine translation of rare words with subword units. *arXiv preprint arXiv:1508.07909*.

Xing Shi, Inkit Padhi, and Kevin Knight. 2016. Does string-based neural mt learn source syntax? In *Proceedings of the 2016 Conference on Empirical Methods in Natural Language Processing*, pages 1526–1534.

Nitish Srivastava, Geoffrey Hinton, Alex Krizhevsky, Ilya Sutskever, and Ruslan Salakhutdinov. 2014. Dropout: a simple way to prevent neural networks from overfitting. *The Journal of Machine Learning Research*, 15(1):1929–1958.

Rupesh Kumar Srivastava, Klaus Greff, and Jürgen Schmidhuber. 2015. Highway networks. *arXiv preprint arXiv:1505.00387*.

Gongbo Tang, Mathias Müller, Annette Rios, and Rico Sennrich. 2018. Why self-attention? a targeted evaluation of neural machine translation architectures. *arXiv preprint arXiv:1808.08946*.

Ashish Vaswani, Samy Bengio, Eugene Brevdo, Francois Chollet, Aidan N Gomez, Stephan Gouws, Llion Jones, Łukasz Kaiser, Nal Kalchbrenner, Niki Parmar, et al. 2018. Tensor2tensor for neural machine translation. *arXiv preprint arXiv:1803.07416*.

Ashish Vaswani, Noam Shazeer, Niki Parmar, Jakob Uszkoreit, Llion Jones, Aidan N Gomez, Łukasz Kaiser, and Illia Polosukhin. 2017. Attention is all you need. In *Advances in Neural Information Processing Systems*, pages 5998–6008.

Lijun Wu, Fei Tian, Li Zhao, Jianhuang Lai, and Tie-Yan Liu. 2018. Word attention for sequence to sequence text understanding. In *Thirty-Second AAAI Conference on Artificial Intelligence*.

A Supplementary Material

A.1 Training details

The majority of our experiments is conducted using the transformer-BASE configuration, with the number of encoder and decoder layers set to 6 each, embedding and attention dimensionality to 512, number of attention heads to 8, and feed-forward sub-layer dimensionality to 2048. We tie the encoder embedding table with the decoder embedding table and the pre-softmax projection matrix to speed up training, following (Press and Wolf, 2016). All trained models are optimized using Adam (Kingma and Ba, 2014) adhering to the learning rate schedule described in (Vaswani et al., 2017). We set the number of warm-up steps to 4000 for the baseline model, increasing it to 6000 and 8000 when adding lexical shortcuts and feature-fusion, respectively, so as to accommodate the increase in parameter size.

We also evaluate the effect of lexical shortcuts on the larger transformer-BIG model, limiting this set of experiments to EN→DE due to computational constraints. Here, the baseline model employs 16 attention heads, with attention, embedding, and feed-forward dimensions doubled to 1024, 1024, and 4096. Warm-up period for all big models is 16,000 steps. For our probing experiments, the classifiers used are simple feed-forward networks with a single hidden layer consisting of 512 units, dropout (Srivastava et al., 2014) with p = 0.5, and a ReLU non-linearity. In all presented experiments, we employ beam search during decoding, with beam size set to 16.

Model	# Parameters	Words / sec.
transformer-BASE	65,166K	29,698
+ lexical shortcuts	71,470K	26,423
+ feature-fusion	84,053K	23,601
transformer-BIG	218,413K	10,215
+ feature-fusion	293,935K	6,769

Table 5: Model size and training speed of the compared transformer variants.

All models are trained concurrently on four Nvidia P100 Tesla GPUs using synchronous data parallelization. Delayed optimization (Saunders et al., 2018) is employed to simulate batch sizes of 25,000 tokens, to be consistent with (Vaswani et al., 2017). Each transformer-BASE model is trained for a total of 150,000 updates, while our transformer-BIG experiments are stopped after 300,000 updates. Validation is performed every 4000 steps, as is check-pointing. Training base models takes ∼43 hours, while the addition of shortcut connections increases training time up to ∼46 hours (∼50 hours with feature-fusion). Table 5 details the differences in parameter size and training speed for the different transformer configurations. Parameters are given in thousands, while speed is averaged over the entire training duration.

Validation-BLEU is calculated using multi-bleu-detok.pl[6] on a reference which we pre- and post-process following the same steps as for the models' inputs and outputs. All reported test-BLEU scores were obtained by averaging the final 5 checkpoints for transformer-BASE and final 16 for transformer-BIG.

A.2 Data pre-processing

We tokenize, clean, and truecase each training corpus using scripts from the Moses toolkit[7], and apply byte-pair encoding (Sennrich et al., 2015) to counteract the open vocabulary issue. Cleaning is skipped for validation and test sets. For EN↔DE and EN→RU we limit the number of BPE merge operations to 32,000 and set the vocabulary threshold to 50. For EN→CS and EN→FI, the number of merge operations is set to 89,500 with a vocabulary threshold of 50, following (Haddow et al., 2018)[8]. In each case, the BPE vocabulary is learned jointly over the source and target language, which necessitated an additional transliteration step for the pre-processing of Russian data[9].

A.3 Probing studies

Cosine similarity scores between the embedding layer and each successive layer in transformer-BASE and its variant equipped with lexical shortcuts are summarized in Figures 6-7.

For our fine-grained probing studies, we evaluated classification accuracy conditioned of part-of-speech tags and sub-word frequencies. For the former, we first parse our test-sets with TreeTag-

---

[6]https://github.com/moses-smt/
mosesdecoder/blob/master/scripts/
generic/multi-bleu-detok.perl

[7]https://github.com/moses-smt/
mosesdecoder

[8]We do not use synthetic data, which makes our results not directly comparable to theirs.

[9]We used 'Lingua Translit' for this purpose: https://metacpan.org/release/Lingua-Translit

ger (Schmid, 1999), projecting tags onto the constituent sub-words of each annotated word. For frequency-based evaluation, we divide sub-words into ten equally-sized frequency bins, with bin 1 containing the least frequent sub-words and bin 10 containing the most frequent ones. We do not observe any immediately obvious, significant effects of either POS or frequency on the retention of lexical features. While classification accuracy is notably low for infrequent sub-words, this can be attributed to the limited occurrence of the corresponding transformer states in the classifier's training data. Evaluation for EN→DE models is done on newstest2014, while newstest2017 is used for EN→RU models. Figures 8-15 present results for the frequency-based classification. Accuracy scores conditioned on POS tags are visualized in Figures 16-23.

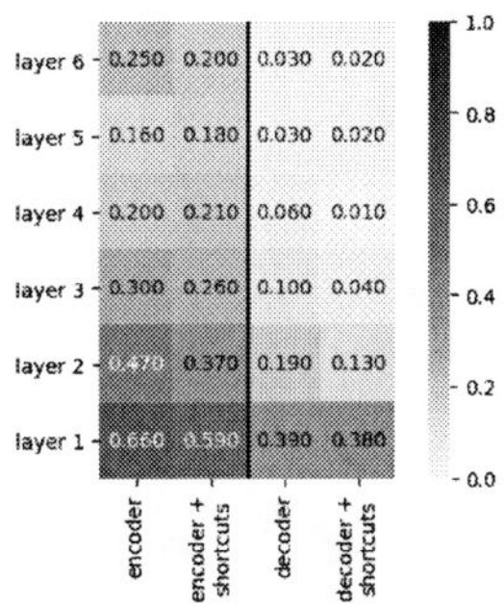

Figure 6: Cosine similarity measured on transformer-BASE for EN→DE (newstest2014).

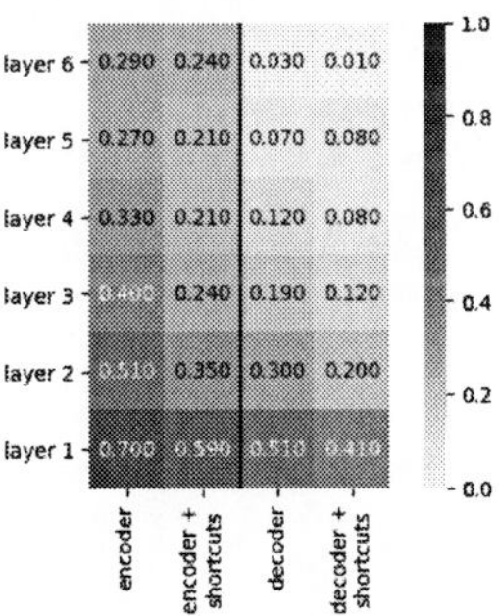

Figure 7: Cosine similarity measured on transformer-BASE for EN→RU (newstest2017).

We also investigated the activation patterns of the lexical shortcut gates. However, despite their essential status for the successful training of transformer variants equipped with lexical connections, we were unable to discern any distinct patterns in the activations of the individual gates, which tend to prioritize lexical and hidden features to an equal degree regardless of training progress or (sub-)word characteristics.

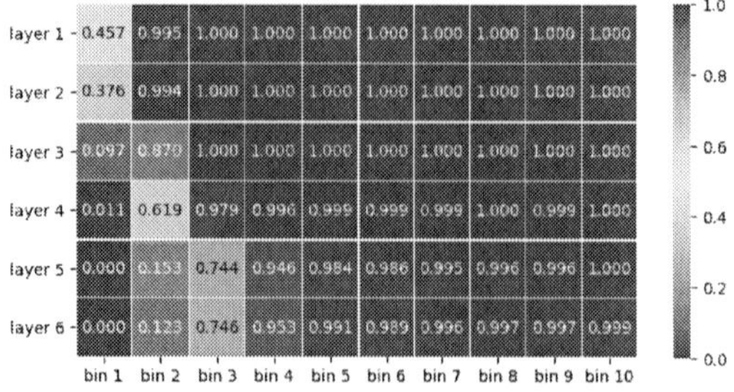

Figure 8: Frequency-based classification accuracy on states from the EN→DE encoder.

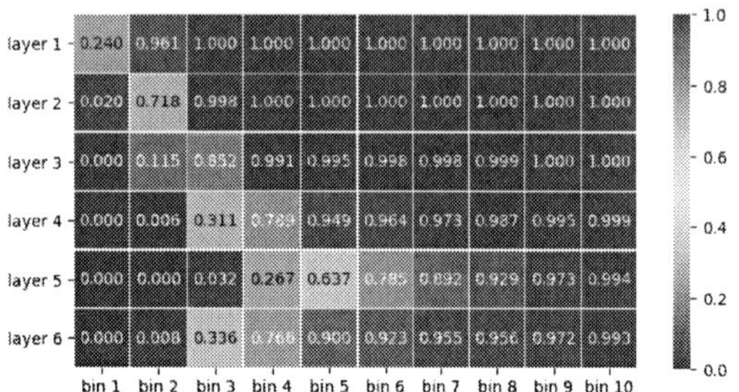

Figure 9: Frequency-based classification accuracy on states from the EN→DE encoder + lexical shortcuts.

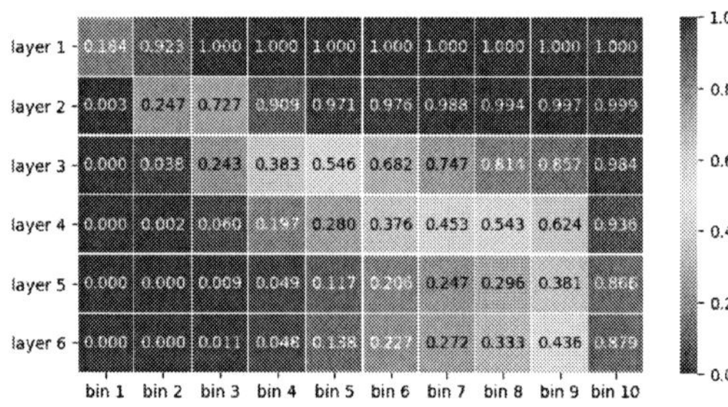

Figure 10: Frequency-based classification accuracy on states from the EN→DE decoder.

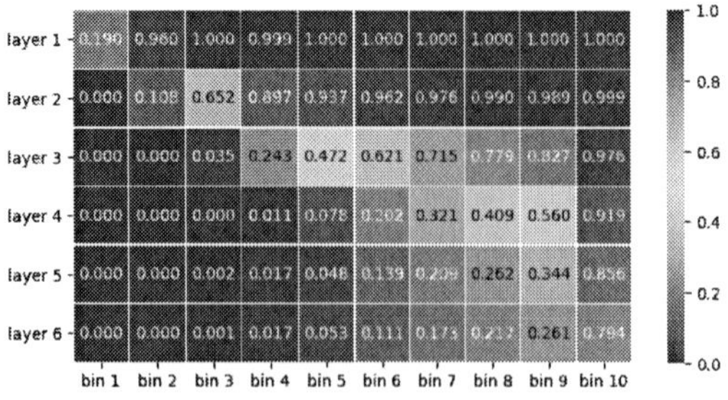

Figure 11: Frequency-based classification accuracy on states from the EN→DE decoder + lexical shortcuts.

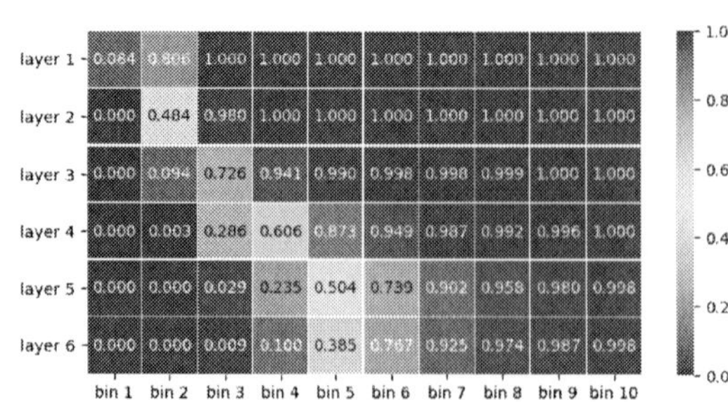

Figure 12: Frequency-based classification accuracy on states from the EN→RU encoder.

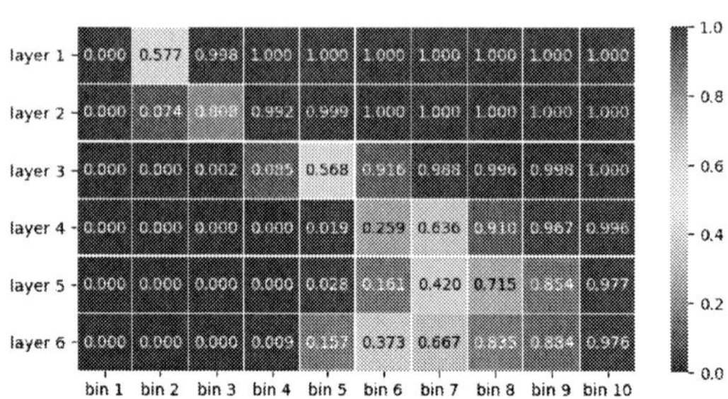

Figure 13: Frequency-based classification accuracy on states from the EN→RU encoder + lexical shortcuts.

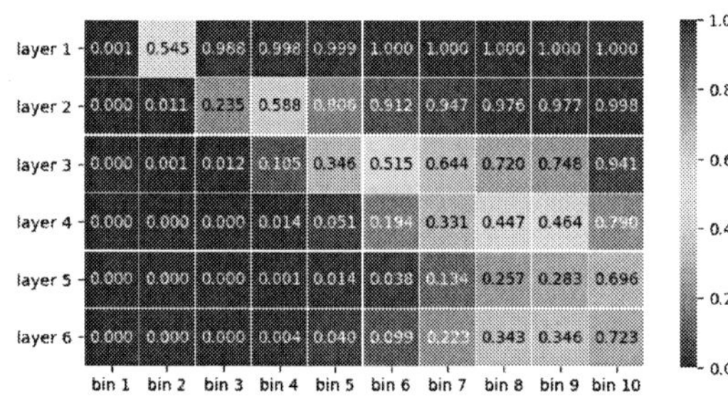

Figure 14: Frequency-based classification accuracy on states from the EN→RU decoder.

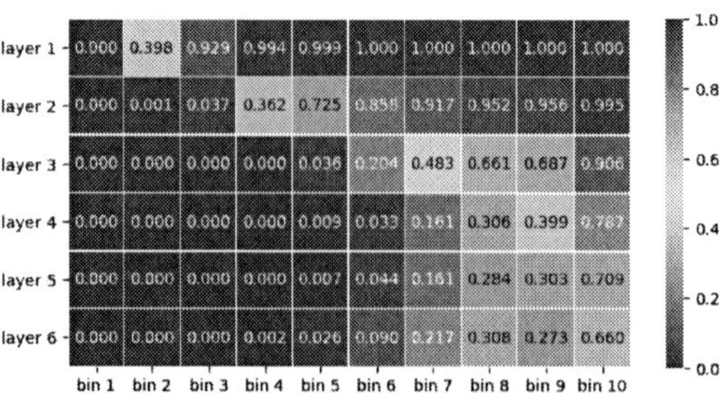

Figure 15: Frequency-based classification accuracy on states from the EN→RU decoder + lexical shortcuts.

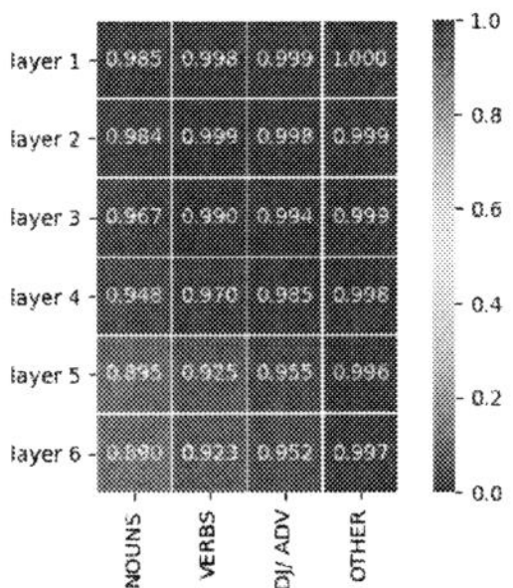

Figure 16: POS-based classification accuracy on states from the EN→DE encoder.

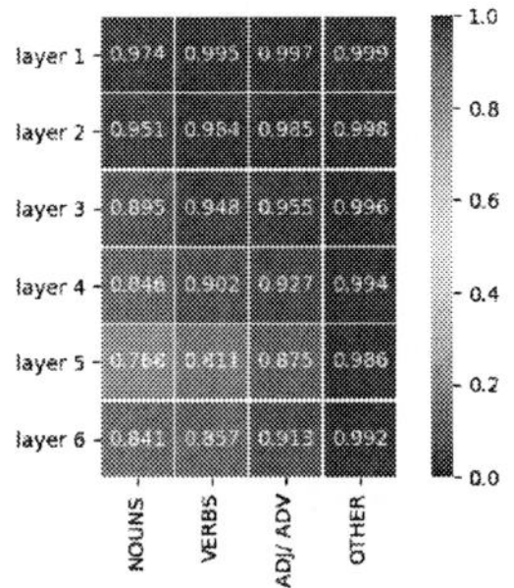

Figure 17: POS-based classification accuracy on states from the EN→DE encoder + lexical shortcuts.

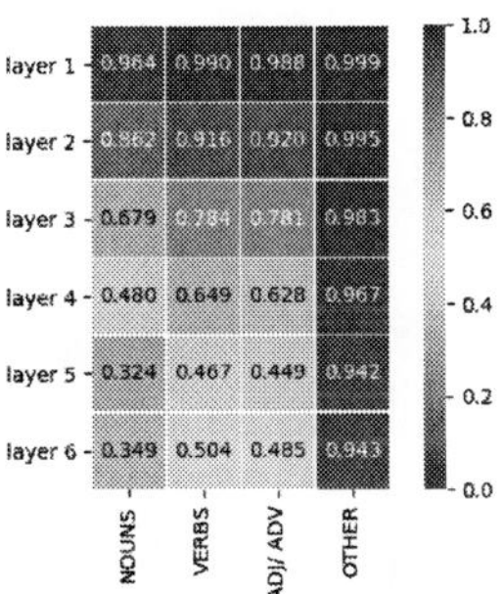

Figure 18: POS-based classification accuracy on states from the EN→DE decoder.

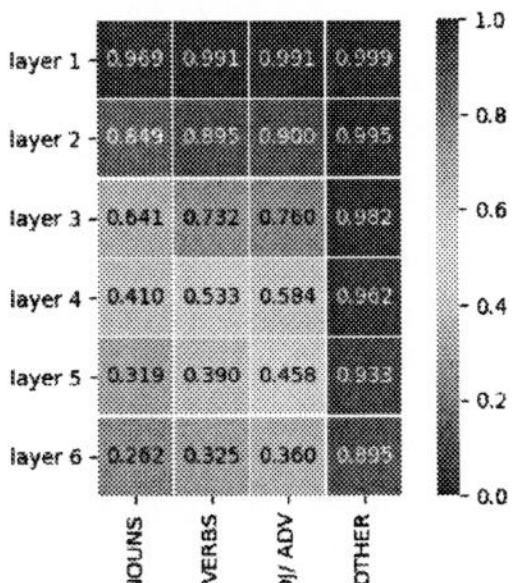

Figure 19: POS-based classification accuracy on states from the EN→DE decoder + lexical shortcuts.

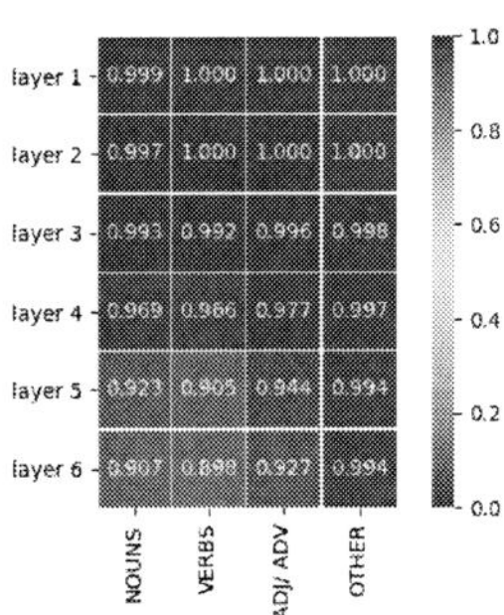

Figure 20: POS-based classification accuracy on states from the EN→RU encoder.

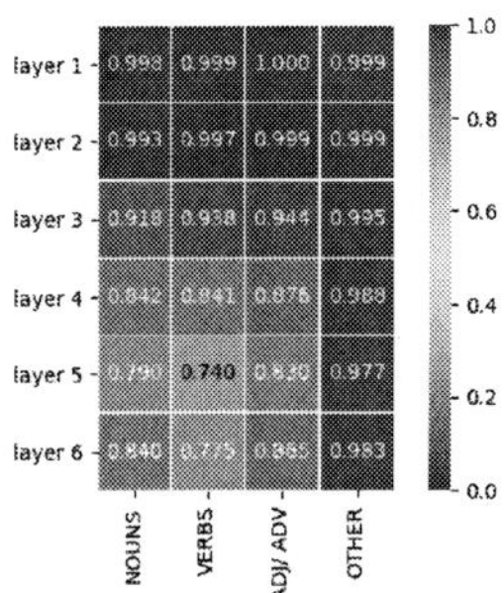

Figure 21: POS-based classification accuracy on states from the EN→RU encoder + lexical shortcuts.

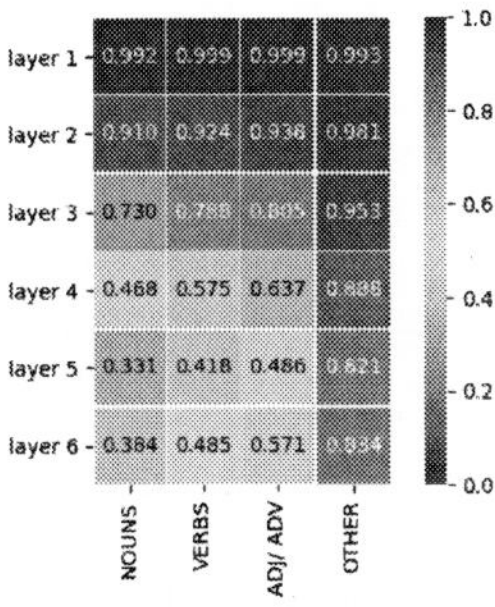

Figure 22: POS-based classification accuracy on states from the EN→RU decoder.

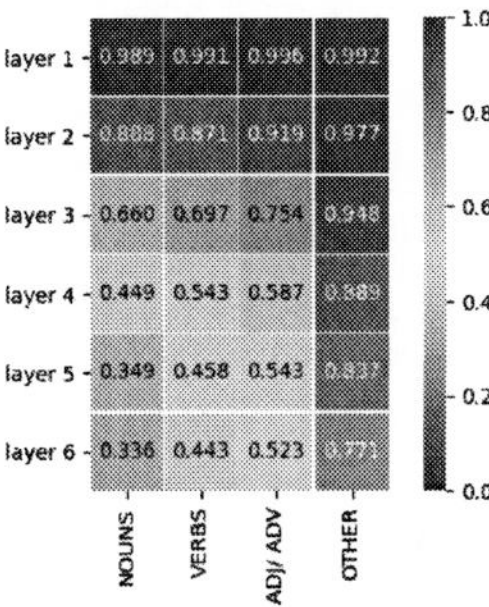

Figure 23: POS-based classification accuracy on states from the EN→RU decoder + lexical shortcuts.

A High-Quality Multilingual Dataset for Structured Documentation Translation

Kazuma Hashimoto   **Raffaella Buschiazzo**   **James Bradbury**[*]
Teresa Marshall   **Richard Socher**   **Caiming Xiong**
Salesforce
{k.hashimoto,rbuschiazzo,james.bradbury,
teresa.marshall,rsocher,cxiong}@salesforce.com

Abstract

This paper presents a high-quality multilingual dataset for the documentation domain to advance research on localization of structured text. Unlike widely-used datasets for translation of plain text, we collect XML-structured parallel text segments from the online documentation for an enterprise software platform. These Web pages have been professionally translated from English into 16 languages and maintained by domain experts, and around 100,000 text segments are available for each language pair. We build and evaluate translation models for seven target languages from English, with several different copy mechanisms and an XML-constrained beam search. We also experiment with a non-English pair to show that our dataset has the potential to explicitly enable 17×16 translation settings. Our experiments show that learning to translate with the XML tags improves translation accuracy, and the beam search accurately generates XML structures. We also discuss trade-offs of using the copy mechanisms by focusing on translation of numerical words and named entities. We further provide a detailed human analysis of gaps between the model output and human translations for real-world applications, including suitability for post-editing.

1 Introduction

Machine translation is a fundamental research area in the field of natural language processing (NLP). To build a machine learning-based translation system, we usually need a large amount of bilingually-aligned text segments. Examples of widely-used datasets are those included in WMT (Bojar et al., 2018) and LDC[1], while new evaluation datasets are being actively created (Michel and Neubig, 2018; Bawden et al.,

---

[*]Now at Google Brain.

[1]https://www.ldc.upenn.edu/

The figure box reads:

- Example (a)
English:
You can use this report on your Community Management Home dashboard or in <ph>Community Workspaces</ph> under <menucascade><uicontrol>Dashboards</uicontrol><uicontrol>Home</uicontrol></menucascade>.
Japanese:
このレポートは、[コミュニティ管理] のホームのダッシュボード、または <ph>コミュニティワークスペース </ph>の <menucascade><uicontrol>[ダッシュボード]</uicontrol> <uicontrol>[ホーム]</uicontrol></menucascade> で使用できます。

- Example (b)
English:
Results with <b>both</b><i>beach</i> and <i>house</i> in the searchable fields of the record.
Japanese:
レコードの検索可能な項目に <i>beach</i> と <i>house</i> の <b>両方</b>が含まれている結果。

- Example (c)
English:
You can only predefine this field to an email address. You can predefine it using either T (used to define email addresses) or To Recipients (used to define contact, lead, and user IDs).
Japanese:
この項目はメールアドレスに対してのみ事前に定義できます。
この項目 は [宛先] (メールアドレスを定義するために使用) または [宛先受信者] (取引先責任者、リード、ユーザ ID を定義するために使用) のいずれかを使用して事前に定義できます。

Figure 1: English-Japanese examples in our dataset.

2018; Müller et al., 2018). These existing datasets have mainly focused on translating plain text.

On the other hand, text data, especially on the Web, is not always stored as plain text, but often wrapped with markup languages to incorporate document structure and metadata such as formatting information. Many companies and software platforms provide online help as Web documents, often translated into different languages to deliver useful information to people in different countries. Translating such Web-structured text is a major component of the process by which companies localize their software or services for new markets, and human professionals typically perform the translation with the help of a *translation memory* (Silvestre Baquero and Mitkov, 2017) to increase efficiency and maintain consistent termi-

Proceedings of the Fourth Conference on Machine Translation (WMT), Volume 1: Research Papers, pages 116–127
Florence, Italy, August 1-2, 2019. ©2019 Association for Computational Linguistics

nology. Explicitly handling such structured text can help bring the benefits of state-of-the-art machine translation models to additional real-world applications. For example, structure-sensitive machine translation models may help human translators accelerate the localization process.

To encourage and advance research on translation of structured text, we collect parallel text segments from the public online documentation of a major enterprise software platform, while preserving the original XML structures.

In experiments, we provide baseline results for seven translation pairs from English, and one non-English pair. We use standard neural machine translation (NMT) models, and additionally propose an XML-constrained beam search and several discrete copy mechanisms to provide solid baselines for our new dataset. The constrained beam search contributes to accurately generating source-conditioned XML structures. Besides the widely-used BLEU (Papineni et al., 2002) scores, we also investigate more focused evaluation metrics to measure the effectiveness of our proposed methods. In particular, we discuss trade-offs of using the copy mechanisms by focusing on translation of named entities and numerical words. We further report detailed human evaluation and analysis to understand what is already achieved and what needs to be improved for the purpose of helping the human translators (a post-editing context). As our dataset represents a single, well-defined domain, it can also serve as a corpus for domain adaptation research (either as a source or target domain). We will release our dataset publicly, and discuss potential for future expansion in Section 6.

2 Collecting Data from Online Help

This section describes how we constructed our new dataset for XML-structured text translation.

Why high quality? We start from the publicly-available online help of a major international enterprise software-as-a-service (SaaS) platform. The software is provided in many different languages, and its multilingual online documentation has been localized and maintained for 15 years by the same localization service provider and in-house localization program managers. Since the beginning they have been storing translations in a translation memory (i.e. computer-assisted translation tool) to increase quality and terminology consistency. The documentation makes frequent use of structured formatting (using XML) to convey information to readers, so the translators have aimed to ensure consistency of formatting and markup structure, not just text content, between languages.

How many languages? The web documentation currently covers 16 non-English languages translated from English. These 16 languages are Brazilian Portuguese, Danish, Dutch, Finnish, French, German, Italian, Japanese, Korean, Mexican Spanish, Norwegian, Russian, Simplified Chinese, Spanish, Swedish, and Traditional Chinese. In practice, the human translation has been done from English to the other languages, but all the languages could be potentially considered as both source and target because they contain the same tagging structure.

2.1 Bilingual Web Page Alignments

In this paper, we focus on each language pair separately, as an initial construction of our dataset. Each page of the online documentation in the different languages is already aligned in the following two ways:

– first, the same page has the same file name between languages; for example, if we have a page about "WMT", there would be `/English/wmt.xml` and `/Japanese/wmt.xml`, and

– second, most of the high-level XML elements are already aligned, because the original English files have been translated by preserving the same XML structures as much as possible in the localization process, to show the same content with the same formatting. Figure 2 shows a typical pair of files and the alignment of their high-level XML elements.

Our dataset contains about 7,000 pairs of XML files for each language pair; for example, there are 7,336 aligned files for English-{French, German, Japanese}, 7,160 for English-{Finnish, Russian}, and 7,927 for Finnish-Japanese.[2]

2.2 Extracting Parallel Text Segments

XML parsing and alignment For each language pair, we extract parallel text segments from XML structures. We use the `etree` module in a Python library called `lxml`[3] to process XML

---

[2] Some documents are not present, or not aligned, in all languages.

[3] `https://lxml.de/`

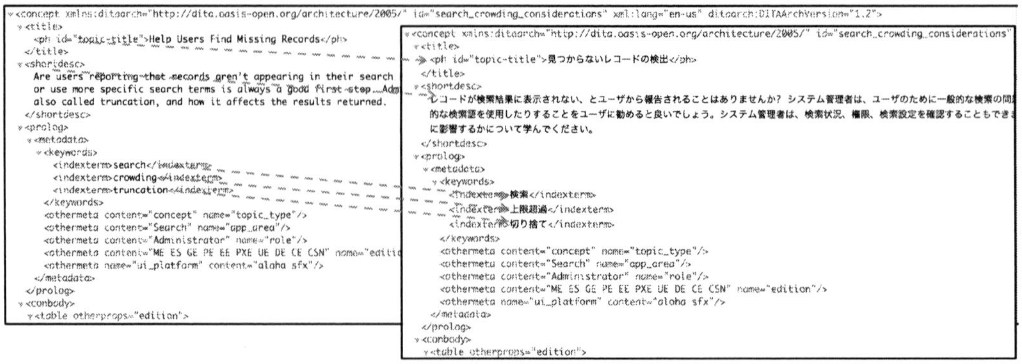

Figure 2: An aligned pair of English and Japanese XML files.

strings in the XML files. Since the XML elements are well formed and translators keep the same tagging structure as much as their languages allow it, as described in Section 2.1, we first linearize an XML-parsed file into a sequence of XML elements. We then use a pairwise sequence alignment algorithm for each bilingually-aligned file, based on XML tag matching. As a result, we have a set of aligned XML elements for the language pair.

Tag categorization   Next, we manually define which XML elements should be translated, based on the following three categories:

– Translatable:

A translatable tag (e.g. `p`, `xref`, `note`) requires us to translate text inside the tag, and we extract translation pairs from this category. In general, the translatable tags correspond to standalone text, and are thus easy to align in the sequence alignment step.

– Transparent:

By contrast, a transparent tag (e.g. `b`, `ph`) is a formatting directive embedded as a child element in a translatable tag, and is not always well aligned due to grammatical differences among languages. We keep the transparent tags embedded in the translatable tags.

– Untranslatable:

In the case of untranslatable tags (e.g. `sup`), we remove the elements. The complete list of tag categorizations can be found in the supplementary material.

Text alignment   Figure 3 shows how to extract parallel text segments based on the tag categorization. There are three aligned translatable tags, and they result in three separate translation pairs. The `note` tag is translatable, so the entire element is

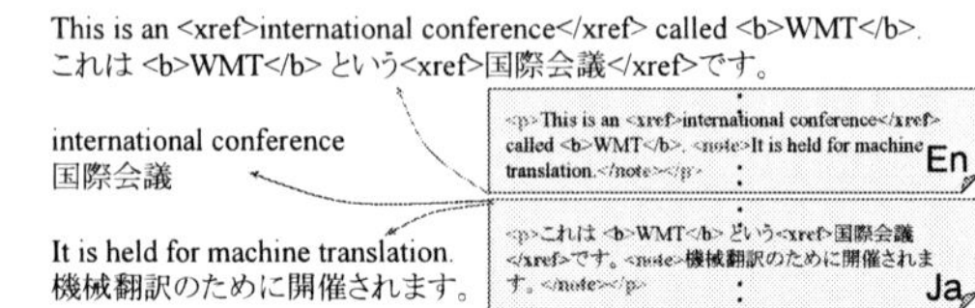

Figure 3: Extracting parallel text segments from aligned XML elements.

removed when extracting the translation pair of the `p` tag. However, we do not remove nested translatable tags (like the `xref` tag in this figure) when their *tail*[4] has text, to avoid missing phrases within sentences. Next, we remove the root tag from each translation pair, because the correspondence is obvious. We also remove fine-grained information such as attributes in the XML tags for the dataset; from the viewpoint of real-world usage, we can recover (or copy) the missing information as a post-processing step. As a result of this process, a translation pair can consist of multiple sentences as shown in Example (c) of Figure 1. We do not split them into single sentences, considering a recent trend of context-sensitive machine translation (Bawden et al., 2018; Müller et al., 2018; Zhang et al., 2018; Miculicich et al., 2018). One can use split sentences for training a model, but an important note is that there is no guarantee that all the internal sentences are perfectly aligned. We note that this structure-based alignment process means we do not rely on statistical alignment models to construct our parallel datasets.

---

[4]For example, the tail of the `xref` tag in the English example corresponds to the word "called."

118

Language pair	Training data	Aligned files
English-		
Dutch	100,756	7,160
Finnish	99,759	7,160
French	103,533	7,336
German	103,247	7,336
Japanese	101,480	7,336
Russian	100,332	7,160
Simplified Chinese	99,021	7,160
Finnish-Japanese	101,527	7,927

Table 1: The number of the translation examples in the training data used in our experiments.

Filtering We only keep translation pairs whose XML tag sets are consistent in both language sides, but we do not constrain the order of the tags to allow grammatical differences that result in tag reordering. We remove duplicate translation pairs based on exact matching, and separate two sets of 2,000 examples each for development and test sets. There are many possible experimental settings, and in this paper we report experimental results for seven English-based pairs, English-to-{Dutch, Finnish, French, German, Japanese, Russian, Simplified Chinese}, and one non-English pair, Finnish-to-Japanese. The dataset thus provides opportunities to focus on arbitrary pairs of the 17 languages. For each of the possible pairs, the number of training examples (aligned segments) is around 100,000.

2.3 Detailed Dataset Statistics

Table 1 and Figure 4, 5, 6 show more details about the dataset statistics. We take our English-French dataset to show some detailed statistics, but the others also have the consistent statistics because all the pairs are grounded in the same English files.

Text lengths Due to the XML tag-based extraction, our dataset includes word- and phrase-level translations as well as sentence- and paragraph-level translations, and we can see in Figure 4 that there are many short text segments. This is, for example, different from the statistics of the widely-used News Commentary dataset. The text length is defined based on the number of subword tokens, following our experimental setting described below.

Sentence counts Another characteristic of our dataset is that the translation pairs can consist of multiple sentences, and Figure 5 shows the statistics of the number of English sentences in the English-French translation pairs. The number of

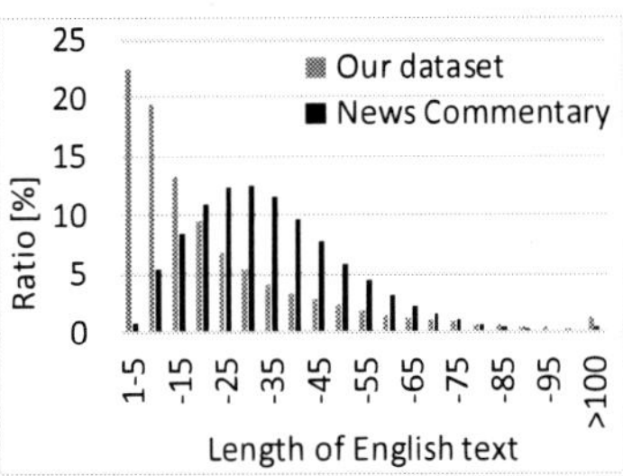

Figure 4: The length statistics of the English text in our English-French and the News Commentary datasets.

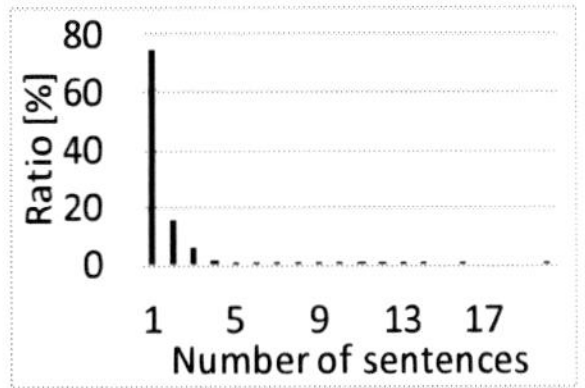

Figure 5: The statistics of the number of English sentences in the English-French translation pairs.

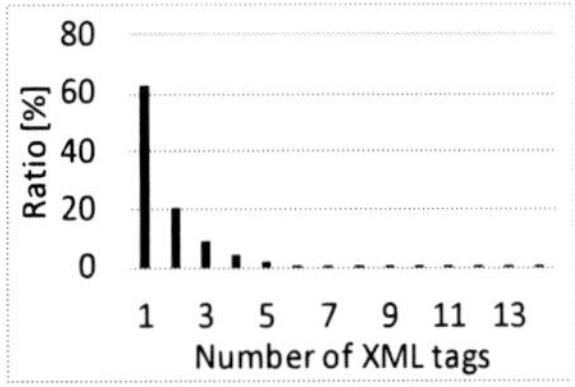

Figure 6: The statistics of the number of XML tags inside the English-French translation pairs.

sentences is determined with the sentence splitter from the Stanford CoreNLP toolkit (Manning et al., 2014).

XML-tag counts As we remove the root tags from the XML elements in our dataset construction process, not all the text segments have XML tags inside them. More concretely, about 25.5% of the translation pairs have at least one internal XML tag, and Figure 6 shows the statistics. For example, Example (a) in Figure 1 has four XML tags, and Example (b) has three.

2.4 Evaluation Metrics

We consider multiple evaluation metrics for the new dataset. For evaluation, we use the *true-cased* and *detokenized* text, because our dataset is designed for an end-user, raw-document setting.

BLEU without XML We include the most widely-used metric, BLEU, without XML tags.

That is, we remove all the XML tags covered by our dataset and then evaluate BLEU. The metric is compatible with the case where we use the dataset for plain text translation without XML. To compute the BLEU scores, we use language-specific tokenizers; for example, we use Kytea (Neubig et al., 2011) for Simplified Chinese and Japanese, and the Moses (Koehn et al., 2007) tokenizer for English, Dutch, Finnish, French, German, and Russian.

Named entities and numbers The online help frequently mentions named entities such as product names and numbers, and accurate translations of them are crucial for users. Frequently, they are not translated but simply copied as English forms. We evaluate corpus-level precision and recall for translation of the named entities and numerical tokens. To extract the named entities and numerical words, we use a rule-based regex script, based on our manual analysis on our dataset. The numerical words are extracted by

"[0-9.,\'/:]*[0-9]+[0-9.,\'/:]*".

The named entities are defined as

"[.,\'/:a-zA-Z$]*[A-Z]+[.,\'/:a-zA-Z$]*"

appearing in a non-alphabetic language, Japanese, because in our dataset we observe that the alphabetic words in such non-alphabetic languages correspond to product names, country names, function names, etc.

XML accuracy, matching, and BLEU For each output text segment, we use the `etree` module to check if it is a valid XML structure by wrapping it with a dummy root node. Then the XML accuracy score is the number of the valid outputs, divided by the number of the total evaluation examples. We further evaluate how many translation outputs have exactly the same XML structures as their corresponding reference text (an XML matching score). If a translation output matches its reference XML structure, both the translation and reference are split by the XML tags. We then evaluate corpus-level BLEU by comparing each split segment one by one. If an output does not match its reference XML structure, the output is treated as empty to penalize the irrelevant outputs.

3   Machine Translation with XML Tags

We use NMT models to provide competitive baselines for our dataset. This section first describes how to handle our dataset with a sequential NMT model. We then propose a simple constrained beam search for accurately generating XML structures conditioned by source information. We further incorporate multiple copy mechanisms to strengthen the baselines.

3.1   Sequence-to-Sequence NMT

The task in our dataset is to translate text with structured information, and therefore we consider using syntax-based NMT models. A possible approach is incorporating parse trees or parsing algorithms into NMT models (Eriguchi et al., 2016, 2017), and another is using sequential models on linearized structures (Aharoni and Goldberg, 2017). We employ the latter approach to incorporate source-side and target-side XML structures, and note that this allows using standard sequence-to-sequence models without modification.

We have a set of parallel text segments for a language pair $(\mathcal{X}, \mathcal{Y})$, and the task is translating a text segment $x \in \mathcal{X}$ to another $y \in \mathcal{Y}$. Each x in the dataset is represented with a sequence of tokens including some XML tags: $x = [x_1, x_2, \ldots, x_N]$, where N is the length of the sequence. Its corresponding reference y is also represented with a sequence of tokens: $y = [y_1, y_2, \ldots, y_M]$, where M is the sequence length. Any tokenization method can be used, except that the XML tags should be individual tokens.

To learn translation from x to y, we use a *transformer* model (Vaswani et al., 2017). In our K-layer transformer model, each source token x_i in the k-th ($k \in [1, K]$) layer is represented with

$$h_k^x(x_i) = f(i, h_{k-1}^x) \in \mathbb{R}^d, \qquad (1)$$

where i is the position information, d is the dimensionality of the model, and $h_{k-1}^x = [h_{k-1}^x(x_1), h_{k-1}^x(x_2), \ldots, h_{k-1}^x(x_N)]$ is the sequence of the vector representations in the previous layer. $h_0^x(x_i)$ is computed as $h_0^x(x_i) = \sqrt{d} \cdot v(x_i) + e(i)$, where $v(x_i) \in \mathbb{R}^d$ is a token embedding, and $e(i) \in \mathbb{R}^d$ is a positional embedding.

Each target-side token y_j is also represented in a similar way:

$$h_k^y(y_j) = g(j, h_k^x, h_{k-1}^y) \in \mathbb{R}^d, \qquad (2)$$

where only $[h_{k-1}^y(y_1), h_{k-1}^y(y_2), \ldots, h_{k-1}^y(y_j)]$ is used from h_{k-1}^y. In the same way as the source-side embeddings, $h_0^y(y_j)$ is computed as $h_0^y(y_j) =$

$\sqrt{d} \cdot v(y_j) + e(j)$. For more details about the parameterized functions f and g, and the positional embeddings, please refer to Vaswani et al. (2017).

Then $h_K^y(y_j)$ is used to predict the next token w by a softmax layer: $p_g(w|x, y_{\leq j}) = \text{softmax}(W h_K^y(y_j) + b)$, where $W \in \mathbb{R}^{|\mathbb{V}| \times d}$ is a weight matrix, $b \in \mathbb{R}^{|\mathbb{V}|}$ is a bias vector, and $\mathbb{V}$ is the vocabulary. The loss function is defined as follows:

$$L(x, y) = - \sum_{j=1}^{M-1} \log p_g(w = y_{j+1}|x, y_{\leq j}), \quad (3)$$

where we assume that y_1 is a special token BOS to indicate the beginning of the sequence, and y_M is an end-of-sequence token EOS. Following Inan et al. (2017) and Press and Wolf (2017), we use W as an embedding matrix, and we share the single vocabulary $\mathbb{V}$ for both $\mathcal{X}$ and $\mathcal{Y}$. That is, each of $v(x_i)$ or $v(y_j)$ is equivalent to a row vector in W.

3.2 XML-Constrained Beam Search

At test time, standard sequence-to-sequence generation methods do not always output valid XML structures, and even if an output is a valid XML structure, it does not always match the tag set of its source-side XML structure. To generate source-conditioned XML structures as accurately as possible, we propose a simple constrained beam search method. We add three constrains to a standard beam search method. First, we keep track of possible tags based on the source input, and allow the model to open only a tag that is present in the input and has not yet been covered. Second, we keep track of the most recently opened tag, and allow the model to close the tag. Third, we do not allow the model to output EOS before opening and closing all the tags used in the source sentence. Algorithm 1 in the supplementary material shows a comprehensive pseudo code.

3.3 Reformulating a Pointer Mechanism

We consider how to further improve our NMT system, by using multiple *discrete* copy mechanisms. Since our dataset is based on XML-structured technical documents, we want our NMT system to copy (A) relevant text segments in the target language if there are very similar segments in the training data, and (B) named entities (e.g. product names), XML tags, and numbers directly from the source. For the copy mechanisms, we follow

the general idea of the *pointer* used in See et al. (2017).

For the sake of discrete decisions, we reformulate the pointer method. Following the previous work, we have a sequence of tokens which are targets of our pointer method: $c = [c(z_1), c(z_2), \ldots, c(z_U)]$, where $c(z_i) \in \mathbb{R}^d$ is a vector representation of the i-th token z_i, and U is the sequence length. As in Section 3.1, we have $h_K^y(y_j)$ to predict the $(j+1)$-th token. Before defining an attention mechanism between $h_K^y(y_j)$ and c, we append a parameterized vector $c(z_0) = c'$ to c. We expect c' to be responsible for decisions of "not copying" tokens, and the idea is inspired by adding a "null" token in natural language inference (Parikh et al., 2016).

We then define attention scores between $h_K^y(y_j)$ and the expanded c: $a(j, i) = score(h_K^y(y_j), c_i, c)$, where the normalized scoring function $score$ is implemented as a single-head attention model proposed in Vaswani et al. (2017). If the next reference token y_{j+1} is not included in the copy target sequence, the loss function is defined as follows:

$$L(x, y_{\leq j}, c) = - \log a(j, 0), \quad (4)$$

and otherwise the loss function is as follows:

$$L(x, y_{\leq j}, c) = - \log \sum_{i, \text{ s.t. } z_i = y_{j+1}} a(j, i), \quad (5)$$

and then the total loss function is $L(x, y) + \sum_{j=1}^{M-1} L(x, y_{\leq j}, c)$. The loss function solely relies on the cross-entropy loss for single probability distributions, whereas the pointer mechanism in See et al. (2017) defines the cross-entropy loss for weighted summation of multiple distributions.

At test time, we employ a discrete decision strategy for copying tokens or not. More concretely, the output distribution is computed as

$$\delta \cdot p_g(w|x, y_{\leq j}) + (1 - \delta) \cdot p_c(w|x, y_{\leq j}), \quad (6)$$

where $p_c(w|x, y_{\leq j})$ is computed by aggregating $[a(j, 1), \ldots, a(j, U)]$. δ is 1 if $a(j, 0)$ is the largest among $[a(j, 0), \ldots, a(j, U)]$, and otherwise δ is 0.

Copy from Retrieved Translation Pairs Gu et al. (2018) presented a retrieval-based NMT model, based on the idea of translation memory (Silvestre Baquero and Mitkov, 2017). Following Gu et al. (2018), we retrieve the most relevant translation pair (x', y') for each source text x

in the dataset. In this case, we set $[z_1, \ldots, z_U] = [y'_2, \ldots, y'_{M'}]$ and $c = [h^y_K(y'_1), \ldots, h^y_K(y'_{M'-1})]$, where M' is the length of y', and each vector in c is computed by the same transformer model in Section 3.1. For this retrieval copy mechanism, we denote p_c and δ as p_r and δ_r, respectively.

Copy from Source Text To allow our NMT model to directly copy certain tokens from the source text x when necessary, we follow See et al. (2017). We set $[z_1, \ldots, z_U] = [x_1, \ldots, x_N]$ and $c = [h^x_K(x_1), \ldots, h^x_K(x_N)]$, and we denote p_c and δ as p_s and δ_s, respectively.

We have the single vocabulary $\mathbb{V}$ to handle all the tokens in both languages $\mathcal{X}$ and $\mathcal{Y}$, and we can combine the three output distributions at each time step in the text generation process:

$$(1 - \delta_s)p_s + \delta_s(\delta_r p_g + (1 - \delta_r)p_r). \qquad (7)$$

The copy mechanism is similar to the multi-pointer-generator method in McCann et al. (2018), but our method employs rule-based discrete decisions. Equation (7) first decides whether the NMT model copies a source token. If not, our method then decides whether the model copies a retrieved token.

4   Experimental Settings

This section describes our experimental settings. We will release the preprocessing scripts and the training code (implemented with PyTorch) upon publication. More details are described in the supplementary material.

4.1   Tokenization and Detokenization

We used the SentencePiece toolkit (Kudo and Richardson, 2018) for sub-word tokenization and detokenization for the NMT outputs.

Without XML tags If we remove all the XML tags from our dataset, the task becomes a plain MT task. We carried out our baseline experiments for the plain text translation task, and for each language pair we trained a joint SentencePiece model to obtain its shared sub-word vocabulary. For training each NMT model, we used training examples whose maximum token length is 100.

With XML tags For our XML-based experiments, we also trained a joint SentencePiece model for each language pair, where one important note is that all the XML tags are treated as user-defined special tokens in the toolkit. This allows us to easily implement the XML-constrained beam search. We also set the three tokens `&`, `<`, and `>` as special tokens.

4.2   Model Configurations

We implemented the transformer model with $K = 6$ and $d = 256$ as a competitive baseline model. We trained three models for each language pair:

"OT" (trained only with text without XML),

"X" (trained with XML), and

"X$_{rs}$" (XML and the copy mechanisms).

For each setting, we tuned the model on the development set and selected the best-performing model in terms of BLEU scores *without* XML, to make the tuning process consistent across all the settings.

5   Results

Table 2 and 4 show the detailed results on our development set, and for the X$_{rs}$ model, we also show the results (X$_{rs}^{(T)}$) on our test set to show our baseline scores for future comparisons. Simplified Chinese is written as "Chinese" in this section.

5.1   Evaluation without XML

We first focus on the two evaluation metrics: BLEU without XML, and named entities and numbers (NE&NUM). In Table 2, a general observation from the comparison of OT and X is that including segment-internal XML tags tends to improve the BLEU scores. This is not surprising because the XML tags provide information about explicit or implicit alignments of phrases. However, the BLEU score of the English-to-Finnish task significantly drops, which indicates that for some languages it is not easy to handle tags within the text.

Another observation is that X$_{rs}$ achieves the best BLEU scores, except for English-to-French. In our experiments, we have found that the improvement of BLEU comes from the retrieval method, but it degrades the NE&NUM scores, especially the precision. Then copying from the source tends to recover the NE&NUM scores, especially for the recall. We have also observed that using beam search, which improves BLEU scores, degrades the NE&NUM scores. A lesson learned from these results is that work to improve BLEU scores can sometimes lead to degradation of other important metrics.

	BLEU	NE&NUM Precision, Recall	BLEU	NE&NUM Precision, Recall	BLEU	NE&NUM Precision, Recall	BLEU	NE&NUM Precision, Recall
		English-to-Japanese		English-to-Chinese		English-to-French		English-to-German
OT	61.61	89.84, 89.84	58.06	94.91, 93.62	64.07	88.64, 85.64	50.51	88.40, 86.55
X	62.00	92.54, 90.51	58.61	94.56, 93.44	63.98	87.48, 86.98	50.96	88.79, 86.43
X_{rs}	64.25	91.64, 90.98	60.05	94.44, 94.27	63.51	88.42, 85.64	52.91	88.00, 86.78
$X_{rs}^{(T)}$	64.34	93.39, 91.75	59.86	93.49, 93.11	65.04	88.98, 88.31	52.69	88.22, 88.45
		English-to-Finnish		English-to-Dutch		English-to-Russian		Finnish-to-Japanese
OT	43.97	87.58, 84.99	59.54	90.89, 88.59	43.28	89.67, 85.26	54.55	90.45, 89.69
X	42.84	83.17, 85.55	60.18	90.41, 90.26	43.44	87.96, 88.35	54.69	93.47, 89.29
X_{rs}	45.10	86.41, 86.49	60.58	88.76, 90.11	46.73	88.65, 89.55	57.92	93.02, 89.03
$X_{rs}^{(T)}$	45.71	87.38, 88.91	61.01	87.66, 90.84	46.44	86.90, 89.59	57.06	93.39, 89.38

Table 2: Automatic evaluation results *without* XML on the development set, and the test set for X_{rs}.

Training data	Our dev set	newstest2014
Our dataset (no XML)	64.07	7.35
w/ 10K news	63.66	14.02
w/ 20K news	64.31	16.30
Only 10K news	0.90	2.66
Only 20K news	2.35	6.72

Table 3: Domain adaptation results (BLEU). The models are tuned on our development set.

Compatibility with other domains Our dataset is limited to the domain of online help, but we can use it as a seed corpus for domain adaptation if our dataset contains enough information to learn basic grammar translation. We conducted a simple domain adaptation experiment in English-to-French by adding 10,000 or 20,000 training examples of the widely-used News Commentary corpus. We used the newstest2014 dataset for evaluation in the news domain. From Table 3, we can see that a small amount of the news-domain data significantly improves the target-domain score, and we expect that our dataset plays a good role in domain adaptation for all the covered 17 languages.

5.2 Evaluation with XML

Table 4 shows the evaluation results with XML. Again, we can see that X_{rs} performs the best in terms of the XML-based BLEU scores, but the absolute values are lower than those in Table 2 due to the more rigid segment-by-segment comparisons. This table also shows that the XML accuracy and matching scores are higher than 99% in most of the cases. Ideally, the scores could be 100%, but in reality, we set the maximum length of the translations; as a result, sometimes the model cannot find a good path within the length limitation. Table 5 shows how effective our method is, based on the English-to-Japanese result, and we observed the consistent trend across the different languages.

These results show that our method can accurately generate the relevant XML structures.

How to recover XML attributes? As described in Section 2.2, we removed all the attributes from the original XML elements for simplicity. However, we need to recover the attributes when we use our NMT model in the real-world application. We consider recovering the XML attributes by the copy mechanism from the source; that is, we can copy the attributes from the XML elements in the original source text, if the XML tags are copied from the source. Table 6 summarizes how our model generates the XML tags on the English-Japanese development set. We can see in the table that most of the XML tags are actually copied from the source.

Figure 7 shows an example of the output of the X_{rs} model. For this visualization, we merged all the subword tokens to form the standard words. The tokens in blue are explicitly copied from the source, and we can see that the time expression "12:57 AM" and the XML tags are copied as expected. The output also copies some relevant text segments (in red) from the retrieved translation. Like this, we can explicitly know which words are copied from which parts, by using our multiple discrete copy mechanisms. One surprising observation is that the underlined phrase "for example" is missing in the translation result, even though the BLEU scores are higher than those on other standard public datasets. This is a typical error called *under translation*. Therefore, no matter how large the BLEU scores are, we definitely need human corrections (or post editing) before providing the translation results to customers.

	BLEU	XML Acc., Match	BLEU	XML Acc., Match	BLEU	XML Acc., Match	BLEU	XML Acc., Match
	English-to-Japanese		English-to-Chinese		English-to-French		English-to-German	
X	59.77	99.80, 99.55	57.01	99.95, 99.70	61.81	99.60, 99.30	48.91	99.85, 99.25
X_{rs}	62.06	99.80, 99.40	58.43	99.90, 99.60	61.87	99.80, 99.50	51.16	99.75, 99.30
$X_{rs}^{(T)}$	62.27	99.95, 99.60	57.92	99.75, 99.40	63.19	99.80, 99.35	50.47	99.80, 99.20
	English-to-Finnish		English-to-Dutch		English-to-Russian		Finnish-to-Japanese	
X	41.98	99.65, 99.25	57.86	99.60, 99.25	40.72	99.60, 98.95	52.14	99.90, 99.30
X_{rs}	43.57	99.50, 99.25	58.51	99.70, 99.30	44.42	99.75, 99.25	55.20	99.65, 98.90
$X_{rs}^{(T)}$	44.22	99.90, 99.65	60.19	99.90, 99.85	44.25	99.80, 99.35	54.05	99.60, 98.75

Table 4: Automatic evaluation results *with* XML on the development set, and the test set for X_{rs}.

- Source to be translated (English)
<xref>View a single feed update</xref> by clicking the timestamp below the update, *for example*, <uicontrol>Yesterday at 12:57 AM</uicontrol>.

- Retrieved source (English)
In a feed, click the timestamp that appears below the post, *for example*, <uicontrol>Yesterday at 12:57 AM</uicontrol>.

- Retrieved reference (Japanese)
フィード内で、*たとえば*、<uicontrol>|昨日の 12:57 AM|</uicontrol> のように、投稿の下に表示されるタイムスタンプをクリックします。

- Output of the X_{rs} model (Japanese)
<uicontrol> |昨日の 12:57 AM| </uicontrol> のように、更新の下にタイムスタンプをクリックして、<xref> 1 つのフィード更新を表示</xref>します。

Figure 7: An example of the translation results of the X_{rs} model on the English-Japanese test set.

	BLEU	XML Acc., Match
w/ XML constraint	59.77	99.80, 99.55
w/o XML constraint	58.02	98.70, 98.10

Table 5: Effects of the XML-constrained beam search.

	Count
Copied from source text	1,638
Copied from retrieved translation	24
Generated from vocabulary	11

Table 6: Statistics of the generated XML tags.

5.3 Human Evaluation by Professionals

One important application of our NMT models is to help human translators; translating online help has to be precise, and thus any incomplete translations need post-editing. We asked professional translators at a vendor to evaluate our test set results (with XML) for the English-to-{Finnish, French, German, Japanese} tasks. For each language pair, we randomly selected 500 test examples, and every example is given an integer score in [1, 4]. A translation result is rated as "4" if it can be used without any modifications, "3" if it needs simple post-edits, "2" if it needs more post-edits but is better than nothing, and "1" if using it is not better than translating from scratch.

Figure 8 shows the summary of the evaluation to see the ratio of each score, and the average scores are also shown. A positive observation for all the four languages is that more than 50% of the translation results are evaluated as complete or useful in post-editing. However, there are still many low-quality translation results; for example, around 30% of the Finnish and German results are evaluated as useless. Moreover, the German results have fewer scores of "4", and it took 12 hours for the translators to evaluate the German results, whereas it took 10 hours for the other three languages. To further make our NMT models useful for post-editing, we have to improve the translations scored as "1".

Detailed error analysis We also asked the translators to note what kinds of errors exist for each of the evaluated examples. All the errors are classified into the six types shown in Table 7, and each example can have multiple errors. The "Formatting" type is our task-specific one to evaluate whether the XML tags are correctly inserted. We can see that the Finnish results have significantly more XML-formatting errors, and this result agrees with our finding that handling the XML tags in Finnish is harder than in other languages, as discussed in Section 5.1. It is worth further investigating such language-specific problems.

The "Accuracy" type covers major issues of NMT, such as adding irrelevant words, skipping important words, and mistranslating phrases. As discussed in previous work (Malaviya et al., 2018), reducing the typical errors covered by the "Accuracy" type is crucial. We have also noticed

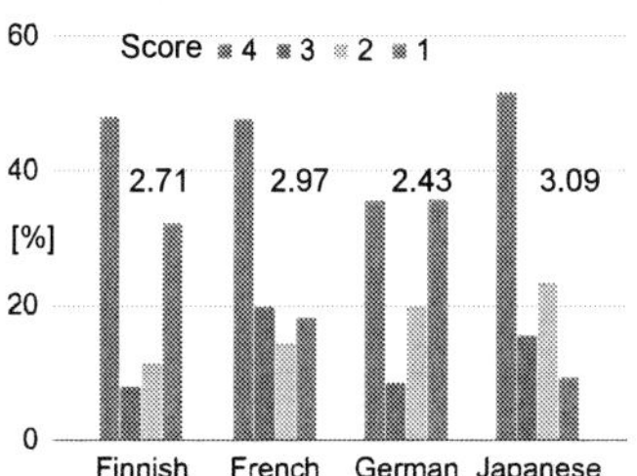

Figure 8: Human evaluation results for the X_{rs} model. "4" is the best score, and "1" is the worst.

	Finnish	French	German	Japanese
Accuracy	30.0	32.8	37.4	37.4
Readability	20.6	20.4	0.8	17.4
Formatting	10.6	0.0	0.8	1.0
Grammar	20.2	10.0	11.4	5.8
Structure	10.2	2.8	2.0	1.2
Terminology	12.0	3.0	2.4	0.6

Table 7: Ratio [%] of six error types.

that the NMT-specific errors would slow down the human evaluation process, because the NMT errors are different from translation errors made by humans. The other types of errors would be reduced by improving language models, if we have access to in-domain monolingual corpora.

Can MT help the localization process? In general, it is encouraging to observe many "4" scores in Figure 8. However, one important note is that it takes significant amount of time for the translators to verify the NMT outputs are good enough. That is, having better scored NMT outputs does not necessarily lead to improving the productivity of the translators; in other words, we need to take into account the time for the quality verification when we consider using our NMT system for that purpose. Previous work has investigated the effectiveness of NMT models for post-editing (Skadina and Pinnis, 2017), but it has not yet been investigated whether using NMT models can improve the translators' productivity alongside the use of a well-constructed translation memory (Silvestre Baquero and Mitkov, 2017). Therefore, our future work is investigating the effectiveness of using the NMT models in the real-world localization process where a translation memory is available.

6 Related Work and Discussions

Automatic extraction of parallel sentences has a long history (Varga et al., 2005), and usually statistical methods and dictionaries are used. By contrast, our data collection solely relies on the XML structure, because the original data have been well structured and aligned. Recently, collecting training corpora is the most important in training NLP models, and thus it is recommended to maintain well-aligned documents and structures when building multilingual online services. That will significantly contribute to the research of language technologies.

We followed the syntax-based NMT models (Eriguchi et al., 2016, 2017; Aharoni and Goldberg, 2017) to handle the XML structures. One significant difference between the syntax-based NMT and our task is that we need to output source-conditioned structures that are able to be parsed as XML, whereas the syntax-based NMT models do not always need to follow formal rules for their output structures. In that sense, it would be interesting to relate our task to source code generation (Oda et al., 2015) in future work.

Our dataset has significant potential to be further expanded. Following the context-sensitive translation (Bawden et al., 2018; Müller et al., 2018; Zhang et al., 2018; Miculicich et al., 2018), our dataset includes translations of multiple sentences. However, the translatable XML tags are separated, so the page-level global information is missing. One promising direction is thus to create page-level translation examples. Finally, considering the recent focus on multilingual NMT models (Johnson et al., 2017), multilingually aligning the text will enrich our dataset.

7 Conclusion

We have presented our new dataset for XML-structured text translation. Our dataset covers 17 languages each of which can be either source or target of machine translation. The dataset is of high quality because it consists of professional translations for an online help domain. Our experiments provide baseline results for the new task by using NMT models with an XML-constrained beam search and discrete copy mechanisms. We further show detailed human analysis to encourage future research focusing on how to apply machine translation to help human translators in practice.

Acknowledgements

We thank anonymous reviewers and Xi Victoria Lin for their helpful feedbacks.

References

Roee Aharoni and Yoav Goldberg. 2017. Towards String-To-Tree Neural Machine Translation. In *Proceedings of the 55th Annual Meeting of the Association for Computational Linguistics (Volume 2: Short Papers)*, pages 132–140.

Rachel Bawden, Rico Sennrich, Alexandra Birch, and Barry Haddow. 2018. Evaluating Discourse Phenomena in Neural Machine Translation. In *Proceedings of the 2018 Conference of the North American Chapter of the Association for Computational Linguistics: Human Language Technologies, Volume 1 (Long Papers)*, pages 1304–1313.

Ondřej Bojar, Rajen Chatterjee, Christian Federmann, Mark Fishel, Yvette Graham, Barry Haddow, Matthias Huck, Antonio Jimeno Yepes, Philipp Koehn, Christof Monz, Matteo Negri, Aurélie Névéol, Mariana Neves, Matt Post, Lucia Specia, Marco Turchi, and Karin Verspoor. 2018. Proceedings of the Third Conference on Machine Translation: Shared Task Papers. In *Proceedings of the Third Conference on Machine Translation: Shared Task Papers*.

Akiko Eriguchi, Kazuma Hashimoto, and Yoshimasa Tsuruoka. 2016. Tree-to-Sequence Attentional Neural Machine Translation. In *Proceedings of the 54th Annual Meeting of the Association for Computational Linguistics (Volume 1: Long Papers)*, pages 823–833.

Akiko Eriguchi, Yoshimasa Tsuruoka, and Kyunghyun Cho. 2017. Learning to Parse and Translate Improves Neural Machine Translation. In *Proceedings of the 55th Annual Meeting of the Association for Computational Linguistics (Volume 2: Short Papers)*, pages 72–78.

Jiatao Gu, Yong Wang, Kyunghyun Cho, and Victor O. K. Li. 2018. Search Engine Guided Neural Machine Translation. In *Proceedings of the Thirty-Second AAAI Conference on Artificial Intelligence*, pages 5133–5140.

Hakan Inan, Khashayar Khosravi, and Richard Socher. 2017. Tying Word Vectors and Word Classifiers: A Loss Framework for Language Modeling. In *Proceedings of the 5th International Conference on Learning Representations*.

Melvin Johnson, Mike Schuster, Quoc V. Le, Maxim Krikun, Yonghui Wu, Zhifeng Chen, Nikhil Thorat, Fernanda Viégas, Martin Wattenberg, Greg Corrado, Macduff Hughes, and Jeffrey Dean. 2017. Google's Multilingual Neural Machine Translation System: Enabling Zero-Shot Translation. *Transactions of the Association for Computational Linguistics*, 5:339–351.

Philipp Koehn, Hieu Hoang, Alexandra Birch, Chris Callison-Burch, Marcello Federico, Nicola Bertoldi, Brooke Cowan, Wade Shen, Christine Moran, Richard Zens, Chris Dyer, Ondrej Bojar, Alexandra Constantin, and Evan Herbst. 2007. Moses: Open Source Toolkit for Statistical Machine Translation. In *Proceedings of the 45th Annual Meeting of the Association for Computational Linguistics Companion Volume Proceedings of the Demo and Poster Sessions*, pages 177–180.

Taku Kudo and John Richardson. 2018. SentencePiece: A simple and language independent subword tokenizer and detokenizer for Neural Text Processing. In *Proceedings of the 2018 Conference on Empirical Methods in Natural Language Processing: System Demonstrations*, pages 66–71.

Chaitanya Malaviya, Pedro Ferreira, and André F. T. Martins. 2018. Sparse and Constrained Attention for Neural Machine Translation. In *Proceedings of the 56th Annual Meeting of the Association for Computational Linguistics, Volume 2*, pages 370–376.

Christopher Manning, Mihai Surdeanu, John Bauer, Jenny Finkel, Steven Bethard, and David McClosky. 2014. The Stanford CoreNLP Natural Language Processing Toolkit. In *Proceedings of 52nd Annual Meeting of the Association for Computational Linguistics: System Demonstrations*, pages 55–60.

Bryan McCann, Nitish Shirish Keskar, Caiming Xiong, and Richard Socher. 2018. The Natural Language Decathlon: Multitask Learning as Question Answering. *arXiv preprint arXiv:1806.08730*.

Paul Michel and Graham Neubig. 2018. MTNT: A Testbed for Machine Translation of Noisy Text. In *Proceedings of the 2018 Conference on Empirical Methods in Natural Language Processing*, pages 543–553.

Lesly Miculicich, Dhananjay Ram, Nikolaos Pappas, and James Henderson. 2018. Document-Level Neural Machine Translation with Hierarchical Attention Networks. In *Proceedings of the 2018 Conference on Empirical Methods in Natural Language Processing*, pages 2947–2954.

Mathias Müller, Annette Rios, Elena Voita, and Rico Sennrich. 2018. A Large-Scale Test Set for the Evaluation of Context-Aware Pronoun Translation in Neural Machine Translation. In *Proceedings of the Third Conference on Machine Translation: Research Papers*, pages 61–72.

Graham Neubig, Yosuke Nakata, and Shinsuke Mori. 2011. Pointwise Prediction for Robust, Adaptable Japanese Morphological Analysis. In *Proceedings of the 49th Annual Meeting of the Association for Computational Linguistics: Human Language Technologies*, pages 529–533.

Y. Oda, H. Fudaba, G. Neubig, H. Hata, S. Sakti, T. Toda, and S. Nakamura. 2015. Learning to Generate Pseudo-Code from Source Code Using Statistical Machine Translation. In *2015 30th IEEE/ACM International Conference on Automated Software Engineering (ASE)*, pages 574–584.

Kishore Papineni, Salim Roukos, Todd Ward, and Wei-Jing Zhu. 2002. BLEU: A Method for Automatic Evaluation of Machine Translation. In *Proceedings of the 40th Annual Meeting on Association for Computational Linguistics*, pages 311–318.

Ankur Parikh, Oscar Täckström, Dipanjan Das, and Jakob Uszkoreit. 2016. A Decomposable Attention Model for Natural Language Inference. In *Proceedings of the 2016 Conference on Empirical Methods in Natural Language Processing*, pages 2249–2255.

Ofir Press and Lior Wolf. 2017. Using the Output Embedding to Improve Language Models. In *Proceedings of the 15th Conference of the European Chapter of the Association for Computational Linguistics: Volume 2, Short Papers*, pages 157–163.

Abigail See, Peter J. Liu, and Christopher D. Manning. 2017. Get To The Point: Summarization with Pointer-Generator Networks. In *Proceedings of the 55th Annual Meeting of the Association for Computational Linguistics (Volume 1: Long Papers)*, pages 1073–1083.

Andrea Silvestre Baquero and Ruslan Mitkov. 2017. Translation Memory Systems Have a Long Way to Go. In *Proceedings of the Workshop Human-Informed Translation and Interpreting Technology*, pages 44–51.

Inguna Skadina and Mārcis Pinnis. 2017. NMT or SMT: Case Study of a Narrow-domain English-Latvian Post-editing Project. In *Proceedings of the Eighth International Joint Conference on Natural Language Processing (Volume 1: Long Papers)*, pages 373–383.

Daniel Varga, Laszlo Németh, Peter Halácsy, Andras Kornai, Viktor Trón, and Victor Nagy. 2005. Parallel corpora for medium density languages. In *Proceedings of the International Conference Recent Advances in Natural Language Processing*.

Ashish Vaswani, Noam Shazeer, Niki Parmar, Jakob Uszkoreit, Llion Jones, Aidan N Gomez, Ł ukasz Kaiser, and Illia Polosukhin. 2017. Attention is All you Need. In *Advances in Neural Information Processing Systems 30*, pages 5998–6008.

Jiacheng Zhang, Huanbo Luan, Maosong Sun, Feifei Zhai, Jingfang Xu, Min Zhang, and Yang Liu. 2018. Improving the Transformer Translation Model with Document-Level Context. In *Proceedings of the 2018 Conference on Empirical Methods in Natural Language Processing*, pages 533–542.

Author Index